George Vallis Garland

The problems of Job

George Vallis Garland

The problems of Job

ISBN/EAN: 9783337735937

Printed in Europe, USA, Canada, Australia, Japan

Cover: Foto ©ninafisch / pixelio.de

More available books at **www.hansebooks.com**

THE PROBLEMS OF JOB

BY

REV. GEO. V. GARLAND, M.A.
AUTHOR OF "THE PRACTICAL TEACHING OF THE APOCALYPSE,"
"NOTES ON GENESIS," ETC.

London
JAMES NISBET & CO., LIMITED
21 BERNERS STREET
1898

PREFACE

THE object of the following treatise on the Book of Job is to place in a consecutive form the apparently disjointed maxims and isolated proverbs used by the various speakers. The chief difficulty in understanding its contents owes itself to the oriental preference for parabolic utterances, instead of continuous argumentative reasonings. It was the mode adopted by our Lord in His parables and discourses, whereby He tested the sincerity of His followers in their desire for Divine knowledge (Matt. xiii. 11). It is also the great characteristic of the Sacred Scriptures. They lay no claim to record consecutive history. They relate only certain salient events and sayings in the lives and utterances of chosen peoples, rulers, and prophets, selected under inspiration to reveal the Divine principles for the regulation of national, social, and individual life, in all successive ages until the end of the dispensation.

As the fundamental subject of the book relates to the mystery of the Divine toleration of pain and sorrow, a chapter has been prefixed descriptive of the revealed nature, object, and relief of affliction. Since several doubts have also been raised concerning its historic veracity and the degree of its inspiration, two chapters have been added on Inductive Biblical Criticism and the Inspiration of the Sacred Scriptures.

The plan adopted has been to treat the contents of the history paraphrastically, whilst adhering as closely as possible to the meaning of the words of the sacred text, at the cost even of crudity of expression.

BOSCOMBE, 1898.

CONTENTS

	PAGE
Preface	v

PRELIMINARY CHAPTER

Affliction and its Causes	1
Introduction	22

CHAPTER I

The History of Job (chap. i. 1–5)	27

CHAPTER II

The Satanic Temptation (chap. i. 6) . . .	35
"Will man fear God for nought?"	

CHAPTER III

Job Reduced to Penury (chap. i. 11) . . .	41
"Will not man curse God on reduction to poverty?"	

CHAPTER IV

Job Exposed to Bodily Pain (chap. ii.) . . .	46
"Will not man curse God on subjection to torment?"	

CHAPTER V

The Personality of the Satan	51

CONTENTS

CHAPTER VI
The Visit of the Three Friends (Chap. ii. 11) . 56

CHAPTER VII
Job's Opening Soliloquy (Chap. iii.) 63
"Why is man born to suffering?"

CHAPTER VIII
Eliphaz's Reply to Job (Chaps. iv., v.) . . . 71

CHAPTER IX
Job's Reply to Eliphaz (Chaps. vi., vii.) . . . 78
"Why is life prolonged to the suffering?"

CHAPTER X
Bildad's Reply to Job (Chap. viii.) 87

CHAPTER XI
Job's Reply to Bildad (Chaps. ix., x.) . . . 91
"Why is unmerited suffering Divinely tolerated?"

CHAPTER XII
Zophar's Reply to Job (Chap. xi.) 101

CHAPTER XIII
Job's Reply to Zophar (Chaps. xii., xiii., xiv.) . 106
"Why do the perfect suffer as if they were wicked?"

CHAPTER XIV
Eliphaz's Second Reply to Job (Chap. xv.) . . 117

CONTENTS

CHAPTER XV
JOB'S SECOND REPLY TO ELIPHAZ (CHAPS. xvi., xvii.) . 123
"Why does God refuse man's plea for relief?"

CHAPTER XVI
BILDAD'S SECOND REPLY TO JOB (CHAP. xviii.) . . 130

CHAPTER XVII
JOB'S SECOND REPLY TO BILDAD (CHAP. xix.) . . 136
"Why does not God vindicate the perfect?"

CHAPTER XVIII
ZOPHAR'S SECOND REPLY TO JOB (CHAP. xx.) . . 142

CHAPTER XIX
JOB'S SECOND REPLY TO ZOPHAR (CHAP. xxi.) . . 146
"Why do the wicked prosper?"

CHAPTER XX
ELIPHAZ'S THIRD REPLY TO JOB (CHAP. xxii.) . . 152

CHAPTER XXI
JOB'S THIRD REPLY TO ELIPHAZ (CHAPS. xxiii., xxiv.) 159
"Why do not the perfect witness the punishment of the wicked?"

CHAPTER XXII
BILDAD'S THIRD REPLY TO JOB (CHAP. xxv.) . . 169

CHAPTER XXIII
JOB'S THIRD REPLY TO BILDAD (CHAP. xxvi. 1-4) . 173

CHAPTER XXIV
JOB'S PARABLE (CHAPS. xxvi. 5—xxxi.) . . . 178

CHAPTER XXV
JOB'S REFLECTIONS ON SHEOL AND CREATION (CHAP. xxvi. 5) 181

CHAPTER XXVI
JOB'S REFLECTION ON THE SUPERIORITY OF DIVINE WISDOM (CHAPS. xxvii., xxviii.) . . . 188

CHAPTER XXVII
JOB'S RETROSPECT OF HIS PAST LIFE (CHAPS. xxix., xxx., xxxi.) 197

CHAPTER XXVIII
THE INTERMEDIATE STATE 212

CHAPTER XXIX
THE INTERVENTION OF ELIHU (CHAP. xxxii.) . . 227

CHAPTER XXX
JOB'S SELF-RIGHTEOUSNESS (CHAP. xxxiii.) . . 231

CHAPTER XXXI
JOB'S IMPUTATION OF INJUSTICE TO GOD (CHAP. xxxiv.) 237

CHAPTER XXXII
GOD'S INDEPENDENCE OF MAN'S HELP (CHAP. xxxv.) . 244

CHAPTER XXXIII
REVELATION OF GOD'S JUSTICE (CHAP. xxxvi.) . . 248

CHAPTER XXXIV
Revelation of God's Omnipotence (Chaps. xxxvi. 26; xxxvii.) 256

CHAPTER XXXV
The Theophany (Chaps. xxxviii.—xlii.) . . . 266

CHAPTER XXXVI
Revelation of God's Omniscience (Chaps. xxxviii., xxxix.) 272

CHAPTER XXXVII
Revelation of God's Omnipotence (Chaps. xl., xli.) 288

CHAPTER XXXVIII
Recapitulation of the Problems 302

CHAPTER XXXIX
Job's Restoration to Prosperity (Chap. xlii.) . . 314

CHAPTER XL
Inductive Biblical Criticism 324

CHAPTER XLI
Inspiration of Scripture 339

THE PROBLEMS OF JOB

PRELIMINARY CHAPTER

AFFLICTION AND ITS CAUSES

The Book of Job contains a Divine revelation of the nature of affliction and its causes, and it indirectly reveals the mode in which it should be met, with a view to its alleviation. Its interpretation will be greatly elucidated by a consideration of the teaching of Holy Scripture in this respect. Since the days of Job, from the contents of the history, such knowledge is shown to have been wonderfully expanded by the revealed character of our Lord's life and example, and by His direct personal teaching. Doctrines only dimly understood by the suffering patriarch, were subsequently brought to his knowledge through the inspired lips of Elihu, and the wonderful revelations conveyed to him by the omniscient voice of Jehovah, seen by him in the Theophany. To believers in Christ, this fundamental knowledge has been yet more fully revealed through the inspired writings of the New Testament. They all reveal the one fundamental lesson, that perfected submission to the will of God is the only method whereby the assaults of Satan can be successfully met; that the fear of God and the keeping of His commandments is the whole duty of man, and that the imitation of our Lord's human example has the assured promise of eternal life; and they further reveal that all affliction either emanates from, or is tolerated by an omniscient and omnipotent personal moral Ruler, with a view to the earthly blessing or future glorification of the sufferers.

For the better understanding of the inner teaching of the history, it may be well to briefly examine what the sacred writings teach as to the nature and objects of affliction.

Holy Scripture teaches the existence of six principal sources from whence it originates, the objects for which it is imposed, and the means to be used for its alleviation. The objects may be described as being (1.) Punitive; (2.) Corrective; (3.) Protective; (4.) Vicarious or Sacrificial; (5.) Disciplinary; (6.) Altruistic.

Its causes originate from—

(1.) The wilful commission of sin, or the wilful neglect of duty.

(2.) The neglect either through inherent ignorance, or fortuitous incapability in the use of the means of grace.

(3.) The necessity of its imposition for the protection of the sufferer from future evil.

(4.) The voluntary love which the sufferers evince by the endurance of the extremes of pain and death in the relief of their fellow-men.

(5.) The importance of the perfectioning of the character through a course of discipline, to enable the sufferer to become qualified for future work in the intermediate state, or in the new heavens and the new earth.

(6.) The promotion of God's glory by the manifestation of the sufferer's disinterested love through his perfect submission to the Divine will.

Self-Examination.

In dealing with the problem of affliction, the first step for its alleviation is to discover the cause for which it has been inflicted. In its true character pain represents an instrument wherewith Christ knocks at the door, in order to draw man's attention to His desire to obtain admission into his heart. For His reception there needs a course of preparation, for "without holiness no man can see the Lord." The condition of the heart must therefore be tested, to show whether it is fitted to receive Him whose name is Holy. This calls for self-examination, which becomes the first step to discover why the affliction has been sent, witnessed by the command of the prophet, "Consider your ways," and that of St. Paul, "Examine yourselves, whether ye are living in the faith of the Gospel; test yourselves" (Hag. i. 5 ; 2 Cor. xiii. 5).

The First Cause—Punition.

The first revealed cause of affliction is personal sin, or the wilful transgression of Divine law. Adam, originally created in a state of innocence and consequent happiness, partook of the forbidden fruit, and at once became subject to suffering and to death, for "the wages of sin is death." Thus suffering, when shown to arise from the wilful commission of sin, or the wilful neglect of duty, is seen to be of a punitive character, sent with a view to the correction of the evil which has been done. This was rightly declared by Eliphaz, "Happy is the man whom God correcteth; therefore despise not thou the chastening of the Almighty, for He maketh sore, and bindeth up; He woundeth, and His hand healeth" (v. 17).

Alleviation must therefore be sought through confession, repentance, and amendment of life. This is confirmed by our Lord in the parable of the prodigal. It is the teaching of the writer of the Epistle to the Hebrews: "No chastening for the present seemeth to be joyous, but grievous; nevertheless afterward it yieldeth the peaceable fruit of righteousness to those who are exercised thereby; therefore make straight paths for your feet." The prophet Isaiah enunciates the same doctrine: "Wash you, make you clean; cease to do evil, learn to do well; if ye be willing and obedient, ye shall eat the good of the land."

The conduct must be tested by its conformity with the principles of the ten commandments, comprehended by our Lord in His two fundamental precepts, "Thou shalt love the Lord thy God with all thy heart, and thy neighbour as thyself. This do, and thou shalt live."

The Second Cause—Correction.

When on sincere self-examination the conscience does not convict the sufferer of wilful guilt, the cause of his affliction must be traced to a want of spiritual vitality or power for the right performance of his duty. It may originate in the unconscious ignorance of man's nature or unintentional remissness in the use of the means of grace, whereby the soul is exposed to loss of spiritual life and vigour. Such spiritual energy is sustained through sacramental channels, for the right use of which a knowledge of God's Word is required. This is inferred from our Lord's claim to be "the bread of life." As the bread of life He imparts Himself to the faithful recipient under three forms: in the sincere milk of the Word issuing from the breast of the mother, or the instruction of the Church; in the breaking of the one bread, or in the practical adaptation of the Word to the exigencies of life, and in the personal study of its contents, and in the sacramental feeding on the body and the blood of Christ, the strong meat of the deeper doctrines of the consummated atonement, embraced by those who have their senses exercised to discern good and evil (1 Pet. ii. 2; St. John vi. 35; vi. 51–57). To this our Lord bears witness in the warning, that "unless we eat the flesh of the Son of Man, and drink His blood, we have no life in us," together with the additional promise, that "whoso eateth His flesh and drinketh His blood has eternal life," or spiritual vitality proportioned to his daily requirements.

Elihu (xxxiii. 23) appears to reveal the importance of ministerial instruction in seasons of trial as one of the means to give the sufferer restoration to peace: "If there be an angel, or an interpreter of God's will, or one of the learned to show man in what his uprightness should consist, he shall pray for him, and God will be favourable to him." He also continues in words which contain a foreshadowing of the doctrine of the Atonement, "Then God is gracious to him, and commands intercession to be made that he should be ransomed, since a propitiation has been found."

Alleviation of the affliction may be expected by

the sufferer proportioned to his increased study of the Word of God, his greater regularity in the use of the means of grace, and his more frequent attendance on the sacraments of the Gospel, which become the tests of the earnestness of his desire for the attainment of increased energy in the performance of the duties of life.

The deliverance of Moses from the threatened danger of death was accorded to him on the recognition of his remissness in the delay of the circumcision of his son, and on his performance of that holy rite (Exod. iv. 24). The ten Samaritan or Nonconformist lepers were cured of their disease, on their obedience to our Lord's command to show themselves to His duly consecrated temple priests, at whose lips the prophet (Mal. ii. 7) was divinely inspired to show how man was "to keep knowledge, and from whose mouth he was to seek the law, as being the appointed messengers of the Lord of Hosts."

The conduct must be tested by its conformity with the laws which govern prayer, study, and worship, comprehended in our Lord's direction to ask, to seek, and to knock, to be read in union with His promise through the prophet Amos, "Seek ye Me, and ye shall live" (v. 4).

The Third Cause—Protection.

When again on sincere examination the conscience does not convict the sufferer of intentional remissness in the use of the means of grace, the affliction may be traced to its being inflicted to guard him from future evil, whereby it assumes a protective character. The victim may have gone through some great spiritual crisis, whether by being delivered from a life of sin or error, or by being vouchsafed deep revelations of a supernatural character, calculated to expose him to the danger of spiritual pride. Permanent or temporary afflictions may at times appear necessary to the Divine wisdom for the preservation of that humility which is needful to render a person submissive to the will of God.

Elihu (xxxiii. 17–30) bore testimony to the protective character of affliction, when he shows how man is chastened on his bed that his ears may be opened to instruction, and that he may be withdrawn from purposes originating in the desires of his will, and may be hidden from the dangers to which pride or spiritual exaltation may expose him. Its object is his enlightenment with the light of life, by reminding him of his past deliverances by the hand of God, and of the continual necessity for his cultivation of that humility of mind which is the essential characteristic of those to whom the most transcendent visions of the Almighty are vouchsafed. Moses, the most favoured of His servants, in being permitted to converse with God face to face, is described as the meekest of men.

Instances appear in the lives of Jacob and of Paul, who, by the shrunken sinew and the thorn in the flesh, were respectively reminded of their conversion from past sin and error, and were recipients of the wonderful visions given to them at Penuel and in Arabia. Similar in character was the protracted delay in the manifestation of our Lord's forgiveness of Peter's denial of his Master, although he had been warned beforehand of the coming Satanic temptation, the full effect of which, in open apostasy, was only averted by our Lord's prayer, that on his being sifted like wheat his faith should not fail. To this eclipse of faith possibly may be traced the reason of his incarceration by Herod, and the afflictions to which he was subjected by the Jewish Sanhedrim, culminating in martyrdom at the hands of the Roman emperor. As chosen vessels for the promotion of the knowledge of God, their subsequent afflictions reminded them of their past weakness, and at the same time made known that perfect humility was the true pathway to success in their work.

Alleviation in such cases is revealed by Paul as being attained in taking pleasure in infirmities, persecutions, and distresses for Christ's sake, whereby weakness is transmuted into strength. The conduct, therefore, must be tested by its conformity with our

Lord's direction to feed His lambs and sheep in the supply of their bodily, intellectual, and spiritual needs, supported by His assurance, through the mouth of Paul, that eternal life is promised to patient continuance in well-doing.

The Fourth Cause—Self-Sacrifice.

A fourth cause of affliction originates in the natural weakness of man's present condition, realised in the pain which accompanies his efforts to relieve the wants of others. By the fall man became exposed to loss of bodily power, of mental vigour, and of control of will, which rendered him liable to affliction, not only in the support of his own life but also in that of others. Such affliction is consequently of a vicarious or self-sacrificial nature. It should be attributed to hereditary defect, and not to any act of personal sin. In these ministrants of mercy it is borne in behalf of others. Thus the mother suffers in bringing her infant into existence; the physician imperils his life in healing the sick; the teacher suffers exhaustion in instructing the ignorant; the priest sacrifices worldly honour in converting the sinner. Even our Lord's miracles were attended by a temporary loss of physical power, witnessed in the healing of the woman with the issue (Luke viii. 46). His continuous instruction of the masses was provocative of exhaustion, seen in the deep sleep on the Galilean Lake, and His weariness at the well of Sychar, whilst the crucifixion bore the culminating witness to the awful character of the vicarious sacrifice endured by our Lord in reconciling man to His Heavenly Father. These are all instances of sacrificial suffering, which is the unavoidable accompaniment of human existence. The concluding portion of Job's last soliloquy (xxxi.), in which he reviews the efforts he made in promoting the welfare of those amongst whom he lived, is a remarkable example of such vicarious suffering.

Alleviation in such cases is revealed by the writer of the Epistle to the Hebrews, as being obtained by the contemplation of the joy set before our Lord in the redemption of the world, and of His promised elevation to the right hand of the throne of God, whereby He was humanly supported in enduring the cross and despising the shame. The apostles were sustained under the loss of the earthly blessings to which they were exposed in preaching the Gospel, by the hope of the heavenly thrones which were being prepared for them in the regeneration, whilst in the parable of the unjust steward men are encouraged to make a due use of their opportunities for vicarious sufferings in the relief of want, by being directed to look forward with joy to their future meeting in the heavenly regions with those for whose well-being they had laboured on earth.

The conduct must therefore be tested by the conformity of men's lives with the doctrine enunciated by our Lord, that all who mitigate the sufferings of their brethren are regarded by Him as having ministered to His own wants, coupled with the promise that by so doing they will become assured of the gift of eternal life.

The Fifth Cause—Discipline.

A fifth cause of affliction is found in its being sent for purposes of discipline in the perfecting of the character for future work, not only in this world but also in the future stages of existence through which men may have to pass to render them fit for the enjoyment of the Beatific Vision. This is witnessed in our Lord's training under the restraint of the cradle, the instruction of the school, and the work of the shop. By such afflictive training He became fitted for the Divine call to the ministry at the Jordanic Baptism, for the plenary, visible, and abiding unction of the Holy Spirit, and for the announcement of His appointment to the Prophetic office through the audible voice of the Divine Father. Our Lord's afflictive training continued during the whole period of His abode in the flesh, until His sufferings were terminated by His sacrificial death upon the cross. This perfectioning of His human character, through learning obedience by the things which He suffered, enabled Him to become the author of eternal salvation to all them that obey Him.

The necessity of such training in believers is taught by our Lord's words, that whosoever would come after Him must voluntarily deny himself, and submissively take up the punitive cross imposed upon him for his offences, and faithfully follow Him in the imitation of His life. By such afflictive training man, like his Divine Master, becomes daily more qualified for the hour of death, to commence the work prepared for him in the Intermediate State. While our Lord's body rested in the grave His human soul, quickened by the Spirit, went and preached to the spirits in prison—to those who beforetime were disobedient in the days of Noah. The existence of work in Hades and its character are thus clearly revealed. It consisted in the arousing the impenitent departed to listen to the Saviour's loving call to conversion, and to reconciliation with their Heavenly Father. The preaching of the gospel to the departed in Hades is made known to us by the apostle St. Peter as well as its object, that "they might be judged according to men in the flesh, and that they should live according to God in the Spirit." Their judgment appears to be the same as that by which those, who have been converted during their earthly existence, will be judged. Their subsequent life is to be of a spiritual character, and in accordance with the revealed will of God.

Such are the subject and the object of the preaching to the departed in Hades. But by whom is this carried on? Is there not great reason for believing that this is the work of departed saints? Such is shown to be the work of Abraham in the history of Dives and Lazarus. It is of a similar character with that of the departed witnesses or martyrs pleading, from beneath the altar of sacrifice, that their blood should be avenged or compensated for by the conversion of those by whom they were injured or slain, and that a white robe of acquittal should be given to each of those for whom they interceded. The ordinary interpretation that they desire the death of their slayers is utterly opposed to our Lord's command to forgive and to pray for our persecutors. These holy departed saints had already received their own white robes of acquittal witnessed by their inward assurance of forgiveness and acceptance. The work of the elect departed saints in Hades appears to be that of their Divine Master and of the holy occupants of the millennial thrones; worship, intercession, preaching, and ruling are their revealed occupation. As priestly intercessors they plead for the conversion of the impenitent in Hades. As prophetic rulers they preach to them the laws of the eternal kingdom, and govern them according to their precepts. Affliction is thus shown to have a disciplinary character to train men for their future work in the Hadean and Heavenly as well as in the Earthly sphere (Rev. vi.).

Alleviation under such affliction will be proportioned to the conformity of the life with the principles of our Lord's command, to sell that we have and to distribute to the poor, to deny ourselves in the pleasures of this life, and to patiently endure the punishment of the crosses imposed upon us for sins, with a view to the right training of ourselves in the use of the treasure which will be committed to our trust in the heavenly home.

The Sixth Cause—Altruistic.

A sixth cause of affliction, which is of an altruistic character, or vicarious suffering, either directly inflicted or indirectly permitted for the promotion of God's glory, is that which forms the fundamental doctrine of the history. It is similar in kind to the account of the death of Lazarus, in which our Lord delayed the display of His miraculous power, in order that, by permitting the sickness to terminate fatally, He might at the end of four days be able to manifest His almighty authority over death itself by the raising of His friend, and thereby make known to the family He loved, and to the Jews present on the occasion of His summoning Lazarus out of the grave, as well as to all succeeding ages, His omnipotent character as the resurrection and the life—the raiser and the life-giver. Thus the sorrow which attended the death was transmuted into the ineffable joy that was caused by His assurance, "Whoso is believing in Me, though he had died, yet he shall live; and every one who is living and is believing in Me shall never die." Therefore Death loses its sting, and Hades its victory.

On a second occasion, when He healed a man born blind, whom He acquitted of any personal sin, either on his own part or that of his parents, our Lord gave as the reason that such sufferer had been specially elected in order that the works of God should be made manifest in him, by enabling Him to show that not only organic defects, but also diseases utterly incurable by man, were subject to the will and power of Jesus for their removal.

In the case of Job a far deeper mystery was revealed, for the instruction not only of the human race, but also of the heavenly hosts. Job was selected as the man through whose reduction to penury and disease were revealed the doctrines of the existence of a personal Satan, of his bitter hostility to man's happiness, of his wonderful power of interference with human events and mundane occurrences, and of the Divinely imposed impassible limitations of his baneful influence, together with a further revelation that through a firm faith on the Divine assistance man is capable of resisting all his incitement to apostacy from his allegiance to his Creator.

The corroboration of the existence and character of altruistic suffering and distress is witnessed in the events of our Lord's human life when exposed to bodily pain from the crown of thorns and the soldier's scourge, to the pangs of sorrow over the world's impenitence, to the temptation to sin from the lips of the Satan, and finally to the unjustifiable condemnation to the punishment of crucifixion, on the false accusation of His being a blasphemer under the Jewish law, and a malefactor obnoxious to Roman law, to all which He patiently submitted, in order that "through death He might destroy him that had the power of death, that is, the devil, and deliver them who through fear of death were all their lifetime subject to the bondage" that accompanies the sense of unforgiven sin. But in either case the glory of God was manifested in the deliverance of the sufferers respectively from organic defect, bodily disease, and the embrace of death. By the resurrection of Jesus Christ from the grave, and His ascension into heaven, the restoration of fallen man to the forfeited Paradise was assured, together with his right to the tree of life, and to enter in through the gates into the city.

The method whereby our Lord was sustained, in bearing His unutterable altruistic sufferings on behalf of man, is witnessed in the words with which He addressed His Heavenly Father on the occurrence of a visit from certain Greeks, typical of those members of the human race who have not as yet been admitted into the kingdom of God. Their advent was the sign of His recognition of the approach of the hour when the Son of Man should be glorified. He shows how the burial of the seed-corn in the earth was essential to the growth of the plant, by giving power of expansion to the living germ. He teaches how the burial of His human body was essential to enable His quickened spirit to emerge from its earthly tenement, to bring forth fruit in the living members of the mystic and spiritual body of the Church, of which He is the glorified Head. Contemplating His approaching sacrifice He recognises that it is the cause of His glorification, according to His sublimely disinterested prayer, "Father, glorify Thy name," to which a voice from heaven was accorded, "I have both glorified it and will glorify it again." Glorified the Father's name had been through life in our Lord's altruistic sufferings attendant on His incarnation; and it was to be glorified again by His restoration to the glory which He had with the Father before the world was.

Alleviation under such altruistic suffering will be proportioned to the conformity of the life to the principle of obedience which governed every action of our Lord's human existence, in His readiness for self-sacrifice in the promoting of God's glory, coupled also with the promise, obedience to which is the test of right conduct, that "he which hateth his life in this world shall keep it unto life eternal." "In your endurance ye shall win your lives."

Affliction is too often regarded as originating from bodily and mental causes, without sufficient attention being given to the spiritual lessons, to which it is Divinely intended that the minds of the suffering should be directed. The miracle of the healing of the palsied man, borne by his four companions into the presence of Jesus, and the method of his cure, enunciates the doctrine, that in cases of affliction originating in the act of personal transgression, remission of sin in its twofold sense of deliverance from its guilt and from its power is the primal step to place the sufferer in a position to commence a new life of renovated capability for the performance of earthly duty. The first words of our Lord were "Son, thy sins have been remitted to thee." On the expression of anger excited in the minds of the bystanders at our Lord's claim to remit sin, He shows that the exercise of His authority in its remission is co-existent with that of His power to raise man from the bondage of weakness, and thereby to give capability for the future carrying out of his work in life.

In all cases of affliction a strict examination into the conduct should therefore be made, in order that the spiritual reason for the infliction of the suffering should be discovered. Affliction is equally traceable to bodily derangement, mental disturbance, and spiritual disquiet. The reproaches of conscience are provocative of unrest of mind, and the two are equally destructive of health of body. Each separate case requires to be accurately diagnosed and spiritually treated with a view to its alleviation. The ordained minister is equally needed with the Christian friend, the intellectual adviser and the learned physician. St. James, under inspiration, has revealed the Divine method whereby alleviation may be obtained under affliction, whether bodily, mental, or spiritual: "Is any afflicted? let him pray. Is any weak among you? let him call for the elders of the church, and let them pray over him, having anointed him with oil in the name of the Lord; and the official prayer of the faith, or of the Catholic Church, will save the sick, and the Lord will raise him up; and even if he should have committed sin it shall be remitted to him. Confess, therefore, your faults one to another, and pray in behalf of one another, that ye may be healed. The energising supplication of a righteous man availeth much" (Jas. v. 14–16.)

These prefatory remarks have been affixed to the following treatise on the Book of Job, in order to draw attention to the practical bearing of its teaching. It is too often read under a mere academic aspect, without regard to the danger which often attends neglect in the observance of these rules of conduct in cases of affliction often ending in chronic weakness, prolonged misery, or even premature death. Our Lord, however, told His disciples that "all things must be fulfilled which were written in the law of Moses, and in the Prophets, and in the Psalms or Hagiographa concerning Himself," of which last section the Book of Job, even in His days, formed a part (Luke xxiv. 44). The mental sufferings recorded in the Book of Job represent the problems by which the human mind of our Lord was tormented under affliction, submission to which formed one of the tests of His perfected humanity. The before-mentioned causes, with their attendant methods for alleviation, represent the inner workings of His human soul under the fierce ordeal. Job's temptations were typical of those of Christ, and are recorded for the support of His followers when similarly afflicted. In this lies the value of this inspired history of a real well-known man, whose endurance under Satanic temptation has been related for the encouragement of all similarly exposed to trials on earth, in Hades, or in the Heavenlies.

INTRODUCTION

THE Book of Job professes to be a Divine revelation explanatory of the mystery which accompanies human suffering. It contains a series of problems which present themselves to the mind of man, originating in the apparently unmerited suffering endured by a most holy and exemplary patriarch.

The question had been raised in the Presence Chamber of the Almighty in the heavenlies, "whether man would fear God for nought?" This is the fundamental problem for the solution of which Job was successively reduced to penury and exposed to physical suffering. The words which the extremity of his misery extorted from his lips represent the various thoughts which arose in his mind, in relation to the causes why the existence of suffering was divinely permitted in the life of one who felt that, to the best of his power, he had endeavoured to regulate his conduct in accordance with the will of God. The replies which were given to his remarks by his three friends show the ordinary reasons, which are advanced by different classes of mankind to account for the existence of suffering.

These are typical men, who, from different standpoints, draw the same conclusion, that suffering is the result of personal sin. They represent the well-to-do man of earthly position, the cold philosophic reasoner, and the superficial talkative man of the world. Their failure to solve the difficulty calls forth the intervention of a man of higher spiritual attainments, who, claiming to speak under direct inspiration from the Almighty, shows that the inability of man to arrive at the perfect knowledge of God precludes the exercise of his right to impugn the righteousness or mercy of any of His acts, both of which will, at the proper moment, be vindicated by the manifestation of His power and justice in the permanent removal of affliction from those who fear Him. In attestation of the truth of this pronouncement, the voice of Jehovah is heard out of the whirlwind directing the attention of Job to the irresistible power and wisdom of God evidenced in the processes of natural order, and indicative of the immeasurable folly of attempting to contend with God, or to dispute the rectitude of His operations either in the universe, or in the life of the individual. Suffering for which no rational cause can be suggested is thus revealed as being a part of the Divine economy, and as such should be patiently endured, in the full assurance that whilst its cause may not be discovered, yet the wisdom of God in its toleration will ultimately be vindicated. Thus an impatient desire for the solution of the problems which it excites in the human mind is realised as being incompatible with the limited knowledge possessed by man of the omnipotence of Jehovah.

In the presence of the revealed omniscience of God, Job's self-justification vanished, and was replaced by the deepest contrition and self-abasement for presuming to question the righteousness of the Almighty in the permission of suffering, the severity of which had appeared undeserved in one who had conscientiously striven to serve God aright. The mystery was moreover to be cleared in the publication of the history, and in the revelation of the spiritual problem, which had been the original cause whereby Job had been exposed to the Satanic temptation. By Job's refusal to curse God it was clearly shown that man was capable of serving God independently of the hope of temporal reward, although, through the weakness of his human nature, he might give utterance to hasty and ill-advised words. The Son of Man was alone able to render all perfect submission to the will of God, "He who did no sin, neither was guile found in His mouth, who, when He was reviled, reviled not again; when He suffered He threatened not; but committed Himself to Him who judgeth righteously." All other men owing to their human infirmity can only approximate to such perfection, but, like Job, they may still adhere to faith in God's love and to allegiance to His rule.

God's dealings with men on earth are here revealed as having a wider sphere of operation than that which is restricted to the mundane system. They are amongst the things which the angels desire to look into, and until the victory of man over Satan is completed through his personal union with his ascended Lord, the toleration of suffering originating in the devices of Satan will remain an unsolved mystery. Many centuries have passed since God revealed to Moses, that though man may see His back parts, yet His face cannot be seen without peril to life, or in other words, that while the revelation of God's work is recognised in what is past, the object and motives of His present operations remain hidden (Exod. xxxiii. 23). "Man walks by faith, not by sight." The agony may be sharp and prolonged, but in due time God's love and wisdom will be fully vindicated by the restoration of the faithful sufferer to reduplicated earthly prosperity, as in the case of Job, or else to the heavenly satisfaction of his soul, as in the case of the all-righteous Servant of Jehovah, whose outpouring of His life upon the cross procured the fruition of the reward for His earthly mission in the justification and salvation of all those who accept Him as their Redeemer.

The Book of Job may be divided into three divisions, and these again into seven parts:—

I. The first division contains the history of Job, and is immediately followed by that of the angelic assembly in the heavenly Presence Chamber of Jehovah.

II. The second division contains the account of the visit of the three friends, and the subject of the discussion between them and Job, followed by the intervention of Elihu. It probably relates to the events of one day.

III. The third division contains the revelation of a Theophany, and is followed by the restoration of Job to his former condition of health and happiness.

The seven parts are :—
1. The history of Job.
2. The revelation of the Satanic temptation.
3. The visit of Job's three friends.
4. The intervention of Elihu.
5. The voice of Jehovah from the whirlwind.
6. The submission of Job.
7. His acceptance by Jehovah, and his restoration of prosperity.

CHAPTER I

THE HISTORY OF JOB

(CHAP. i. 1-5.)

THE writing should not be regarded as a biography, but only a history of certain selected events which took place in the life of a man who, by the blamelessness of his conduct and the earthly prosperity with which he had in consequence been Divinely rewarded, had incurred the enmity of the Satan or the apostate spiritual accuser of man in the Presence Chamber of the Almighty. The fact of Job's existence is attested by the prophet Ezekiel (xiv. 14) and by St. James (v. 11), "the servant of God and of the Lord Jesus Christ," by both of whom he is referred to as an historic personage. Ezekiel associates him with Noah and Daniel as the most prevalent intercessors with the Lord God in times of universal desolation, of national apostacy, and of individual misery in virtue of their personal righteousness. St. James classes him with the prophets, who have spoken in the name of the Lord, as an example of endurance in suffering unmerited evil, and of patience.

The record opens with the affirmation that "There

was a man in the land of Uz, and that his name was Job." The theory that the book is only a religious fiction impugns the veracity of the prophet and of the writer of the epistle. Outside the book itself and the two passages referred to nothing more in Scripture is known of his history.

The meaning of his name Job, the "one exposed to hatred," as is common in the use of Scripture names, may be considered emblematical of the object of the writing, suggestive of its internal claims to inspiration, and to admission into the Canon of Scripture. It seems intended to reveal to man the spiritual support and consolation whereby he may be enabled to sustain the apparently unmerited sufferings, to which his earthly existence is at times exposed, and to refer their true origin to the hostility of the Satanic opponent of man's happiness.

The home of Job was in the land of Uz, a name probably derived from that of the son of Aram and grandson of Shem (Gen. x. 23). Its locality may, therefore, be placed in some portion of Syria, which, from the contents of the history, was remarkable for a high state of civilisation, the intellectual attainments of its educated classes, the religious character of its people, and the recognised worship of God. The purity of the Noachical faith had not there been corrupted by the worship of the other gods, to which the progenitors of Abraham had fallen victims, though the existence elsewhere of the

Chaldean nature cult of the heavenly hosts may be inferred from the words of Job, xxxi. 26.

The period when Job lived may possibly be discovered in the name of one of his friends, Eliphaz, the Temanite, or the Southerner, expressive of the Edomitish home of the son of Esau (Gen. xxxvi. 11). Under the supposition that Eliphaz was the son of Esau, Job would have been cotemporary with the patriarchs Isaac, Esau, Jacob and his sons, and possibly with Abraham, whose conversion from the fire worship of Ur of the Chaldees may thus be traceable, under the Divine superintendence, to his recognition of the greater purity of the patriarchal worship of Job in the other division of the land of Syria.

The two names of these divisions of Syria may be emblematic of the two forms of ancient patriarchal worship. That of Ur, or Light, would represent the materialistic fire worship of the Chaldees originating in the traditional remembrance of the Shekinah of glory, the visible memorial of the presence of Jehovah at the gates of Eden in the Antediluvian age. That of Uz, or counsel, would represent the true worship of God, based upon wise advice or counsel in recognising the invisible glory of God, even His eternal power and Godhead by means of the things which He has created. The contemplation of created matter necessarily leads to the worship of a Creator in all those whose minds are not devoid of counsel and knowledge, which are the peculiar attributes of those upon whom the spirit of Jehovah rests.

From the mention of Rahab, an ancient name for Egypt, in two of Job's replies to his friends, a later date appears also possible as representing the period when he lived (ix. 13; xxvi. 12). He alludes to the wounding of Rahab, and the piercing of the fleeing serpent by the direct intervention of the hand of God (Ps. lxxxvii. 4; Isa. li. 9). These expressions appear to refer to the overthrow of Pharaoh and his hosts in the Red Sea, for the fleeing serpent is revealed by the prophets as being another emblem under the form of the crocodile of the Egyptian devil worship (Isa. xxvii. 1; Ezek. xxxii. 2). Under this supposition Job would appear to have lived at the time of the Exodus, when great advances had been made in the civilisation of the East, not only in Egypt and Assyria, but also in Edom, to the wisdom of whose elders and the extensive commerce of its trading caravans several allusions are also made in the sacred writings (vi. 19; Jer. xlix. 7).

The history proceeds with the description of Job's character. "He was perfect, or blameless and upright, fearing God and turning from evil." These four qualities represent the principles by which his life was regulated. Such conduct was attended with its normal result in the earthly prosperity which accompanies "growth in wisdom and in favour with God and man." He was blessed with a large and united family, having seven sons and three daughters. His wealth in flocks and herds, and his extensive household, caused him to be regarded as the greatest of the men of the East or of the former patriarchs. The social and domestic life of his family was witnessed in the intercourse by which the mutual love of its members was sustained. His sons feasted each one in his day, and sent for their sisters to unite in their festivity. It was further sanctified by a strict attention to their religious duties, evidenced by the purity of their worship of God, and the weekly burnt offerings, which Job, as the priestly head of the clan, offered for the purification of any secret reproaches against the Divine will, which might have been called forth by the events of their current lives.

In the worldly prosperity of Job was witnessed the nearest revealed approximation to that uninterrupted happiness which would presumably have been the inheritance of man, had not Adam caused its forfeiture by eating of the fruit of the forbidden tree. Since that unhappy moment, experience however shows that right conduct is not invariably attended with earthly success, and one of the objects of the history is to account for this apparent infraction of natural law, by revealing the invisible, spiritual influences which at times interfere with its general action. For this purpose it was necessary that the biography should be that of a well-known historic personage, one who had actually experienced the temptations and trials therein related. The supposititious words of an imaginary sufferer would not carry the same weight as those of one who had in his own person endured the affliction.

One of the objects of the incarnation of the Divine Word, whereby our Lord has prevailed to establish His supremacy over the mind of man, was to enable Him to appeal to His own sufferings, as a plea to encourage men in their endurance of those to which they themselves are exposed. "Having Himself suffered being tempted, He is able to succour them that are tempted." To treat therefore the Book of Job as a mere dramatic poem is destructive of its influence, and reduces the problems which it contains to the commonplace platitudes of some philosophic or poetic mind, in the exclusion of the traditional view that they are the actual agonised utterances of one pressed above measure, and incapable of finding relief through the ordinary channels of human consolation, but who, under the spiritual instruction of an inspired teacher, corroborated by the voice of Jehovah out of the whirlwind, is led to realise, in the contemplation of natural order, that the operations of the Almighty in the spiritual as well as the natural sphere, are beyond the range of the human intellect to be fully understood. These utterances, as all others contained in the Sacred Scriptures, must therefore have been imparted to the mind of the writer of the history under the direct guidance of the Holy Spirit, without whose Divine inspiration he would have been incapable of committing to writing, as matters of fact, events or words which had not occurred or had not been spoken in his presence. Except under such inspired direction, the ascription of words to the Almighty, expressive only of the thoughts of the writer, becomes an act of presumption. None can with truth dare to say "God said," excepting those unto whom the word of God has actually been revealed.

The events recorded appear to have extended over several months, and the accompanying dialogues are generally supposed to have been only an infinitesimal selection of numberless other actual utterances. If this theory be correct, such selection must also have been made under the same direct inspiration of the Holy Spirit, who was the alone witness of some of these events, and therefore alone cognisant of the words which were then uttered. Who but an inspired writer would have allowed his imagination to conceive the toleration of the Satan in the Presence Chamber of the Almighty? or who but such an one would have been permitted to reveal the Satan as publicly challenging the integrity of the holy patriarch before the assembled sons of God in the heavenlies? The subsequent dramatising of heavenly mysteries by modern poets is but an imitative development of imaginary ideas, of which the history of Job is the Divine original.

The prolongation of the discussion, however, over many days appears doubtful. The true solution seems to show that it commenced and was concluded on one day, and was immediately followed by the Theophany; but of this later.

CHAPTER II

THE SATANIC TEMPTATION

(CHAP. i. 6.)

Problem—"Will man fear God for nought?"

THE Satanic temptation is divided into two sections. It witnesses to the existence of three distinct though kindred problems, arising out of the Divine toleration of suffering in man, for which no adequate cause can be suggested in the cases of those who have conscientiously regulated their lives in accordance with their knowledge of the will of God.

These problems are—

I. "Will man fear God for nought?"

II. Will he not curse or reproach God on being reduced to a state of abject penury?

III. Will he not equally curse God when exposed to the extremes of bodily pain and disease?

The first of these is the fundamental problem for the solution of which the history appears to have been written. The remaining two represent respectively subsidiary aspects of the same problem in its action upon the mind and body of the sufferer. They find a counterpart in our Lord's temptation, related only in reverse order. The closing offer of the kingdom of the world by the tempter necessarily carried with it the two antecedent offers of the supply of bodily support and the grant of intellectual position, analogous to the bodily suffering and lost secular pre-eminence of the holy patriarch.

For the solution of these problems the history is transferred from the sphere of earthly events to that of heavenly mysteries. "There was a day when the sons of God came to present themselves before Jehovah, and the Satan also came amongst them." This is a revelation of the worship of the angelic orders before God, and of the then unforfeited permission which had been granted to the Satan to accuse man of his failure of duty before the throne of Jehovah, prior to his final expulsion out of heaven at the ascension of the glorified Son of Man (Rev. xii.). The Sons of God appear to be one of the highest of the angelic orders (xxxviii. 7). They are named by the Almighty as witnesses of the creation of the earth, uniting with another celestial order, that of the Morning Stars, in hymning His praises on this marvellous manifestation of His omnipotence. An earlier record, which had been divinely collated by Moses, reveals how some of their number, forsaking their first estate through lust for the earthly, intermarried with the daughters of men, whereby they exposed themselves to reservation in invisible chains under darkness unto the judgment of the great day. This Divine revelation gives a wonderful insight into the intimate, though now to man invisible, intercourse that exists between heaven and earth by means of the angelic hosts, so long before revealed in vision to Jacob at Bethel of the ladder set upon earth whose top reached to the heavens. This scene is recorded as having actually occurred in the heavenlies, and consequently it could only be made known to man under the direct inspiration of the Spirit of God. To treat this narrative as a work of human imagination is destructive of faith in the records of all unseen heavenly mysteries universally accepted as inspired.

Wonderful, indeed, are the truths revealed in the history. Notwithstanding the existence of the millions of responsible beings with which the earth is peopled, it is shown that not one individual escapes the recognition of the all-seeing eye of God. His character, his conduct, and his inner motives are known to his Creator. God's words to the Satan affirm this truth. " Hast thou considered my servant Job, that there is none like him, perfect and upright, fearing God and turning from evil ? " The Satan, fresh from going to and fro in the earth, at once challenges the disinterestedness of Job's motives. " Doth Job fear God for nought ? " This is the primary problem of the writing. The true character and continuous malice of the Satan is revealed as the personal accuser of man before God. The doctrine of the personality of the Satan is placed on the same assured foundation as that of the faithful and holy Sons of God, amongst whom he came into the Presence Chamber of the Almighty.

The doctrine of an impersonal malign influence tempting man to sin is neither inconsistent with reason, nor with the revealed energising of the Satan, provided his actual personality is admitted, as the principal source from which it emanates. It is simply one of the modes by which the personal Satan carries out his evil designs against man. But when an impersonal malign influence is represented as acting upon Jehovah, productive of suffering to man, such a theory would impugn His love or His omnipotence. "God cannot be tempted with evil, or is incapable of temptation by what is bad, neither tempteth He any man by what is evil." Yet man is often tempted by the direct permission of God, as in the case of Abraham. Such temptation does not, however, spring from a malign influence. Its origin and object are the promotion of increased blessing for the sufferer.

The doctrine of the personality of the Satan affords a reason to account for the toleration by God of Job's suffering. The Satan had raised the question of Job's disinterestedness, affirming that the loss of physical health and worldly wealth would provoke him to apostatise. Such a question, raised by a personal opponent of God, could best be answered by exposing the subject to the trial of his faith under suffering. Such trial must not be limited to the case of Job. Its force embraces the entire human race. The problem is, "Will man serve God for nought?" It was propounded by the arch opponent of God and the enemy of mankind. A practical solution was required. It was granted in the exposure of the most perfect and the greatest of the sons of the East, or of former times, to the fiery ordeal. Notwithstanding many hasty expressions of astonishment and indignation at God's toleration of his apparently unmerited sufferings, Job's faith in His wisdom, and admission of God's right to do all things according to His own will, remained unshaken. Whilst retaining the conviction of his integrity under the sharpest inducements to apostatise, Job never wavered in his allegiance to God. He boldly stated that he considered "the denial of God to be iniquity, punishable by the judges" (xxxi. 28). Thus God's omnipotence was vindicated in the formation of an intelligent being, endowed with the faculty of free will, yet in the midst of the acutest affliction capable of retaining faith in his Maker's love and wisdom, to make all things work together for good in those who love Him. Job's answer to the Satanic challenge, and his disinterested obedience to the will of God, are realised in his words, "Shall we receive good at the hand of God, and shall we not receive evil?"

These words are the expression of his full reliance on the wisdom of the Almighty, and of his implicit willingness to submit himself to the Divine Will. They are Job's unconscious answer to the challenge of Satan, and its arrogant author was subjected to defeat by Job's submissive endurance of the most aggravated suffering.

CHAPTER III

JOB REDUCED TO PENURY

(CHAP. i. 11.)

Problem—" Will not man curse God on reduction to poverty?"

THE problem, raised by the Satan, was placed before the sons of God in the heavenlies under two definite forms. At first, the Satan asked that Job's disinterestedness should be tested by his reduction to a state of penury. He pointed out how the happy result of his work, and the vast increase of his wealth, was due to the protection and blessing of God, and affirmed that on their withdrawal, attended with the loss of his earthly pre-eminence, Job would "curse or reproach God to His face," expressive of apostacy from the allegiance which is due from man to his Maker. To show the fallacy of the Satan's assertion, and to prove that man is capable of retaining faith in God when subjected to the greatest earthly loss, the possessions of Job were delivered into the hands of the Satan, limited, however, by the injunction that his person should remain inviolate.

Upon this the Satan went forth from the Divine

presence to carry out his evil purpose. His departure was shortly followed by malicious action. By four successive attacks the vast wealth of Job was scattered, and his family destroyed in the overthrow of the house in which they lived, by the simoon or the desert wind. The Cushite Sabeans captivated his oxen and asses. The lightning from heaven burnt up his sheep, and three bands of the Syrian Chaldees carried away his camels. His numerous servants were consumed by these respective destructions, with the exception of a single survivor in each class, reserved to convey the message of desolation to the bereaved patriarch. Stroke followed stroke in appalling rapidity. Before the first messenger had finished his tale of woe, he was followed by the others in immediate succession, so that within the space of a few hours the greatest man of former days was reduced to a state of abject poverty.

The Satanic opponent of God and man was, however, foiled in his expectation. Job, neither by act or word, betrayed unfaith in God's love or failed in submission to His will. The clothing himself with the signs of mourning was followed by an act of adoring worship in his prostration on the ground, and his lowly words witnessed to his mental resignation to the hand of God, "Naked came I out of my mother's womb, and naked shall I return thither; the Lord gave, and the Lord hath taken away;

blessed be the name of the Lord." These words represent the mental condition of Job during the protracted interval that elapsed between this and the second gathering together of the Sons of God in the Presence Chamber of Jehovah, when his Satanic foe asked for an extension of his power to expose Job to intense personal suffering.

The length of his trial through poverty is nowhere recorded before it was intensified by that which followed. Job's utterances give frequent intimations that it was of long continuance. He speaks of the hedging in of his way by God. He mournfully compares the present incapability to which he was condemned by the loss of worldly riches and secular position, with his former honourable opportunities in the relief of the poor, the defence of the oppressed, and his wise counselling of the nobles who consulted him in their social difficulties. He sadly contrasts the insolent treatment which he experienced from the very outcasts of society, with the honour in which he was held by the surrounding princes. The keenest sorrows which accompany the loss of wealth and eminence are realised by the good in the restriction of their power and influence to promote the welfare of their fellow-men. This was one of Job's sharpest trials: "If I have withheld from the poor his desires; if I have feared a great multitude, and kept silence in restraining them from evil, then let my land cry out against me, and let thistles grow instead of wheat." With such words he ended his defence, resigning himself into the hands of his Heavenly Father.

The solution of the problem is accompanied with the revelation of many hidden mysteries. It is thereby disclosed that earthly prosperity is regulated by the will of God. The good man and all his possessions are fenced around by the Divine protection. His work is rendered successful and productive by the Divine blessing. Except by the permission of God no harm can happen to himself or his belongings. For wise purposes the Divine restraint may be withdrawn for a time, but the injury so permitted is always restricted within definite limits. The action of Satanic influence in the disturbance of social events is clearly revealed in the hidden causes of Job's earthly ruin, tolerated, but at the same time limited, by the Divine will. They are indicative of the doctrine that to the same Satanic influences man is still universally exposed, both in his individual and social life. As a relation of facts which have actually occurred, the history explains many an otherwise insoluble mystery, and is calculated to give comfort and support to all who may be exposed to losses for which no adequate causes may be assigned. But as a work of simple imagination, emanating only from the mind of man, it will be of little assured efficacy to strengthen the faith of any so suffering in the wisdom and love of God, so as to enable them to resign themselves in the spirit of Job into His hands. Unless composed under the plenary inspiration of the Holy Spirit, so precise a statement, professing to reveal the concealed realities of the heavenly regions and the secret reasons actuating the Divine purposes, becomes an act of human conceit, and takes rank only with the poetic dreams of Milton or Dante, excited by the perusal of the Book of Job, from which they probably acquired their subsequent ideas.

CHAPTER IV

JOB EXPOSED TO BODILY PAIN

(CHAP. ii.)

Problem—" Will not man curse God on subjection to torment ? "

AFTER a lengthened interval another presentation of the Sons of God before the throne of Jehovah is revealed, at which also the Satan is again permitted to appear. After the Lord's inquiry into the Satan's earthly work, the conduct of Job under his bitter deprivation of worldly prosperity is again submitted to his consideration, " Hast thou considered my servant Job, that there is none like him in the earth, perfect and upright, fearing God, and turning from evil, who, notwithstanding his exposure to the loss of earthly wealth, has still held fast to his integrity of conduct ? " The Satan then alleges that man will sacrifice anything for the preservation of life; that to protect his own skin from suffering, he will yield up the skin or body of any one over whom he may be possessed of protective power; and that he will sacrifice the happiness and comfort of any other to preserve himself from bodily evil. He insinuates that the death of his children, and the slaughter of his servants, may have been regarded by Job with stoical indifference in the consideration of his own personal deliverance from the hand of the destroyer.

The Satan then propounds a second test, "Touch his bone and his flesh, and he will curse or reproach Thee to Thy face," evidenced by apostacy or the denial of allegiance to the Divine will. The challenge is again accepted by the Almighty. "Behold he is in thy hand, but his life must be preserved inviolate." Again the Satan departs to carry out his evil purpose, and he smites Job with the fearful leprous boils which accompany elephantiasis, the worst form of Eastern leprosy. The intensity of his sufferings is manifested in the remedy to which he has recourse. On Job's loss of wealth he appears to have been reduced to such an extremity of poverty that his habitation had become that of one of the poorest class, with its attendant Metzbele, or heap of ashes for the deposition of all the refuse with which such dwellings were accompanied. These ash-heaps appear to have been used by the ancient lepers as places where they sat for the removal of the leprous ulcers, and the application of the sun-dried ashes of which they were composed to allay the irritation of the disease. This recorded event shows that a prolonged period had been passed by Job before the infliction of the second temptation to render such heap available for the purpose.

The history of the disease by modern writers witnesses to the sufferings to which the lepers are exposed. The utterances of Job are full of expressions in which its character and attendant pains are pointed out. His longing for death, his continuous sighs, and his roaring extorted by the excruciating pain, are vividly revealed in his first recorded monologue, after the agonised silence of his friends had witnessed to their utter inability to comfort him under his grief. He compares the action of the disease to that of the poisoned arrow, productive of the awful terrors of expected severer tortures as death became imminent (vi. 4). He describes the painful constriction of the skin, succeeded by its becoming cracked, whilst these multiplying wounds become the abode of the evolving worms and of the irritating dust. His nights are rendered sleepless through agony, and the short intermittent intervals of rest are scared by horrible visions, one of the many miseries which accompany this terrible malady (vii. 4, 14; ix. 17). The horrors of his position are intensified by his isolation from man, caused by their dread of infection, and of witnessing the hideous appearance of the loathsome sores and the victim's painful sufferings. Again and again does he plead for death, which continuously appears to evade his grasp.

A fresh motive to apostatise from the will of God is suggested when his wife appears to have counselled suicide as a relief from his agony: "Dost thou still retain faith in the value of thine integrity?" She exhorts him to "curse God and die," presumably by his own hand. This seems to be the climax of his trial, that the wife of his bosom should counsel unfaith in God, and this also urged upon him from motives of the greatest human love in her desire for his release from pain. Had Job succumbed to the temptation the Satan would have been triumphant, for suicide is the denial of a Heavenly Father's love. The patriarch's faith was, however, proof against the temptation. Job reveals the true character of suicide in his rebuke of his wife's suggestion, "Thou speakest as one of the vile women." To sacrifice eternal life for the preservation of earthly existence is one of the sins of the flesh, for it is a corruption of the temple of the Holy Spirit. "Know ye not," says St. Paul, "that your body is the temple of the Holy Spirit?"

Job then proceeds to reveal the inner steadfastness of his faith: "Shall we receive good at the hand of God, and shall we not receive evil?" This was the thought which sustained him through the whole trial. He recognised that, however his sufferings appeared to be unmerited, they were directed by the hand of an all-wise and an Almighty God, whose word was to be obeyed, and to whose will submission was to be rendered. The extremity of his suffering was often provocative of language that testified to angry impatience, bordering at times on arrogant presumption; yet, even in his most tried moments, he never lost his trust in God. The underlying principle of his life in every moment of his temptation is revealed in his words, "Though He slay me, yet will I trust in Him." His trust was grounded on his assured conviction that "the fear of the Lord was wisdom, and that to depart from evil was understanding" (xiii. 15; xxviii. 28).

CHAPTER V

THE PERSONALITY OF THE SATAN

On his departure from the presence of Jehovah to afflict Job with the extremes of bodily suffering, all further mention of the Satan disappears from the writing. His introduction into the history appears to have had for its object the revelation of his assured personality, and of the malignant character of his operations in the heavenly as well as in the earthly sphere. These two doctrines are affirmed in the original record of the fall, where he is represented as assuming the form of a serpent, verified by the revelation given by God to Jesus Christ, and also by St. Paul, for the purpose of deceiving Eve to take of the fruit from the forbidden tree of the knowledge of good and evil (2 Cor. xi. 3). The prophet Isaiah (xxvii. 1) speaks of him as the Leviathan, the fleeing and perverted serpent, the dragon in the sea, whose destruction as the devil, by being cast into the lake burning with fire and brimstone, is also revealed in the Apocalypse (xx. 10). In the vision of Zechariah (iii.) the typical high priest Joshua is seen standing before the angel of Jehovah, and the Satan standing at his right hand, to accuse him of the sins of the Jewish high priesthood, so as to resist the removal of his iniquity, and to deprive him of the continued enjoyment of the priestly office. The vision is apparently emblematic of the judgment of souls on their separation from the body at the hour of death, whereby their respective positions of bliss or torment in the Intermediate State is determined, and the Satan is represented as endeavouring to deprive the faithful saints of their hoped-for rewards in their new sphere of existence, by pleading their unfitness for the promised blessing in consequence of their earthly defilements.

These two doctrines are corroborated in the history of our Lord's temptation in the wilderness, into which He was cast out, according to St. Mark, to be tempted by the Satan. It was probably under the human form that the Satan tempted our Lord to provide for the supply of His bodily wants as man by the miraculous transmutation of stones into bread, whilst possibly under his transformation into an angel of light he tempted our Lord to cast Himself from the pinnacle of the temple, so as to compel faith in Himself as the Son of God from the assembled multitudes, by manifesting His control over the angelic hosts sent for His preservation. Thereby He would have anticipated the period assigned by the Divine Father for the manifestation of the sign of the Son of God, coming with the clouds of heaven with power and great glory to send forth His angels to gather together His elect. It is also probable that the Satan assumed the royal and superhuman dignity of the prince of this world, referred to by Ezekiel (xxviii. 14), as the protecting cherub or emblematic prince of Tyre, better rendered "the rebel king," when he demanded from our Lord Divine worship on the promise of delivering into His hand the immediate possession of all the kingdoms of the world.

The mode by which the Satan carries out his evil designs appears to be by the delegation of the work to his subsidiary demons, similar in degree to one of the processes by which the Almighty delegates the performance of the Divine purposes of His will to the various angelic orders by which He is attended. Such is the fiery stream which, in the prophet Daniel's dream, issued and came forth from before the Ancient of Days (Dan. vii. 10). The Apocalypse reveals the existence of the war in heaven between Michael and his angels successfully contending with the devil and his angels in a vision wherein he is identified with the Great Dragon, that old Serpent called the Devil and Satan (xii. 7). The exorcism of the demons out of their victims suffering under infirmity of body, aberration of mind, and disturbance of spirit, was of frequent occurrence in our Lord's ministry, witnessing to their secret power over man as well as beast, as in the case of the swine at Gadara. It was doubtless owing to their occult influences that the bands of Sheba and Chaldea were incited to their raids upon the herds of Job, and that the lightning and the desert wind were directed to the destruction of his children and household. The afflictions of Job, though tolerated but yet limited by the Almighty, originated in the action of the Satan, and were probably effected by his demons in the same way that the Law was ordained at Sinai by the disposition of angels. The miracles wrought by the Egyptian magicians in the days of Moses are apparently beyond the range of human skill, for to refer them to mere sleight-of-hand appears to contravene the revealed doctrine that at times human beings were satanically endowed with power for evil, evidenced in the cases of the witch of Endor and of the lying spirit which was Divinely permitted to energise in the minds of the prophets of the groves in the days of Ahab (1 Kings xxii. 23). Thus Judas was used by the Satan as the agent for the betrayal of our Lord. Even Peter's loving anxiety to dissuade Him from submission to death was met by its being attributed to the same evil influence: "Get thee behind me, Satan, for thou savourest not the things which be of God, but those which be of man." Men, therefore, appear at certain times to be utilised by the Satan for the carrying out of his wicked intentions through the evil influences with which, as the prince of the power of the air, he now energises in the sons of disobedience.

The mode, therefore, by which Satan works appears to be of a threefold character, by his direct personal action, by the delegation of his powers to the demons, and by the influence which he exercises over the minds of wicked men, who yield themselves to his wiles.

CHAPTER VI

THE VISIT OF THE THREE FRIENDS

(CHAP. ii. 11.)

THE exposure of Job to the miseries of earthly penury and physical suffering appears to have extended to a lengthened period. In his first reply to Eliphaz he is represented as saying, " I am made to possess days of vanity, and nights of toil are appointed to me" (vii. 3). His sufferings, therefore, must have been very prolonged before the visit of his three friends, when the discussion as to the causes of his affliction and of the best methods for his relief took place.

The general idea is that this discussion continued during the whole time of his illness, and that certain salient portions of it were, under Divine inspiration, selected and committed to writing under the form of a dramatic poem. There is, however, nothing in the record which necessitates the acceptance of such an idea. The language in which the visit is described leads, moreover, to a different conclusion. It is related that when they heard of Job's misfortunes, they came each one from his place of abode, and that they made an appointment to go together and comfort him, for his misery appears to have become before this period greatly aggravated, as witnessed by the wife's incitement for him to commit suicide, to procure relief from his agonies.

The homes of the three men appear to have been at a distance from one another. Eliphaz is described as a Temanite, or dweller in Tema, a town or district of Edom. Bildad is called the Shuhite, an inhabitant of Shuah, supposed to be a district west of Chaldea, bordering on Arabia, the people of which appear to have been descended from Shuah, a son of Abraham by Keturah. Members of this race may be identified with the Tsukki, who at one time dwelt near the Euphrates. Zophar is spoken of as the Naamathite, or dweller in Naamah, a place elsewhere unknown in the Scripture record. In the Septuagint he is called the king of the Minaei, a people supposed to have settled in the north of Arabia, on the borders of Syria. This gathering together by appointment, from localities separated by wide desert tracts, must have required time before they could have been collected at one point of meeting, and this raises the question whether their visit did not take place immediately before the vindication of Job, and his delivery from his captivity to the Satan. Under this theory the discussion may be regarded as the event of a single day, and the writing in which it is recorded may be considered as a revelation of words which were actually uttered by the respective speakers, and then under direct Divine inspiration entrusted to the mind of the writer, to be by him inscribed in a roll or book similar to those of other prophetic messengers.

The purport of the writing in recording this discussion is apparently to reveal the inner working of the human mind under affliction, and the different problems which suggest themselves as to its causes, together with the best methods to be adopted for its relief. The thoughts of the sufferer are represented by the words of Job. The three friends are typical of three different classes of mankind, who, witnessing the afflictions of their fellow-men, endeavour to alleviate them by the investigation of their probable causes. On their failure to convince Job of the correctness of their views, another person intervenes, who points out the defects of their advice, and the errors into which Job himself had fallen in imputing injustice to God in tolerating his sufferings, without also enabling him to understand the reasons for their existence.

The names of the three friends are emblematical of the classes to which they apparently belong, and show the character of the respective reasonings which are generally held by such persons in the presence of sufferings undergone by others. Eliphaz, the Temanite, represents the wealthy man occupying a position of acknowledged influence, qualified by secular wisdom.

His name, Eliphaz, means "Gold is my god;" and his dwelling in Teman was a place noted for worldly wisdom (Jer. xlix. 7), and descriptive of official authority, from its derivation from the Hebrew root, "the right hand." Bildad, the Shuhite, represents the cold materialistic philosopher, and the critical scientific investigator of secular causes and their results. His name, Bildad, means "without love;" and his home was in Shuah, from its root-sense of "meditation," descriptive of study. Zophar, the Naamathite, represents the shallow, talkative man of society. His name, Zophar, describes "the chattering sparrow;" and his abode was in Naamah, whose root-meaning is "pleasant or sociable."

These three friends, on receiving the tidings of Job's illness in their distant homes, appear to have made a mutual arrangement to go together to comfort him. On approaching the place where he was sitting on the Metzbele or ash heap, and beholding the inroads which the terrible disease of elephantiasis had made in his personal appearance, so as to render him almost incapable of recognition, they were reduced to such a state of mental amazement, as to be unable to do anything beyond lifting up their voices and weeping, rending their garments, and casting ashes towards the heavens, which again returned upon their heads. They who came to sympathise and condole with him were themselves, by excess of grief, deprived for seven days of power to give utterance to what they felt, and could only sit on the ground without voice, contemplating his misery.

This silent expression of agonised inability to render him any consolation intensified his wretchedness, and caused him at last "to open his mouth and curse his day." These words of Job became the cause and commencement of a discussion, which appears to have continued throughout the whole day, by introducing the first problem issuing from the human mind, for the solution of which, in addition to those originating with the Satan in the heavenlies, the history appears to have been divinely revealed. "Why is light given to him that is misery, and life unto the bitter in soul," to one undergoing suffering for which no adequate cause appears capable of being assigned? The three friends, at the conclusion of Job's soliloquy, state their several opinions, which are respectively replied to by the patriarch, showing their failure to give any efficient solution to the problem. After three separate discussions by the three respondents, they are reduced again to a state of silence. This is again succeeded by fresh lamentations uttered by Job over his present miserable condition, as contrasted with his past prosperity and happiness, concluding with a final appeal to God to vindicate his integrity, and to admit the inequality of his suffering when compared with the blamelessness of his past life.

This claim to self-justification causes a fourth person to intervene in the discussion. His name Elihu, meaning "he is God," appears to be typical of the inspired character of his utterances. In these he shows that all attempts at self-justification before God are opposed to real righteousness, and that the only true position which a man can occupy in his relation to God is one of faithful reliance on His justice and mercy. In support of this doctrine, he receives a divine corroboration from the mouth of Jehovah answering Job out of the whirlwind. He shows how the processes of nature, and His wisdom in the regulation of sentient as well as intellectual beings, proclaim His omniscience and omnipotence, whereby He convinces Job of the comparative vileness of finite man, and of his ignorance in understanding the workings of the Divine purposes. The repudiation of any pretension to question the acts of God, and repentance in dust and ashes for the manifold transgression and sins which stain the lives of all mortal men, are shown to be necessary qualification for acceptance with God.

The recorded events of the day on which the discussion took place appear to have terminated with another Divine utterance, in which Jehovah vindicated the fundamental rectitude of Job's conduct, "in speaking that which was right or established in respect of the Almighty." This was followed by a command from the Lord to the three men, that they should take seven bullocks and seven rams, and go to Job for him to offer them as a burnt-offering to avert the punishment of their folly. The alleged reason was that Jehovah would accept Job's intercession in their behalf. To this historic incident the prophet Ezekiel appears to refer when he was inspired to unite the name of Job with those of Noah and Daniel as the most prevailing intercessors with God in social and national distress. The record of the events for which this day had been remarkable closes with the offering of these holocausts and the freeing of Job from his captivity under the hand of the Satan.

The renewed intercourse with his brethren and acquaintance would probably have commenced with the succeeding morning, which witnessed the beginning of the ever-increasing restoration to prosperity and wealth for which, during his subsequently prolonged life of 140 years, the aged patriarch became remarkable.

CHAPTER VII

JOB'S OPENING SOLILOQUY

(CHAP. iii.)

Problem—" Why is man born to suffering ? "

THE next division of the history commences with the outward manifestation of Job's increasing suffering. The feelings of his three friends at the sight of the poor afflicted leper sitting upon his Metzbele or ash-heap, so overcame them, that for a whole week they were incapable of giving any acceptable comfort or support. They themselves required consolation to assuage the grief to which they were unable to give utterance except by outward signs of woe. Thereby Job's realisation of his misery was intensified, and their silent agony extorted from his lips the first recorded words of impatience and despair. His case now seemed hopeless. There appeared no possible hope of alleviation, and the more so because the cause of his sufferings was concealed from him. He had endeavoured faithfully to do his duty in life, with the apparent result that God was angry with him, and refused to acquaint him with the cause of His displeasure.

Agony of body was rendered more insupportable by mental disquietude. "Without were foes, within were fears." Such increasing sufferings at last overcame him, and he burst out into angry invectives against the night of his conception and the day of his birth. He pleads for their divestment of God's blessing, for their erasure from the records of existence, for their absorption into darkness and isolation, and for their deliverance into the pitiless hands of the Satanic leviathan, or as expressed in the two Anglican versions, to be cursed by those "who curse the day and are ready to raise up their mourning, or to rouse up leviathan," or in other words, are ready to raise up their mournful execrations, or to invoke the intervention of the serpent's power.

In such pleadings the selfishness which often accompanies extreme misery becomes apparent. Only the holy Jesus could undergo vicarious suffering without uttering a prayer for deliverance. The realisation of His agony as a propitiation for the sin of man closed His lips against asking for any alleviation. Even the stupefying mixture of wine and myrrh, kindly provided on the way of sorrows by the pitying women to deaden the pangs of His approaching crucifixion, was declined. The cup which His Father had given Him must be drained to the dregs to procure man's deliverance from eternal death.

Job's thoughts, however, were at the moment

confined to a desire for exemption from suffering at the cost of even non-existence. "Why died I not from the womb? Then should I have been at rest, as an infant who never saw the light." His mind was concentrated on himself. His mother's joy at his birth to compensate for the bitterness of her birth throes was forgotten. The wish savours of the Buddhist hope of absorption into the concrete Nirvana, destructive of all individual existence. He contemplates the bodily quietude and rest that is the lot of the departed, whatever has been their earthly condition, whether mighty kings, wise counsellors, wealthy princes, still-born babes, master or slave, wicked oppressors or honest toilers, small or great, all are visibly at rest.

At this stage of the discussion the feelings of Job are entirely confined to the consideration, that the body by death is in a state of rest. He does not here make any reference to the condition of the soul in Sheol. But its unconsciousness after death does not appear to form any part of the creed of Job, for elsewhere, when expressing his desire that God would cut him off, the recognition that death would bring him comfort is based on the remembrance that "he had not concealed the words of the Holy One;" on another occasion he clearly implies that death will not destroy his faith in God, "though He slay me, yet will I trust Him;" and on a third occasion he looks forward to the resurrection of his body, because he knows "that his Redeemer liveth, and that after his awaking from the sleep of death, he will from out of his reanimated flesh see God with his own eyes." These passages bear evident testimony to his faith in the continuity of the soul's existence in Sheol (vi. 10, xiii. 15, xix. 25).

The problem naturally presents itself to his mind, as it does to that of every thoughtful person suffering under apparently unmerited affliction, "Why should a man be conceived and born into the world so as to become a prey to suffering, and why should his life be prolonged to be exposed to intense misery, for which no adequate cause can be reasonably assigned?" The largest proportion of human affliction may be traced to the wilful commission of sin, or the wilful neglect of duty, and its object is admittedly correction of evil. Unavoidable ignorance and inherent weakness of will are also fruitful causes of suffering, and apparently sent to stimulate the mind to the quest after increased knowledge, or to quicken the soul by the impartition of Divine life through the more earnest study of the Word, and the more frequent use of Sacramental agencies. Another cause of affliction is realised in the painful restraint which is often divinely imposed after the occurrence of certain important events in men's lives, and is apparently appointed to preserve their remembrance, so as to avert a relapse into past mistaken courses. Instances of such restricted action appear in Jacob's shrunken sinew after his wrestling with the angel at Penuel, and in Paul's thorn in the flesh, after the mysterious visions of the third Heaven and of Paradise. In such cases the causes which have led to the imposition of suffering may generally be discovered, and the sufferer made acquainted with the means whereby it may be alleviated, either by amendment of life or increased attention to intellectual and spiritual privileges, or by the enjoyment of a sense of protection realised in the recognition of the Divine care in the past. Much suffering also is of a vicarious character. Persons willingly expose themselves to danger, for the impartition of blessing to others. Such was the nature of our Lord's crucifixion, "I, if I be lifted up from the earth, will draw all men unto Me." Parents undergo great toil and pain, and often death, in order to supply the requirements of their children. Such sufferers are supported in their trials by the assured hope of seeing the travail of their soul compensated for in the future prosperity of those for whom they suffer.

None of these causes were applicable to the circumstances of Job. The intensity of his misery was increased by his failure to discover any satisfactory reason which would meet the requirements of his case. His revealed character proved that in his past conduct he had been blameless, yet still he found himself exposed to what appeared to him to be unmerited penury and physical pain; hence his bitter cry, "Why is light given to him that is in misery, and life unto the bitter in soul; who longs for death, and it comes not: who is glad when he can find the grave? Why is light given to him whose way is hidden, whom God hath hedged in?"

He illustrates this in his own present condition, by his words, "When a feeling of awe seizes me, it comes upon me, and whatever I dread happens to me; I have neither prosperity, nor quietude, nor rest, and thus trembling takes hold of me."

This is the fundamental problem which forms the basis of the discussion. Job propounds it for the solution of those around him, and his three friends vainly endeavour to supply reasons which may satisfy his inquiry. Its true solution is beyond the range of man's unaided reason. A revelation from God can alone explain the mysteries of the heavenlies. The history itself is therefore the solution of Job's problem. It shows that the Almighty, for the instruction of the heavenly hosts, at times allows mortal man to suffer pain for which no earthly cause can be alleged. Our Lord, in the kindred case of the man born blind, declared that his blindness was not to be attributed to sin, either in himself or in his parents, but that it was permitted for the manifestation of the works of God. The sufferings of Job were similarly divinely permitted to teach the doctrine, not only on earth but also in the heavenlies, that man has been created capable of resisting all the efforts of the Satan to incite him to withdraw from his allegiance to his Maker, and that a temporary deliverance into the hands of his Satanic accuser, limited however in time and degree, is one of the methods whereby his faith and endurance are to be tested.

As a mere vehicle to enable an unknown author of the exilic period to expound his own views of the hidden causes of suffering, the writing would carry little weight. The first thought of the reader would be to challenge the veracity of one who presumed, without accredited authority, to reveal the mysterious purposes of the Almighty in the Presence Chamber of the heavenlies. The whole solution of the problem is dependent on the truth of the events in the two first chapters of the history. The acceptance of the Book of Job into the Hebrew Canon in the days of our Lord, witnessed by the appeal to its contents by the apostle St. James, the writer of the epistle, testifies however to its veracity. It is apparently beyond belief that a writing claiming to form an integral part of those Scriptures, to which our Lord referred His disciples for instruction in matters concerning eternal life, would have been allowed to retain its position in the Sacred Canon unchallenged by Him unless the mysteries therein revealed were in accordance with the truth. Although the verification by St. James was given some centuries after the publication of the history, yet the reference to Job's exalted character by the prophet Ezekiel shows that it must be traced to a far earlier period than that of the exile, to allow time for the dissemination of the knowledge of Job's sufferings and of their causes, so as to be quoted in the prophetic record as a source of consolation and support to the Jews under the Babylonish captivity. The allusions it contains to the commerce and power of Sheba appear to connect it with the time of Solomon and the visit of the Queen of Sheba. It was the period when, according to the historic Scripture, the prosperity of Israel and its territorial extent and influence were at their zenith. It was an age noted for wisdom, commerce, luxury, and art. The linguistic objection to an early date, owing to the admixture of Aramaic, Arabian, Greek, and Persian words, may possibly be accounted for by the theory that under its present form the writing is a copy of an archaic autograph, long since lost, into the vernacular language in general use when the copyist lived, similar to the ancient Toldoth, or books of generations compiled and transcribed by Moses in the Book of Genesis, or to the versions of the Scriptures made by missionaries and published by our Bible Societies.

CHAPTER VIII

ELIPHAZ'S REPLY TO JOB

(CHAPS. iv., v.)

THE impatient character of Job's soliloquy attracted the attention of Eliphaz, and inspired him with a desire to attempt to alleviate his wretchedness by leading him to the consideration of its causes. From the root meaning of his name, and that of his abode, he is the representative of the prosperous and influential men of the world, conditioned by the practical soundness of their ordinary opinions. He states that suffering is due to the existence of some personal sin or error, recognised or otherwise, into which the sufferer has been betrayed, and then proceeds to show that the true remedy for its relief is the discovery of its primary cause. In the discussion that follows he gives three replies to the problem that Job has proposed for solution, respectively supporting his views by arguments drawn from his own experience, from the general experience of mankind, and from the inconsistency of imagining that God would afflict any man without some definite reason in harmony with the Divine justice and mercy.

The fundamental problem that had presented itself to the mind of Job was,—Why light, through conception and birth, should be given to any undergoing suffering for which no adequate reason could be assigned ?

Eliphaz commences his reply with a courteous request for Job's permission to address him, adding how difficult it was to witness aggravated suffering without making an effort to afford some consolation and relief. At first he refers to the conduct of Job in his assistance to others similarly afflicted, expressing his wonder that he had not derived support from the reasonings that had dictated his advice to them. He attributes his fear to foolishness in failing to recognise that hope for relief must not be expected from a too confident reliance on his integrity of life or conduct. " Is not the cause of thy fear, thy past foolishness; and the cause of thy hope, the former perfection of thy way ? He asks if he can remember any case when the innocent perished or the upright were cut off. He appeals to his own experience, that they who ploughed or made preparation to do iniquity, and who sowed or committed wickedness, passed away under the anger of God. He supports his opinion by the fate of lions, who, by the action of natural law, become incapable through age or other accidents of obtaining the prey necessary for the support of their lives." They are the emblems of cruel tyrants, who fail in their efforts to preserve their own existence, and the continuity of their families, from their want of power to avert the dangers to which they are exposed by their oppressive character and the growing infirmities of age.

Eliphaz then proceeds to adduce another argument, equally drawn from his own experience, in support of his views that sin is the cause of suffering. It originated in the impressions produced on his mind by a night vision, in which a spirit passed before his face; he could not discern its form, but a likeness incapable of definition was before his eyes. There was a mysterious stillness, followed by a voice, revealing man's inherent imperfection: "Is mortal man more righteous than God? or a strong man more pure than his Maker? So in His servants he puts no faith, and he imputes not praise even to His angels. Surely those who tabernacle in houses of clay, whose foundation is in the dust, are crushed before the moth. From morning to evening they are broken in pieces, yet they perish without any of the survivors permanently laying it to heart. Even the reputed excellency that was in them has also passed away; they died, and that not in the enjoyment of wisdom." This utterance of the spirit should be regarded as an inspired revelation of God's Spirit, and not the mere imagination of a dreamer. Thus Eliphaz professes to draw his third experience from the borderland, where the quickened soul is still united to the insensible body, and whence the spirit voice proclaims the defectibility of man as the cause of human suffering. Sooner or later the earthly tenement perishes, whatever be the excellency of its intellectual occupant, or his pre-eminence over all other earthly created beings. This passes away. Men die, and that because in their unwisdom they lay not God's past visitations to heart. Natural death, the common lot of all, is hastened by the suffering that originates with the defective life. The elect servant, and the angelic spirit, have still the taint of imperfection when compared with the infinite perfection of the All-holy One. How much more then is mortal man liable to suffering of which death is but the culmination.

It is quite possible, as suggested by a modern commentator, that the words of Eliphaz may have caused increased exasperation in the mind of Job at his implied imputations of past failure in the performance of duty, as well as anger at his assumed pretension to superior judgment. These feelings the patriarch appeared incapable of concealing, and a temporary pause in the discussion may have resulted. The silence, however, seems to have been soon broken, by an attempt of Eliphaz to strengthen his arguments by challenging Job to declare "whether he knew of any earthly man capable of giving an answer to his question? or of any saints in the heavens on whom he could call for a solution of the problem, at the same time warning him that such exasperation and anger were productive of danger to life."

Reverting to his statement that suffering is the result of sin, he now adduces an example which had come under his own observation, in which the short-lived prosperity of a foolish wicked man had suddenly been cursed, when both he and his family were reduced to the extremes of degradation and poverty. The reason alleged for such a change of circumstances was due to the fact that the evolution of affliction is not to be attributed to automatic action, but to the intervention of a Higher Will; "for affliction goeth not out of the dust, and painful toil sprouteth not out of the ground, for man is born to toil as the sparks fly upward." Like all earthly events, the result is governed by antecedent causes. It becomes, therefore, the duty of a wise man "to inquire of God, and to commit the matter into His hands." To show the wisdom of such action, he refers to the Divine omnipotence visible in the realm of nature, and in His governance of man, realised in His exaltation of the humble and in the overthrow of the froward, whereby hope is given to the poor, and the mouth of iniquity is stopped.

The contemplation of God's omniscience, and of His infinite wisdom in the regulation of the universe for the promotion of the eternal happiness of all who unfeignedly love and fear Him, inspired Eliphaz to declare the blessedness of receiving reproof and correction at the hand of God: "Happy is the man whom God convinces of his errors, therefore reject not thou the chastisement of the Almighty." The intellect requires instruction by the rebukes of conscience, and the body needs chastisement through the pains which it endures. He proceeds to declare the curative effects of suffering to those who are exercised thereby: "God maketh sick, and bindeth up; He woundeth, and His hand healeth. He shows how God will deliver man in his trouble, whatever be its character, whether famine, or war, or the scourge of men's evil tongues, or disease; how the metalliferous stones of the field will be productive of support to promote his prosperity, whilst the carnivorous beasts will fail to destroy him. Peaceful will be his tabernacle. Numerous will be his progeny, until finally he will come to maturity, as a shock of corn in its due season."

Such is the result which is attained by investigations drawn from their own experience by the powerful, prosperous, and intelligent men of the world, into the mysterious problems which accompany the infliction of suffering on the perfect and upright man, who fears God and turns from evil. Eliphaz concludes by counselling Job to accept this statement as the answer to his question: "Lo, this we have searched out, and found it true. Do thou, therefore, hear it, and recognise its correctness for the promotion of thy well-being."

To a certain degree the views to which he gives utterance are in accordance, not only with the general experience of mankind, but also with the revealed laws of God. As a general rule sin is productive of suffering. But these reasons are insufficient to meet the case of Job, the representative of the godly who are exposed to suffering for which no adequate earthly cause can be assigned. The revelation of the supermundane events which took place in the Presence Chamber of the Almighty in the heavenlies, shows that the afflictions of Job were not to be referred to any personal sin under its twofold aspect of either moral wrong or inherent imperfection. Their origination can be traced to no earthly cause. Apparently, before the publication of this history, no prior revelation had been given of the doctrine, that, as in the case also of the man born blind in our Lord's days, men are at times, without any fault of their own, Divinely selected to undergo sufferings in order that the works of God should be made manifest in them. The words of Eliphaz fail, therefore, to afford a solution to the problem which presents itself to all thoughtful minds of all ages, as it did also to the mind of Job. "Why are the perfect born to suffer?" remains an unanswered question to all who look only to earthly conditions as the cause of suffering.

CHAPTER IX

JOB'S REPLY TO ELIPHAZ

(CHAPS. vi., vii.)

Problem—"Why is life prolonged to the suffering?"

THE arguments advanced by Eliphaz in reply to Job's first problem, "Why is man born to undergo apparently unmerited suffering?" did not commend themselves to his understanding. Judging by his own experience, he could not admit that that of his friend had been so much wider in its extent, as to allow him to agree with his assertions that suffering was invariably the result of sin. In his own case he could not remember that he had been guilty of sin of sufficient magnitude to account for his being visited with so much misery, as to cause him to wish that he had never been born. This leads him to propound for solution a second problem, "Why is life prolonged to one undergoing suffering for the infliction of which no adequate reason can be assigned?"

He introduces the subject by showing that the exasperation, for which Eliphaz had reproved him, was to be traced to the inequality of his suffering when weighed in the balances with his woeful condition, which would then appear to be heavier than the sand of the seas, and that when men scorned his words they did so from their neglect of this consideration. He compares the state of his feelings to the inflammation caused by the wounds of the poisoned arrow of the savage, productive of physical pain, and mental terror of the impending evil of which it is the precursor. He shows that even in the animal kingdom the pangs of hunger excite the braying of the wild ass, and the lowing of the ox. He therefore asks whether the utterances of a man, struck down by extreme want, are to be reproved; or even the words which issue from the spirit of a mortally sick person, whose soul refuseth the unsavoury and loathsome food, which alone he can procure for the supply of his necessities?

Such thoughts excited the expression of his longing desire that God would grant his petition, even that He would remove His hand and crush him. It is the prayer of many an agonised sufferer whose feelings are described by the words of the stricken patriarch, "Then I shall have comfort; I would exult in the death throes." He gives an additional reason why God should not spare him, or restrain His hand from giving the final stroke. He looks forward with confidence to the moment of its infliction. He has no fear of death, for "he has not concealed the words of the Holy One." His whole life had been one of courageous confession of faith in God by word and deed, being fully convinced that whoso confesseth God before men, shall himself also be confessed before the Heavenly Father, an assurance long afterwards corroborated by the lips of the incarnate Word. To such an one the hope of continuance in life offered no consolation. "What is my strength, is it that of stones; or has my flesh the insensibility of copper, that I should desire to wait? What better end can there be for me that I should desire to prolong my life? Is it not true that there remains for me no human help, and that God has thrust from me all hope of prolonged existence?" Such words seem to be almost those of despair. Yet underlying them there is still the recognition of God's omniscience witnessing his faithful endurance of suffering under the temptation to end his misery by his own hand. The feelings of Job, as of all others suffering as he did, find their fulfilment in our Lord's all perfect resignation to His Father's will, when on the cross He gave utterance to the agonised words, "My God, My God, why hast Thou forsaken Me?"

Job now again turned his attention to his friends, and his words reveal the Divine method whereby comfort may be afforded to those sinking under the sorrows of life: "To him whose life is melting away mercy should be shown, lest he should forsake the fear of the Almighty." Inattention to mercy was the cause of the failure of Eliphaz to give consolation. Not a word of pity appears in his address. All his thoughts are directed to the discovery of the causes of Job's sufferings. The acceptance of advice is often beyond the power of the afflicted. They need at first physical support and words of tenderness. The mollifying oil must be first poured into the gaping wound before the stimulating wine can be applied. The mercy and the love of God should be whispered into their ears before the call to self-examination and repentance is pressed upon the conscience. The reverential fear of God, the beginning of wisdom, starts from the recognition of His love. "There is mercy with Thee, therefore Thou shalt be feared." The realisation of God's mercy is the surest protection from the sin of suicide, so often the temptation of those wretched in body or mind.

Job proceeds to show the dismal failure of his friends to console him. At first, in silent impotence, they had sat on the ground for seven days and seven nights. Eliphaz then approached him with his self-sufficient advice. We read nothing of any act of mercy being shown to the poor sufferer. He describes his disappointment, "My brethren have dealt treacherously with me." Their ostentatious grief, their rent mantles, their dust-besprinkled heads, all of them outward signs of mourning, were powerless to assuage the torments of the excommunicate leper, who continuously required the skilful hands of some self-sacrificing attendant to supply his wants. Their failure in bodily relief was followed by failure in intellectual reasoning and spiritual consolation. "Elihu's anger was subsequently kindled against them because they found no answer to his words, and yet had condemned Job." Thus Job compares them to the channels of a torrent whose waters quickly pass away, at one moment congealed into ice, at another again melting and drying up under the action of the solar heat. The travelling caravans approach its banks, —they hope to find water in its channels, and are thrown into confusion by its absence.

Turning to his friends, Job (vi. 2) says, "Ye also are useless; ye see my casting down, and are afraid to touch the infectious leper. Did I ask you to bring ought to me, or to hire another to nurse me? Did I entreat you to deliver me from the hand of an enemy or to ransom me from the power of the oppressor? Your proffered help when needed you failed to give. In silence and inaction ye sat beside me. Teach me where I have erred, and I will be silent, for words of uprightness carry weight." He does not ask to be shown where he had sinned, for this would have impugned his reliance on the conscientious integrity of his conduct, but he challenges them to say of what evil they had convicted him beyond the utterance of a few hasty words spoken to the wind. He contrasts their treatment of orphans taken captives in war, over whom they cast lots to receive them into their houses, whereas they treated their friend as an alien in a strange land. These words of Job represent the feelings of many under affliction, when confronted with the ostentatious offers of consolation from acquaintances ever ready to give advice, but backward in self-denying assistance to their suffering friends. They reveal the character of true help in sorrow and sickness, correlative with that taught by our Lord in the parable where the personal and pecuniary assistance of the good Samaritan is favourably contrasted with that of the Pharisaic priest or the critical student of Levitical law.

Possibly at the conclusion of Job's words, complaining of his friends' unkind imputations of wrongdoing, a pause may have been given for their reply, but on their continued silence he appears to have requested them to return to their own place: "Now therefore be content; look upon me: surely I have not lied to your face. Return home. Let not this be considered an act of wrong. You have failed to convict me, therefore leave me and return home again, for the sense of my integrity remains unshaken in my mind. There is no iniquity in my tongue, and my reason is still capable to discern what is perverse."

Then Job again reverts to his pleading with God for his deliverance from suffering by the hand of death. He had before stated his preparedness to die, being supported in his confidence by a sense of the faithful performance of his duty, and of his present feebleness destructive of all hope of recovery. He now advances other reasons for a favourable answer to his prayer for death. He compares his earthly struggles to the labours of an hired servant, longing for the close of the day to receive the hire of his work. He looks forward in earnest hope to receive after death compensation for the endurance, month after month, of profitless existence and painful nights of restless disturbance. He pleads the loathsomeness of his bodily sores, the hopelessness of his quickly passing days and the transitory character of his earthly life, incapable of the enjoyment of prosperity, as reasons for his speedy consignment to Sheol, where no mortal eye will see his misery, and from whence there is no return to the sorrows of the world. In impatient terms he refuses to refrain his mouth from urging the acceptance of his prayer, extorted as it is by anguish of spirit and bitterness of soul, resentful of the restraint in which he is held as the raging sea is held back by the rocky shore, or as a captive dragon or an apostate angel is detained by everlasting chains in darkness. He alleges as a reason for his repudiation of the blessings of life, the terrible dreams of earthly dangers and the worse visions of imaginary horrors to which the leprous disease exposes its victims, or the supernatural darkness in the land of Egypt subjected the hardened despisers of Moses' warnings: "My soul chooses strangling, and death rather than this skeleton. I reject life; I would not live alway; let me alone, for my days are vanity." These words express in principle the thoughts of many when tried by intense sorrow. Terrible are the temptations to which aggravated suffering exposes a man. Forgetfulness of God's past mercies, hopelessness in His abiding protection, and faithlessness in His eternal love, are often the results of prolonged endurance of evil.

Yet, in the midst of these utterances of wretchedness, a supporting thought presents itself to Job's mind. Surely man, with all his high privileges, is not intended only for suffering. God must have some better thing provided for him. "What is man that Thou shouldst magnify him, or that Thou shouldst set Thy heart upon him, that Thou shouldst visit him every morning with renewed existence, though Thou triest him every moment. These pains surely cannot be the result of vindictive punishment. Some unknown mysterious reason must exist for their infliction. I must have sinned, though I knew it not."

The doctrine that personal moral evil is not the only cause of suffering is forcing itself on Job's mind. He realises that involuntary nescience of law is a form of sin equally with voluntary transgression of law, in being productive of wrong action. Such sinful action through ignorance of law shows itself in the babe and the idiot. These, as all others, have sinned, and come short of the glory of God. In such cases suffering ceases to be punitive; its object is discipline, so as to lead to a search for perfection and capability of work for God, whether in this life or in Sheol. Hence he asks, "How shall I work for Thee, Thou keeper of souls? Why hast Thou set me as a place of meeting where Thy presence reveals itself, so that I become a burden to myself, distracted with fears and doubts, which I am utterly unable to overcome and resolve? Why dost Thou not take away my transgression, and cause my iniquity to pass away?" This is a prayer for enlightenment in the removal of involuntary transgression and unintentional iniquity, without which he perceives that he must sleep in the dust; and when sought for in the morning of the resurrection, he fears that his name will not be found written in the pages of the book of life. He was willing to admit the possibility of having unconsciously fallen into error, but he appears to deny the rectitude of its being punished with such intense suffering.

CHAPTER X

BILDAD'S REPLY TO JOB

(CHAP. viii.)

THE impatient character of Job's language excited the anger of Bildad, whose words, according to the root meanings of his name and of his place of abode, appear to represent the thoughts which arise in the mind of the dispassionate philosopher meditating on the causes to which suffering may be traced. He briefly reproves Job for the violence of his words, comparing them to the action of a strong wind. He points out their impropriety by asking, whether it is not inconsistent with the nature of God to act perversely either in judgment or righteousness? The character of Job's reply to Eliphaz had been to charge God with cruelty in the infliction of wretchedness which seemed to be unmerited. Bildad appears to affirm that the absence of pity is opposed to the character of God, and consequently that all suffering is thus proved to be necessarily in accordance with the principles which regulate the automatic action of Divine law, and of the laws that govern the free intervention of His righteous will. From this reasoning Bildad draws the conclusion that some sinful action on the part of Job must exist to account for the infliction of the suffering. As the papyrus reed cannot grow without mire, so misery cannot subsist without some antecedent cause. He attributes the death of his children to some unknown transgression on their part. He exhorts him to be warned by their fate, and to make supplication to God to reveal to him where he had failed in purity or uprightness, concluding with the assurance that if his claim to pureness were established, " God would rise up over him as his protector, and restore peace to his dwelling, and greatly multiply his posterity."

In support of his views, this calm reasoner on metaphysical subjects appeals to the teachings of tradition and antiquity in the same way that Eliphaz, the man of high earthly position, appeals to his own experience: " We are of yesterday and know nothing, but inquire of former generations and trace out the knowledge of the fathers. Shall not they teach thee?" He draws a simile from the banks of a river: " The sedge cannot grow without water; and while yet in the thicket, the failure of the waters of the stream causes it to wither quicker than any other herb." This he compares to the fate of the hypocrite, who, under the pretence of piety, forgets the presence of the all-seeing eye of God, which detects his sin, and by the withdrawal of His grace causes his hope to perish as quickly as the spider's web. He may rely on the firm foundation of his house, but it will not stand, however much he may endeavour to strengthen it. The support may be strong, but the web itself is weak. He appears to insinuate that the piety of Job is of an hypocritical character, which, like the succulent green herb, may appear to be flourishing under the solar warmth of earthly prosperity, in sending out fresh offshoots in the garden; but as its roots are only interwoven on a stone heap, without any deepness of earth, it will soon be swallowed up in its place and leave no trace of its existence. This, he adds, is the joy of the hypocrite, whose principles being deeply rooted in worldly considerations, cause him quickly to pass away, and to make room for others.

Bildad, as the representative of tradition, teaches that human suffering only evolves out of personal sin, is developed by intellectual weakness, and originates in the hardness of the human heart. He affirms that God will not cast away a perfect man until He has filled him with restored joy and renewed honour. He argues that suffering therefore bears witness to the presence of sin or error, and that while these remain unforsaken, the help of God will not be granted to those who do evil, until at the last their dwelling-place will no longer be found. To reconcile the recognised uprightness of Job's outward conduct with the wretchedness to which he has been reduced, and taking advantage of his admission that he may have sinned, though unconsciously, he proceeds to attribute his misery to hypocrisy, regarding his assertions of innocence as the words of one who is forgetful that the Divine Omniscience is able to detect the hidden evil motives of the heart. But the misfortunes to which the godly are manifestly exposed, are of too frequent occurrence to be accounted for by the allegation of unproven hypocrisy, whilst the pains of innocent infants, unconscious of good and evil from the very moment of their birth, proclaim the fallacy of the doctrine, that suffering is always to be traced to the personal act of sin.

The failure of Bildad to prove the correctness of this imputation, therefore deprives his reply of any claim to the solution of the problem propounded by Job, Why should life be prolonged to one undergoing suffering for which no adequate cause can be assigned, and whose earthly life is too short for compensation to be made to him? The records of the past and the traditions of the ancients are thus seen to be unable to answer the question, Why should the perfect suffer?

CHAPTER XI

JOB'S REPLY TO BILDAD

(CHAPS. ix., x.)

Problem—"Why is unmerited suffering Divinely tolerated?"

JOB in his reply to Bildad admits the truth of his statement, that "God cannot pervert judgment or righteousness," and that He will not reject the perfect man or preserve the dwelling-place of the wicked. "I know that it is so," he says. Yet, when he regards his own wretched condition, he asks whether it is possible for a man to appear righteous in the eye of God, so as to establish a claim to the blessings promised to the perfect man? If God contends with a man in respect of his life, he realises that not one of the learned, however wise or mighty, can make any pretension to absolute perfection, or harden himself against the Divine decisions with any hope of attaining unto peace.

To show the utter impossibility of resistance to the will of God, he appeals to the infinite power of the Almighty over the whole realm of nature in the earthly and heavenly spheres: "By His command the mountains are removed, men know not how; the earth is shaken, the light of the sun and stars is sealed up; the atmospheric heavens are spread abroad by His word, the constellations are grouped together at His will. He does great things and wonderful, which are incapable of being traced out or numbered; His invisible presence pervadeth all space. None can resist His power or question His right of action. Under the weight of His anger, the proud abettors of the Egyptian Rahab, or of the Satanic dragon, are caused to bow themselves." Therefore he asks, "How much less shall I answer Him? I would therefore choose my words, and abstain from hasty expressions when reasoning with Him. If I were perfectly righteous, I would only make supplication for a sentence of acquittal. If He answered my prayer, I should scarce believe that He had given ear to my voice, for He still bruiseth me with the tempest, and multiplieth my wounds, incessantly filling me with bitterness, and all this without any revealed cause. If it were a matter of strength, He is infinitely strong; if it were a matter for adjudication, who is able to appoint me a time to plead? If I attempt to justify myself, my very mouth through its impatient words would condemn me. If I should claim to be perfect, even again my mouth would prove me to be perverse; and even if I were absolutely perfect, I should not recognise my soul as such, but I should even despise the apparent defectibility of my life when contrasted with His infinite perfection." Job's defence against Bildad's accusation, of his having attributed perverseness of action to God in causing him to suffer, appears to be directed to establish the utter impossibility of his venturing to assert that the omnipotent Creator could be convicted of error in the governance of the universe, and that the omniscient Judge could be convicted of injustice in His dealings with any of the intelligent beings which He has called into existence. Whilst firmly asserting his integrity and conscientiousness, Job lays no claim to absolute perfection of life, but at the same time he repudiates with scorn his friend's imputation of conscious hypocrisy: " Thou knowest that I am not wicked, for none can deliver out of Thine hand."

Job then proceeds to the consideration of Bildad's affirmation, that God will not reject the perfect man, but will bring to nought the dwelling of the wicked. He controverts the traditional theory that the reward of the good and the punishment of the evil always takes place in this life: "This is one thing concerning which I will speak. God causes both the perfect and the wicked to come to an end." He supports his argument by two examples. He shows that the scourge of the taskmaster is often, by God's permission, destructive to the innocent slave. He points out that the earth appears at times to be given into the hands of the wicked, whose misdeeds remain unpunished, through the intellectual blindness of which God allows the judges to become victims in the seat of justice. A man's innocency cannot always therefore be impugned on account of the suffering to which he may be exposed. He therefore demands of his opponent, "If God does not permit this miscarriage of justice, where and who is he that promotes it?" A pause may be imagined to have taken place in the discussion, but the question remained unanswered.

Job then again gives way to his sad repinings: "He sees his days passing away with the speed of a running postman, they glide quickly by as the swift boats of reed, or as the eagle swooping upon its prey. If he tries to forget his bitter meditations, or to change the sad expression of his face, and for a while to attempt a smile, then his grief terrifies him anew, for he fears that God will not hold him innocent. He thinks that if he admitted himself to be wicked it would be vain labour to attempt to amend, for he fears that, even if he should bathe himself in snow-water and cleanse his hands at the well, God would dip him in the pit of corruption, so that his enveloping burnoose would abhor him."

Such despairing thoughts cause a fresh problem to present itself to his mind: "Why does God give no clear reason for the toleration of such apparently unmerited suffering, or appoint some person to act as mediator, so that man may justify himself before God?" He says, "God is not a man as I am, for then I would interrogate Him, and we could come together before the judgment-seat, and then the cause could be interpleaded between us; neither is there a pleader or advocate betwixt us, who could lay his hand upon us both, and thereby reconcile our differences." In these words of Job there is a foreshadowing of that which was subsequently fulfilled in the Divine Mediator, who, in the person of the Word made flesh, laid His sacred hands on God and man. Job gave utterance to two earnest wishes. First, he desired "that as a man pleads with man so he might be rendered capable of holding communion with God." In the man Christ Jesus human nature was enabled to answer for all the sins with which it stood charged before the judgment-seat of God. "In the days of His flesh He offered up prayers and supplications, with strong crying and tears, unto Him that was able to save Him from death, and was heard, in that He feared to relax his submissive faith in God's mercy." All believers who are truly united with Him can through Him plead their cause with God, and in proportion to their sincerity and faith obtain an answer of peace. Secondly, Job desires that there should be an advocate between him and God, who, partaking of the nature of both, might lay His hands on both. This was one of the principal objects of the incarnation of Christ. Begotten of the Father, He was perfect God; born of the Virgin, He was perfect man. This He revealed to Nicodemus when He said, "No man hath ascended into heaven except He that came down from heaven, the Son of Man, the existing One in heaven." As man on earth, and the existing One in heaven, He acted as Mediator to make atonement between God and man, by reconciling man to his forgiving God.

Later on Job's eclipse of faith partially passed away. For the moment he had been sorely tried by his friends' false reasoning and his own intense suffering; but when true faith in God exists in the heart, as in the case of Job, it must soon again shine forth, and the darkness of the soul will be dispelled by the remembrance that "its Vindicator liveth, and that hereafter He shall rise up over the dust, and, after reawaking from the sleep of death, man shall see God."

Realising the impossibility of having his wishes immediately gratified, Job now looks around for some other form of relief. He regards his sufferings as punitive for some unknown fault, and he therefore prays "that the uplifted sceptre should be withdrawn, so that he might not be terrified by this display of God's infinite majesty. He thinks that then he might fearlessly give utterance to his inmost thoughts in a way of which at present he feels himself to be incapable." But it is all in vain. "He is so borne down by the weight of his misery as to be weary of life. He can only complain to himself, and speak in bitterness of soul. He therefore implores God not to consider him as being wicked, but to cause him to know why He contends with him, and why He so oppresses a conscientious man whom He has formed, although He still shines upon the counsel of the wicked. Surely the eye of the Omniscient God cannot be deceived by the outward appearance as the eye of man. The days of the Eternal are not so limited as to require an immediate search to be made after secret lusts before they have been developed into open sin. Thou knowest, he says, that I am not intentionally wicked, and that if I become so none can deliver me out of Thine hand." As an argument for God's forbearance, he pleads the inconsistency of His destroying one whom He has created and preserved, to whom in time past He has granted life and mercy, whose spirit also owes its protection to His oversight.

He then traces his afflictions to the hand of God: " I know that they are the hidden purpose of Thine heart; that if I sin Thou wilt observe it and not acquit me from my guilt; that if I be wicked it will be woe to me; that if I be righteous I shall even then be unable to lift up my head." Yet, full of vileness as he may appear, he prays that God would look at his affliction as it increases in its intensity: "Thou huntest me as the fierce lion, Thou dealest marvellously with me; Thou findest fresh witnesses against me. Thou hast multiplied

Thine indignation upon me. Changes of attack and continual warfare are upon me." Such is the pitiful cry of his sorrow-stricken heart; yet all seems unavailing—he receives no answer, he experiences no relief.

Finding therefore no possible solution to his inquiry, why God refuses to give a reason for the toleration of such suffering, Job again reiterates his former question: " Wherefore hast Thou brought me out of the womb ? I should have expired, and no eye would have seen me. I should have been as though I had not been. I should have been carried from the womb to the burying place. Thus I should have been free from misery." Death therefore appears to be the only way of release from all his wretchedness. He then goes on to contemplate the fewness of his remaining years, and pleads this as a reason why God should cease from afflicting him, and should turn away from him, so that he might smile (ix. 27), or have some gleam of cheerfulness before he went whence he should not return, " to a land of darkness and of the shadow of death; a land of faintness, as of gloom without order, whose brightness is as the gloom of the nether world."

These concluding words of Job appear to define the view which in his days prevailed as to the nature of Sheol. It has already been shown that several passages in his replies testify to his faith in the continuity of the existence of the soul when separated by death from the body, which, in consequence of its dissolution into dust, ceases to be a source of suffering. This was the cause of Job's desire for death. He realised that the bodies of the departed are in a state of unconsciousness and of consequent freedom from all pain. But the same cannot be said of the soul, and his gloomy description of the Intermediate State conveys the impression that Job regarded Sheol as a place in which the sorrows of existence under other conditions might possibly be continued independent of its bodily environment. Hence it is described as a place of gloom and darkness, modified in proportion to the position of the individual at the moment of his entrance into such disembodied state. This pessimistic view possibly underlies the statement of Solomon—" where the tree falleth, there it shall be "—implying that the soul enters the unseen state in the same mental condition by which it was distinguished at the moment of death. This is in accordance with the words of the angel to St. John recorded in the Apocalypse: "He that is unjust, let him be unjust still; he that is filthy, let him be filthy still; he that is righteous, let him be righteous still; and he that is holy, let him be holy still." To the mind of Job, Sheol, while recognised as a means of deliverance from bodily suffering, would still be regarded as a place of darkness and of the shadow of death, in consequence of the fear and anguish with which he was oppressed from a sense of the loss of God's favour, and his ignorance of its cause, accompanied by a feeling that he had no assurance of restoration to the light of God's countenance when he entered the Sheol. The believer in Christ has alone the full revelation that it is better to depart and to be with Christ, whereby he is enabled to endure with resignation the sufferings for the infliction of which he can discover no adequate reason.

The new problem which Jöb lays before his friends for their solution is embodied in his question, " Why does God give no clear reason for the toleration of unmerited suffering, or appoint a mediator to act as an advocate between Himself and man ? "

CHAPTER XII

ZOPHAR'S REPLY TO JOB

(CHAP. xi.)

Job's claims to purity of doctrine and integrity of life gave offence to Zophar. By the root meaning of the name and that of his abode he is the representative of the superficial man of society, ever ready to treat garrulously the ordinary topics of the age. He commences with an allusion to the language used by Job, whom he offensively describes as "a man of lips, and his utterances as mere babblings." The deep problems which his sufferings had caused to arise in his mind were beyond the shallow intellect of the frivolous man of pleasure to understand. Zophar was unable to distinguish between impatient words extorted by pain and the fundamental truth of the doctrines held by Job concerning God's nature and wisdom. Job's difficulty lay in the apparent hardship that affliction should be permitted by God where its cause was unknown to the sufferer, and the more so if, as in Job's case, his life had been characterised by the purity of his doctrine and the integrity of his conduct. Zophar offers no solution of this mystery. He merely appeals to God to reprove Job by words directed against him, so as to reveal to him that wisdom has a twofold aspect, the character of which he does not attempt to define. His statement is a mere truism that the full understanding of the Divine wisdom is beyond man's apprehension. On this basis he utters the uncharitable judgment that God has forborne much punishment which was strictly due to Job's iniquity. The theories held by the prosperous man that suffering must be traced to wickedness, and by the philosopher that in those apparently good it must be attributed to their hypocrisy, are regarded by the vain talker as insufficient, for he holds that such suffering is less than was deserved. These are the narrow, uncharitable views in which those who labour under affliction are generally judged by worldly-minded men.

Zophar next proceeds to rebuke Job's desire that it were possible to be brought face to face with God to plead his own cause. He argues as if Job were ignorant of the invisible nature of God: "Wilt thou by searching find out God? Wilt thou find the limit of the Almighty's infinitude? Higher than heaven is He—deeper than Sheol. What wilt thou do or know concerning one whose measure is longer than the earth, and wider than the sea?" He goes on to describe God's secret mode of action, and its reasons: "If He glides by unseen, or shuts men in confinement, or convokes them to judgment, who can turn Him from His purpose? For He sees who are vain and He sees their wickedness, therefore He must take cognisance of both, so as to restrain the self-willed nature of man, untamed as the wild ass." In these words Zophar implies that Job's misery must be attributed to mistaken reliance on his own wisdom, which requires to be shaken by the hand of God, to deliver him from the errors and sins into which it has betrayed him. He therefore advises him "to prepare his heart to return to God with prayer and self-examination, so that he may put far away iniquity from his own daily conduct and from amidst those who dwell in his tents. Then will he again be able to lift up his face without spot, and even when in straitened difficulties he will have no fear, for he will soon forget his misery as the quickly-gliding waters of a river. The pathway of his life will shine forth with greater brilliancy than the noonday, and his dark hours will be as the morning. Thus he will become confident, because he has hope. He will dig his land and sleep safely; he will lay down, and no one will cause him to tremble. Many will entreat his favour." Such are the blessings promised to the penitent, to him who forsakes his past errors and transgressions. These Zophar contrasts with the fate of the bad: "But the eyes of the wicked shall fail, their place of refuge will perish from them, and their hope shall be as the breathing out of the life of the soul."

The reply of Zophar entirely failed to explain Job's problem that God destroys both the perfect man and the wicked without any discrimination. The reiteration of the statement, that the wicked will always be punished in this life, is not only inconsistent with general experience, but even if it were invariably true, it would afford no consolation to sustain the perfect under their apparently unmerited suffering, since the sight of pain in others distresses them. Job's misery had been intensified by a temporary loss of hope that restoration to happiness would be accorded to him in the Intermediate State. This, to his troubled vision, had assumed the character of gloom and darkness more terrible than even death itself, in which the dissolution of the body gave evidence that its sensibility to all suffering had necessarily been destroyed. Job appears to have dreaded that the soul at death would depart into another state of conscious existence, in which the mental sorrows of life would be perpetuated even in the perfect man. But this eclipse of faith was only transient, for in his next reply to Bildad he records his conviction that "his Redeemer liveth, and that after his awaking from the dust he should with his own eyes again see God from his reanimated body." Faith in the future vindication of the integrity of his life is the main support through which the earthly sufferings of the perfect can be sustained. It was the joy that was set before Him in the accomplishment of His work in man's salvation and the hope of subsequent glorification which enabled our Lord to bear the trouble of His soul, and to abstain from praying to the Father to be saved from the dark hour of its endurance.

CHAPTER XIII

JOB'S REPLY TO ZOPHAR

(CHAPS. xii., xiii., xiv.)

Problem—" Why do the perfect suffer as if they were wicked ? "

THE discourteous words of Zophar, accusing him of ignorant and foolish talking, excited the anger of Job. He had failed in proving the fallacy of Job's statement, that "God destroyed the perfect and the wicked," and only reiterated the advice of the other two friends, that "if he put away iniquity he would forget his misery." Job naturally denied the inferiority of his own knowledge, and regarded himself as an object of mockery to his friends, who, when he was calling on God for a solution of his difficulties, presumed to answer him with scornful laughter. He feels that "one ready to slip with his feet is regarded by those at ease as a despised lamp unfit to guide their steps." He then re-affirms his statement, that "the tents of robbers prosper, and that confidence to obtain the plunder which God brings to their hands is enjoyed by those who rage furiously against His laws." In support of this he appeals to animated nature, in which suffering appears to be the necessary consequence of the means used by the wild beasts to supply their requirements. Yet "who knoweth not that this unavoidable pain to which the animals are subjected, has been permitted by an All-merciful God, in whose hand is the soul of every living creature and the spirit of all mankind." He goes on to show that as meat is tasted by the palate, so he has tested the words which his ear has heard spoken by his friends, and, comparing them with the wisdom of the ancient, he has found them unprofitable. He states "that with God alone is infinite wisdom and irresistible might, and that to Him belong infallible counsel and illimitable understanding." This he illustrates in His governance of the world: "He breaketh down a house, and it is not rebuilt. He shutteth men up, and the prison door cannot be opened. He withholdeth the rain waters, and the earth becomes dry. He sendeth the deluge, and earth is submerged. With Him is force and matter. To Him belong ignorance and its cause. He permits wise counsellors to become a prey to destruction, and He makes judges to be praisers of vain things. He looses the bond of captive kings, and then bindeth their loins with the girdle of fidelity to their royal duties. He causes profane priests to go away spoiled, and He overthrows the idolatrous Baalim, or false gods. He turns aside the eloquent lip of the faithful, and perverts the intriguing policy of the elders. He poureth shame on the nobles, and weakens the belt of the wrestlers. He uncovereth the depths of darkness, and bringeth the shadow of death to light. He increases the nations, and then causes them to perish. He scatters nations, and then comforts them. He turns away the heart and dissolves the courage of the heads of the peoples of the earth, and causes them to wander in chaos where there is no way. They grope in darkness, where there is no light, and He causes them to stagger as a drunkard. Lo this I have seen with mine eyes, and mine ear hath heard and understood it. As ye know I also know. I have not fallen away from knowledge any more than you."

Thus Job asserts his own position and the utter failure of his friends to reply to his inquiry. As yet they have made no attempt to prove the correctness of their theory, that the cause of suffering must invariably be traced to the commission of sin. He has shown the fallacy of this doctrine in the examples which he has drawn from the cruelties to which animals are exposed from the hand of man, and from the events which take place amongst men under their threefold individual, social, and national aspects. He shows that in the cases referred to it is impossible to affirm that their sufferings are always the result of sin. He therefore calls them "inventors of false theories and incompetent physicians. Their intellectual reasonings were shown to be inapplicable to solve mental doubts, and their spiritual instruction failed to give comfort to the disturbed soul. He points out therefore that silence was their truest wisdom, whilst he pleaded his own cause with God.

He gives additional reasons for this advice. He appears to charge them with false motives for the character of their language when revealing the will of God: "Will you speak words of iniquity or deceit in advocating God's cause? Will you hypocritically be partial when contending for God's honour in giving utterance to words concerning His doings in which you do not believe? Are you open to His investigation of your real motives, or, as men deceived by their fellow-men, are you only mocking Him with words proceeding from the lips and not from the heart?" He exposes the dangers to which they are thus exposing themselves: "Know, therefore, that if you are thus partial He will surely reprove you. Does not His infinite exaltation cause you to fear in so doing, and does not the dread of Him fall upon you?" He shows them the extreme weakness of their arguments: "Your remembrances of intellectual theories are mere parables of ashes from which all spiritual illumination has been eliminated. Your very bodies are mere bodies of clay without any mental vigour." He therefore again calls upon them "to hold their peace, so that he may give outward expression of his feelings to God

Himself, without any regard to the risk to which he may be exposed from His anger. For this he is willing to imperil his very existence, by proverbially taking his flesh between his teeth, and by putting his soul into the palm of his hand." Yet, underlying all his feelings of indignation at the apparently harsh and undeserved treatment to which he has been subjected by the will of God, there is still a firm determination to "trust God even if He should slay him, and to wait upon Him for a vindication of his conduct." The Satan is still unable to force Job to apostatise, and the accusation, that man will not serve God for nought, still remains divested of proof.

Job, however, refuses to renounce his claim to conscious integrity of life. He therefore looks to God for salvation, because he is fully convinced that any confession of sin—of the commission of which he is unconscious—would not only fail to obtain God's favour, but would also cause him to forfeit admission into the Divine presence, whereinto no hypocrite can obtain an entrance.

He now calls upon the friends " to hear his speech, and to receive into their ears what he has to declare; for he adds, I have now ordered my cause before God, with the full assurance that I shall be acquitted and that my conduct will be vindicated; for who is there that will contend with me? If so, and if there were any one able successfully to convict me of sin, I would at once remain silent and give up the ghost."

A fresh problem appears to have presented itself to the mind of Job: "Why is man treated as an offender without having revealed to him the character of his sin?" For the solution of this he addresses himself to God, asking "that two favours should be granted to him, so that he may not be tempted to hide himself from God. He prays that God's afflicting hand should be drawn away, and that the dread of God's majesty should not terrify him." Twofold rest of body and mind would thus be secured to him, so that he might be ready to be arraigned before God and to make reply to any charge brought against him. In the event of God's refusal to grant this petition, he further prays that he might be allowed to state his grievance and humbly await God's answer. He proceeds on the latter assumption. "He prays that God would cause him to know what, and how many were his transgressions and sins, and that He would give him a reason why He hides His face from him, and holds him for an enemy. He compares himself to a leaf torn from its parent branch, and to the dry stubble driven to and fro by a mighty wind, without power of resistance. He complains that bitter things are recorded against him of which he has no cognisance, and that in old age he is apparently caused to inherit the evils which result from the forgotten iniquities of his youth. The burden of his prayer is that the immediate causes of his misery should be revealed to him, that by their removal relief might be obtained. He describes his condition as that of a culprit whose feet are confined within the stocks, depriving him of progressive movement, whose paths through life are being sharply observed by his harsh jailer, and upon whose heels a brand has been placed, so that any future footstep may be clearly traced. Thus, as a rotten thing whose outward character, like a moth-eaten garment, is marked by increasing deterioration," the unhappy victim consumes away, though utterly unconscious of the sources whence his corruption has proceeded, and therefore unable to seek for inward reformation, or to protect himself from open enemies.

He proceeds to contemplate the natural condition of humanity. He observes that "man born of woman is of few days, and full of bodily and mental disturbance. He cometh forth like a flower, and is cut down; he fleeth as a shadow, and continueth not." He questions whether one so shortlived is a fit subject for the infinite God to mark all his steps, and to bring him into judgment, without giving him time to amend. He then traces out the origin of man's trouble. It is seen to be hereditary: "Can a clean thing come out of an unclean?" Hence man's liability to trouble. Thus he feels the hardship that continuous suffering should be the lot of any who have been born under such conditions.

He advances another reason why the cause of suffering should be speedily revealed, in the limited determination of man's life within bounds which are impassible. He pleads that he should be treated as the hireling servant who rests after the accomplishment of his daily labour. Job has already shown that by the very nature of his disease he is deprived of such rest; night and day he suffers agony, and this is intensified by its hopeless character and his reduction to penury. He contrasts this sad condition with what happens "to a tree, which, when cut down, will again sprout, and perpetuate its existence by means of its suckers, which will bud and bring forth branches, when the scent of water is applied to its old root and its decayed stock. It is different with man. When man wastes and dies, where is he? none can perceive where he goes. He is like the waters, which, by evaporation out of the sea, are distilled into rain till they form a river, which glides away and then dries up. So the body of man lies down, and rises not till the heavens are no more. Till then it wakens not, and is not raised out of its last sleep."

The continuity of life in Sheol is fully recognised: "Oh that Thou wouldst hide me in Sheol; that Thou wouldst keep me secret till Thy wrath be past; that Thou wouldst appoint for me a set time to remove me to Sheol, and remember me in the midst of my present sufferings." Such existence

H

in Sheol is regarded as a deliverance from all his misery. Job desires to remain there till God's anger is appeased, whereby he will be freed from his bodily suffering. But at times even a moment of despair seems to come upon him, and he almost doubts whether he will be preserved alive in Sheol: "If a man die, will he live?" Such a cry, like the bitter utterance from the Cross, "My God, My God, why hast Thou forsaken Me?" is extorted from his agonised feelings. Ignorance of the cause of his sufferings is provocative of unfaith in the continuity of life after death. Everything seems hopeless. Were I fully assured of life, "all the days of my warfare would I patiently wait in eager looking forward to my passing away into Sheol." But this eclipse of faith is only temporary. His assured hope of life in Sheol is realised in the next words, "Thou shalt call, and I will answer; Thou shalt call me to resign life on earth, and I will answer by resigning my spirit into Thy hands, for by such a call Thou bearest witness of Thy desire for the work of Thine hands." It is an anticipation of our Lord's promise, "He that cometh unto Me I will in no wise cast off."

He again reverts to his present misery. He imagines that every step is numbered with a view to recording his imperfect progress, and in abject fear he expresses a feeble hope that God will not observe him for purposes of punishment. The intensity of his suffering suggests "that the remembrance of every transgression and iniquity is sewn up in a bag and sealed for future reference." This permanent memorial of his unknown errors intensifies his dread. Nothing seems to remain but to expect destruction. Inorganic nature appears to teach the same lesson: "The continuous landslip imperils the existence of the mountain, and leads to the removal of the rocky superstructure from its very foundation. The stone is worn away by the perpetual drip of the water, which in time washes away all that grows out of the dust of the earth. The earth itself bears witness to the denudation which follows perpetual abrasion; and so the hope of man perishes."

The reply of Job to Zophar witnesses to some of the feelings that arise in the hearts of those exposed to prolonged pain and grief, for which they can find no adequate cause. They examine their past lives, and seek in vain for some forgotten sins to which they may be attributed. They question their hearts why God should hide away His face, and treat them as enemies. They mentally regard their youthful follies as being the cause of such continuous harsh treatment, implying that if God will for ever manifest His power over them, they must go away from life, when, after changing their faces by the death throes, He will send them to the grave. Then if their sons are honoured they will not know of it, or if they are brought low they will not perceive it. It is only in their own flesh that they feel pain, and their souls only mourn for themselves. Such is the egotism of feeling that is produced by apparently causeless misery.

Even conscience does not convict them of sins proportionate to the suffering. Despairingly turning from the contemplation of the past, they mournfully look forward to the future, to the passing away in death into the invisible Sheol, with its dimly revealed conditions of existence. Hope of a future revival seems almost to forsake them, whilst doubts intrude themselves into their minds, whether the apparently causeless wrath of God will in this new existence have passed away.

The full solution of such deep problems was beyond the understanding of the patriarchs, or even of those living before the incarnation of the Divine Word. Christ Jesus alone could explain such deep and hidden mysteries, and by His perfected submission to the Father's will, witnessed in the agony of Gethsemane, and followed by the resurrection from the grave, bring peace and assurance of acceptance to the troubled souls of all faithful sufferers. In the knowledge of Christ's resurrection, and the contemplation of His perfected submission to the Father's will, man becomes better able to endure apparently unmerited suffering without impatiently demanding the solution of the problem, "Why is man treated as an offender without having revealed to him the nature of his sin?"

CHAPTER XIV

ELIPHAZ'S SECOND REPLY TO JOB

(CHAP. XV.)

On the conclusion of Job's answer to Zophar, Eliphaz makes a second reply. In his first address to Job he had based his arguments in support of the theory, that suffering was to be attributed to some act of sin, upon his own personal experience. He now proceeds to show that this view is also a matter of general experience confirmed by the prevalent depravity of humanity: "I will show thee that which I have seen, which wise men have received from their fathers, and have told it and not hid it." He commences by pointing out to Job "the unwisdom of giving utterance to inflated language, of filling his mind with antiquated knowledge, and of reasoning upon unprofitable subjects. He accuses him of casting off the fear of God in pleading to be allowed to defend himself against the apparent injustice of unmerited suffering, and thereby substituting the expression of his own wishes instead of offering up submissive prayer to God. He thereby reveals the existence of some hidden iniquity in his heart, witnessed by the subtlety of his language. Thus he stands self-condemned. But this judgment of Eliphaz was not only harsh, but also undeserved, for Job never presumed to dispute the inherent wisdom and counsel of God. His words, extorted by his pain and sorrows, were directed to the discovery of their cause. His faith in the fundamental love of God was never shaken, his only difficulty was to reconcile God's treatment with his sense of conscious integrity.

Eliphaz, as the wealthy man of position, taunts the poor afflicted leper sitting on the ash-heap, with presumption in claiming equality of knowledge with the three friends, " I have understanding as well as you." He scoffingly asks, " Art thou the first man that was born, so as to be able to speak with such assurance? Has the secret counsel of God been committed to thy cognisance, as if wisdom was thy peculiar gift? Canst thou know or understand any things which the aged and grey-headed, and those older than thy father, do not know? Are the ordinary consolations which God gives man too few for thee, or are there with thee any subtler words than those spoken by us? Why does the wish of thy heart carry thee away, and why do thine eyes roll with anger, so that thou turnest thy spirit against God, and permittest such words to go from thy mouth? Thou boastest of thine integrity, but what is man that he should be pure, or one born of woman that he should be righteous? Lo, God trusts not in His saints. Even the heavens are not clean in His eyes. How much more abominable and filthy, then, is the man who drinketh iniquity as water?"

After this arraignment of his friend, Eliphaz proceeds to give him the result of his investigation into the causes of suffering, derived from the general experience of mankind. He traces it to the primeval knowledge which was originally possessed and transmitted by the wise men to whom the earth was first given, before any strangers, possibly deriving their origin from the apostate angels, passed among them (Gen. vi.). He seems to distinguish between the purity of primeval doctrine held by man, and entrusted to the body of elect elders, who in patriarchal ages appear to have received the title of wise men, and the corruptions which afterwards through liability to error attended its transmission by means of oral tradition, as well as those to which in later days it became exposed by Satanic influences.

Eliphaz next enlarges on the evils to which transgressors are exposed: "All the days of the wicked he travails in pain, and the number of his years is reserved for the oppressor to afflict him. A voice of dread is in his ears, and the robber comes upon him when he is in peace. He believeth not that he will ever come out of the darkness into which his guilt has cast him. He feels the sword of God waiting for his destruction. He wanders alone everywhere for bread. He knows that a day of darkness is prepared for him. The anticipation of distress and anguish terrifies him. They overpower him as a king equipped for a siege." Eliphaz then goes on to describe the character of the wicked in his opposition to the Divine will, and gives a reason for his fear. It is because he stretches out his hand against God, and strengthens himself to resist the Almighty.

Under the powerful symbolism of an ancient warrior fighting against his foe, his determined opposition to the purposes of God is shown in his running with a stiff neck, descriptive of his callous insensibility to danger, revealed in his rushing forward under the shelter of the thick backs of his protecting shields of carnal security. He covers his face with fatness and adds fat to his loins, to symbolise the crass stupidity in which he has encased his mental and bodily faculties so as to render them impermeable to spiritual influences.

He dwells in desolate cities and deserted houses, ready to become ruins amongst the once organised associations and homes of men whom he has driven from the presence of their brethren, like the Arab slave raiders pillaging the dwellings of their wretched captives: "But he will not become rich; his wealth will not increase, and his possessions will not extend upon the earth. He will not be turned away from obscure darkness, for the flame will consume his sucking babes, and by the breath of God he will be removed."

Eliphaz concludes his words with a warning: "Let him not trust in vanity. He is deceived, for vanity will be his recompense. Before his time his fate will be fulfilled, and his branch or posterity shall not flourish. He will shake off his unripe grape as the vine, and cast off his immature flower as the olive. Thus his ill-matured wishes and plans will fail, for the congregations of the hypocrites shall become solitary, and fire shall consume the tents of bribery. Men conceive mischief, they beget vanity and bring forth deceit."

Such warnings are not calculated to afford consolation to any labouring, as Job, under a sense of unmerited suffering, and a feeling of injustice in God's refusal to acquaint him with their cause. He observed that the innocent were equally exposed to pain and sorrow as the bad, and the mere reiteration, that even in the time of prosperity the destruction of the wicked might be expected, offered no solution to the problem why the perfect should undergo suffering for which no adequate cause could be given, or why God should refuse to acquaint them with any transgressions or sins into which they had been unconsciously betrayed. Until such knowledge has been attained, hope of relief appears to be very distant, and such hopelessness only aggravates their wretchedness. The true source of comfort lies in the recognition of the assurance that with his Divine Master every righteous servant of Jehovah participates in the prophetic promise, that he shall see the happy fruits of the travail of his soul and shall be satisfied, and that all things are promised to work together for good to those who love God. Patient endurance of whatever suffering it pleases God that man should undergo is the true solution of Job's problem. "It is the Lord's hand, let Him therefore do what seemeth Him good."

CHAPTER XV

JOB'S SECOND REPLY TO ELIPHAZ

(CHAPS. xvi., xvii.)

Problem—"Why does God refuse man's plea for relief?"

ELIPHAZ had reproached Job for turning his spirit against God, and had insinuated that his sufferings were due to sin, by the description which he had given of the punishment of the wicked. Job commences his reply by showing the unsuitableness of his remarks. He says that he had advanced no fresh argument in support of his theory of the cause of suffering, and he therefore entreats him "to give up speaking words valueless to give comfort. He expresses his wonder at his boldness in so addressing him. He contrasts the harsh character of his words with that of those which in a similar position he himself would have spoken, for he would have endeavoured to give the sufferer strength by the words of his mouth, or else have withheld the moving of his lip."

Having thus relieved his feelings in respect of his friend's harshness, he reverts to the agonised condition of his own mind. Nothing seems to give relief. The giving utterance to his woe does not assuage his grief; and if he is silent the pain does not leave him. In very despairing words he therefore proceeds to give expression to the thought, that all his sufferings must be attributed to the direct action of God. Unconsciously he is thus stating one of the great truths which this history was designed to reveal. Though the trial was necessitated by the craft of Satan in propounding his problem as to Job's disinterestedness, yet, as he himself states, it was God who delivered him into the power of Satan, and permitted a large portion of his sufferings to be inflicted by man. The robbers despoiled him of his goods; he was erroneously accused of sin by his friends, and insolently treated by the abject classes to whom he had before been the greatest benefactor. All this he describes in highly symbolical language, the impatience of which must be attributed to the intensity of his misery. Thus he proceeds: "God has worn me out with weariness from my pain. He has deprived me of association with the company of my friends. The very wrinkles arising from my disease with which He has filled me, and the leanness that increases upon me, bear witness that He accuses me with the unconscious commission of some unrecognised sin. Therefore He tears me in His anger and hates me; He gnashes upon me with His teeth, and fixes His eyes sharply upon me to scrutinise all my faults.

The very abjects gaped upon me with their mouths; they have smitten me on the cheek as they uttered their reproaches upon me; they have filled themselves with insults and revilings against me, for God hath delivered me into the hands of the ungodly. I was prosperous, but God has utterly frustrated my purposes. He has seized me by the neck and dashed me aside. He has set me as a target against which the encircling archers direct their arrows, even their scornful words. He cleaveth my reins and scrutinises my inmost thoughts. He breaketh me with breach upon breach, with sorrow added to sorrow. He runs upon me as a mighty warrior." Then in allusion to his terrible disease, he shows how his ordinary raiment has been exchanged for " the common sackcloth, and the ornamental horn of official honour has been lowered to the dust, whilst his face is marred with weeping, and on his eyelids is to be seen the near approach of the agonies of death."

Every instant the tension produced by his wretchedness increases. For a few moments he appears to pause in his impatient arraignments of God's permission of his misery.

Then a fresh problem appears to present itself to his mind. He asks himself, why should God witness undeserved suffering in one who has lived a conscientious life without giving relief, or the opportunity to plead his cause with Him, so that his only hope is in the grave? He remembers how Eliphaz, by his strong denunciation of the evils to which the wicked are exposed, has insinuated that Job's wretchedness must be traced to the commission of sin. The desire to clear himself becomes paramount, and he indignantly affirms that all the sufferings to which he has been exposed are due to "no violence committed by his own hand. Even the desires of his heart are free from sin. My very prayer is pure." Mistaken imputations of the commission of evil are some of the bitterest sorrows which a godly person has to bear. This is realised in the prophetic Psalm treating of the sufferings of our Lord. "The ungodly gaped upon Me with their mouths and said, Fie on Thee, fie on Thee, we saw it with our eyes, extorting the Divine prayer: This Thou hast seen, O Lord; hold not Thy peace then, go not far from me, O Lord."

He despairingly looks around for some one to vindicate his life from the imputation of evil. He finds no one to undertake the office. Possibly calling to remembrance the tradition of God's words to Cain after the murder of his brother, he makes a sublime appeal to the earth itself: "O earth, cover not my blood, let there be no place on thy surface where my cry can remain unheard, and from whence it can be hindered in its ascent to the heavens; for he further affirms, my Witness is there, my Watcher is on high. He appeals from man to God: my earthly friends scorn me; mine eye therefore pours out her tears to God." Then, again, he bursts out with an imploring cry, "Oh that one might plead for man with God, as a son of man for his friend." Then he would feel safe, that his integrity would be vindicated, when the number of his years should be completed, and he should go the way whence there is no return. Even now, he adds, "My spirit is in travail, my days are become extinct, the graves are ready for me. Though I am thus at the point to die, yet surely my friends are mocking me, and mine eye is fixed upon their provocations." This he alleges as a reason for asking God to give a pledge and to make Himself a surety or mediator between Job and Himself; for he has none other to whom he can apply to answer for him, for God has hidden their hearts from understanding, so that God will not accept them in justifying their assertion of his guilt. At the same time he warns them that whoever speaks in flattery to his friends, will imperil the eyes or the prosperity of his own children. He again gives utterance to his feelings of misery, when he contemplates how God has made him a byword to the people, who was once a judge amongst them, so that his eyes are dim with sorrow and his very bodily form is reduced to a shadow. Far different, however, are the thoughts of the godly who are astonished at this apparent misprision of justice, and of the innocent who stir themselves up to expose the falsehood of such hypocritical accusations, being convinced in their own minds that the righteous man will hold on his way, and that he who is clean-handed will become more and more courageous.

At this point of the discussion Job again counsels his friends to return to their own homes, as he does not find amongst them one possessed of sufficient wisdom to give him any efficient consolation or support. Your methods of consolation are as if you put night for day, in making the cause of my misery more difficult of apprehension through your erroneous arguments rather than by the weakness of my own reasoning, so that light, or the hope of relief, can only be looked for out of the darkness of the grave. " If I have any hope it is for Sheol to become my house, that I may spread my couch in darkness. I have called to corruption, Thou art my father; and to the worm, Thou art my mother and sister. Where then is my hope? As for my hope who can see it? It goes down to the bars of Sheol, where together with myself it rests in the dust."

In such despairing language does he support his prayer for permission to plead his own cause with God, whom he knows to be the witness not only of his misery but also of his conscientious efforts in the performance of his duty.

The words of Job as their Divinely revealed representative, express the feelings of those who are undergoing great and prolonged afflictions of mind and body for which they can discover no adequate reason. Fully believing that their Heavenly Father, without whose knowledge not a sparrow falleth to the ground, must be fully conscious that they have faithfully endeavoured to conform themselves to His will, a sense of injustice is engendered in their minds when they contemplate the prosperity of the wicked, and see no way out of their own troubles except by submission to the hand of death. Failing to obtain from man a sufficient reason to account for such an apparent inconsistency in the Divine dealings, a desire arises in their heart to be allowed to vindicate their conduct before God, feeling assured that an All-just God would not fail to make known to them any hitherto unrecognised error into which they had been betrayed, by the forsaking of which they might hope to be placed in a way whereby peace and happiness might be restored to them.

CHAPTER XVI

BILDAD'S SECOND REPLY TO JOB

(CHAP. xviii.)

THE opening words of Bildad suggest the idea that he had interrupted Job as he was describing his hopeless condition, "How long wilt thou be in putting an end to thy utterances? consider, and let another speak." He had been angered when Job complained of the unkind language of his friends, and showed the unsuitableness of their arguments to meet his case. He calls upon him to give greater consideration to his choice of words, and to allow them better opportunities for reply: "Why do you treat us as if we were carnal and profane persons," actuated by animal passions and interested or distorted motives? In illustration of this he refers to the complaint of Job that "God tore him in His anger," whereas Bildad retorts that the true cause of his mental disturbance must be traced to his own fury: "Job tears his own soul by his anger." It was due to opposition to the will of God, humble submission to which would have been attended with peace, whereas impatient reliance on his own integrity was only productive of increasing misery, through his charging God with injustice.

By such arguments he accuses Job of misunderstanding the laws whereby the world was governed: " Do you expect that the earth will be rendered desolate, or the rock removed out of its place, for thy sake?" Job had complained of God's toleration of the ill-treatment which he had received from men, not only from the harsh treatment of his friends, but also from the insults of the abject crowds who visited him in his misery: "God has delivered me into the hands of the wicked. My friends scorn me. I am become a byword to those by whom aforetime I was regarded as a judge. They gape upon me with their mouth, and smite my cheek reproachfully." These words assume the character of a prayer for their punishment. But according to the theory of Bildad, that his suffering is the result of sin, it would be a reversal of natural law to punish them for so doing, and thereby to make the earth more desolate by depriving it of their presence. Moreover it would be opposed to the invariable fixity of the moral law, unless retribution should follow sin, of which the immovability of the rock is the emblem.

The difference between the two replies of Bildad is but small. Both are based on the doctrine that affliction is caused by sin. He grounds his argument at first by an appeal to the tradition of the fathers, whereas in the present instance he does so

by an appeal to the invariability of natural law.
Both these appeals fail in their application to the
action of the Creator. The tradition of the fathers,
by its transmission through human channels, is at
all times liable to error. This was shown by our
Lord when reproving the Pharisees for teaching
that the dedication of the Corban, or gift to God,
freed the offerer from his duty to support his starving
parents. The action of natural law, which is only
the outward expression of the Divine will, is at all
times liable to be changed by the intervention of
some higher purpose of God, but until such intervention has been revealed, the law itself remains
unrepealed and its action invariable. This is witnessed in the evolution of a child from the mother's
womb, in which it has been conceived by being
begotten of the father. The invariability of this
law has since the creation remained unbroken except
on two occasions—when Eve was first brought into
existence out of the side of Adam, and when Jesus
was conceived in the womb of the Virgin by the
Holy Ghost. The invariability of the law, therefore, that restricts suffering to the punishment of evil,
is equally liable to the intervention of God. It not
only may be, but is repeatedly broken in this life,
when in accordance with the Divine will the wicked
prosper and the righteous suffer. The faithful Abel
perished by the hand of the unbelieving Cain. The
life of Barabbas, the insurgent murderer, was spared,

while that of the innocent Son of Man was taken away upon the cross. Man's knowledge of law is limited by the capabilities of his mind, so that what appears invariable to the child is recognised as only transitory by the philosopher. The theory of the existence of eternal law which does not originate with God, to which God, though not subject, yet with which God's will is identical, deposes God from His position as Creator, for law presupposes the existence of two entities whose relationship is governed by law. Their existence can only be attributed to God as their Producer. One of these as God is self-existent, the other is man or matter, of which God is the Creator. The laws governing their relations must therefore emanate from God Himself, unless the exploded Zoroastrian doctrine of two eternal independent principles of good and evil is revived, a theory subversive of the unity of God, which forms the basis of the problem which the Book of Job was intended to reveal.

Bildad then proceeds to illustrate the invariability of law in the punishment of the wicked. He shows " how the light or prosperity of the wicked is extinguished both in his tent and in his life; how the firmness of his footsteps or his progress in the world becomes straitened, and his own counsel casts him down, so that he is taken in various kinds of snares. He points out how causeless terror therefore seizes him, and drives him into exile; how enfeebled he becomes by famine, so that destruction only awaits him." He states "that the ravages of disease which come upon him, and the dreaded leprosy, the firstborn of death, will devour his inward strength and the outward protection of his skin. Thus he loses confidence even when dwelling in his tent, and realises the gradual approach of death, the king of unseen terrors, which will take up its abode in his tabernacle from which he is excluded, whilst the desolating brimstone is scattered about his homestead. His roots, or the attractions which hold him to his dwelling, lose their power, and the harvest or profit of his labour is cut off. The remembrance of him perishes, and his name is forgotten. He is driven away from the light of the sun into the darkness of the grave. He is chased out of the world. He leaves behind him no posterity nor any survivor in his place of sojourn. They that come after him are astonished at the day of his visitation, and those who were formerly his contemporaries are seized with horror at his fate." With such unsupported assertions Bildad concludes by affirming that "such are the dwellings of the wicked, and that this is the place of him that knoweth not God."

Bildad entirely evades the indisputable fact that the wicked are often seen in the enjoyment of the greatest earthly prosperity, which frequently accompanies their lives to the moment of their death.

His arguments, drawn from natural evolution, fail therefore to give any support to his contention, that suffering is the invariable result of sin, and offer no solution to Job's question, "Why the perfect are exposed to suffering equally with the wicked?"

CHAPTER XVII

JOB'S SECOND REPLY TO BILDAD

(CHAP. xix.)

Problem—" Why does not God vindicate the perfect ? "

THE words of Bildad, endeavouring to show from the invariability of natural order that suffering should be traced to the commission of sin, and his evasion of any attempt to account for the afflictions to which the perfect are exposed, increased the irritation under which Job was labouring. He at once rebukes him for thus vexing his soul and crushing him with unjust accusations and groundless calumnies: "These ten times ye have reproached me." Then he adds, that even on the supposition "that he had erred, it was a matter that concerned himself alone, and gave no reason why Bildad should magnify himself so as to give utterance to reproaches against him." He declares that he had not been overthrown from his former prosperous position by man, but by the direct action of God, who had encompassed him with impassible barriers, and who remained deaf to his cries for deliverance from violence, and to his prayer for justice. He goes on to describe how deeply he feels the restraint which his leprous disease had laid upon him, and the consequent darkness that had impeded his progress in life. He shows how his reduction to poverty had deprived him of the glory which, as a crown, was attached to his former honourable position. He speaks of himself as utterly broken down and thrust out of the current concerns of life, so that his case was as hopeless of revival as that of an uprooted tree. He points out the mode in which God had manifested His anger in treating him as an enemy, collecting His troops and causing them to encamp near his tent, possibly in allusion to the robber bands and atmospheric agencies by which he had been deprived of his wealth and family. He complains of His having produced the estrangement of his friends and acquaintances, of His allowing him to be regarded with neglect by his former servants, of His alienating the affections of his wife, and of making him an object of contempt to the young, and of abhorrence to those who formerly shared his most secret counsels, owing to the terrible condition to which his loathsome disease had reduced him: "My bone cleaveth to my flesh, and I am escaped with the skin of my teeth."

The contemplation of his misery extorts a cry, "that pity should be accorded to him by his friends. Deal favourably, deal favourably with me, oh my friends, for the hand of God has troubled me."

With the best intentions their words only increased his sufferings, though spoken with a view to his relief. Their insinuations, that these were due to some sin of which he professed himself to be unconscious, were destructive to his peace. They added mental disturbance to his bodily torments: "Why do you persecute me as God? are you not satisfied with the pains to which my flesh is exposed?" Your reproaches are as much without foundation as the affliction which God has laid on me appears to be without cause.

Such thoughts only increase the intensity of his desire for his vindication, and a fresh problem presents itself to his mind. He asks himself the reason "why God should refuse to vindicate his innocence before he departs into Sheol?" He then ponders on the best mode whereby it may be attained. God is apparently deaf to his prayers for a hearing of his pleadings. His friends are unable to give him any consolation. He feels himself gradually passing away, and appears to dread his departure into Sheol before his integrity has been made manifest. Hence his desire that "his words should be written and engraven in a book, that they were hewn in the rock as a witness, and filled up with iron and lead for safe preservation." His sorest trial is the mistaken accusation of personal sin which has been laid against him by his friends, and the erroneous imputations of ill-doing to which his miserable condition has exposed him from those who once respected and honoured him. Until his past conduct has been freed from these calumnies nothing seems capable of affording comfort to his troubled soul.

He has no fear in presenting himself before God. He looks forward to the future judgment with the calm assurance of acceptance, for he knows that "his Redeemer liveth, One who will hereafter rise up and stand over the dust of his perishing body ready to vindicate his character before God." Job was a firm believer in the resurrection of the body, for he goes on to affirm that this appearance of his Redeemer will be the signal for the awaking of his mortal body out of the sleep of death, so "that his dust will again take form, and in the presence of those who will encompass it, he will with his own eyes be permitted to see God from out of his re-animated flesh." Under such concise terms does Job describe the resurrection of the body, and reveal his faith in the future vision of the Divine Being by whom it is to be effected.

The doctrine of a redeeming Goel, or Vindicator, forms one of the clauses of the patriarchal creed. The Divine Angel of Jehovah, who had been formerly revealed to Jacob at Penuel, and was afterwards referred to by the aged patriarch as the Angel who had redeemed him from all evil, is here described under the same Godlike nature. His divinity and unity with God is clearly affirmed. Job appears to have been possessed of a very deep insight into His divine offices: not only was He the protector of the faithful during their earthly lives, but also the witness of their conduct from the heavenly sphere; and here He is revealed as coming to be the vindicator of their innocence at the close of the dispensation, when the dead are to be called out of their graves to stand before the judgment-seat of God: "I know that my Redeemer liveth, and that He will rise up at the last over the dust, and after my awaking this dust shall become consolidated, and from my flesh I shall see God, whom I shall see for myself, and mine eyes shall behold, and not a stranger."

The desire for the written record of his words originated with the desire that his posterity on earth should know of the claim he made to integrity of life. He appears to have had no doubt of his acceptance in the heavenlies. Like St. Paul, he knew in whom he had believed, and was persuaded that He was able to keep that which he had committed to Him against that day. This confession of faith was attended with such exaltation of spirit that he makes a short pause, and then gives expression to his excited feelings: "My reins consume within me." My heart is entirely absorbed with a burning desire for the manifestation of this promised blessing, and of the glorious revelation of My Divine Mediator.

He now turns again to his friends with words of warning. Far from reproaching me as you have been doing, you should examine and ask yourselves, why we have indulged in such persecution? what proof have we alleged for the reproaches which we have uttered? what definite sin have we convicted him of having committed, or what certain error have we shown that he has holden? You should have asked yourselves, "What are we persecuting in him? seeing that the root of the matter is found in me. The suffering itself as well as its cause is my affair. Beware, therefore, of the sword, the sword of sharp words, productive only of anger which often provokes the retaliation of the sword, the sword of bitter answers, which are often permitted by God to be uttered so as to convince men that judgment attends unjust and mistaken reproaches."

From this reply of Job to Bildad it appears that two special problems were pressing themselves upon his mind—

1. Why does God refuse to vindicate a man's innocency before his death, and his departure into the Intermediate State?

2. How will the vindication of such innocency after death be revealed to his friends upon earth?

CHAPTER XVIII

ZOPHAR'S SECOND REPLY TO JOB

(CHAP. XX.)

Job's warning, of the danger of judgment being pronounced on those who were thus falsely accusing him of the commission of personal sin, excited the anger of the shallow-minded Zophar. The irritation felt by the man of pleasure, when he assumes the *rôle* of the censor, rarely fails to cause him to display his intense ignorance about solemn subjects. "My own opinion," he says, "prompts me to give an immediate answer. I have heard the calumnious reproof that has been uttered against us, and the spirit of my mind forces me to an immediate reply." It takes the form of a simple reiteration of the dangers to which the wicked expose themselves. No fresh argument is advanced to show why a perfect man may be subjected to misery, or why a wicked person may escape the earthly punishment of his sins. Zophar only affirms that "the triumphant shout of the wicked is short, and that the mirth of the hypocrite is only momentary. However high may be his exaltation, yet his rolling down will be permanent. Men will ask where is he? Like a dream or a night vision, he will utterly pass away, so that the eye will see him no more, and his place on earth will not again behold him. The poor will oppress his children, and their hands will restore his ill-gotten wealth. His bones may be full of youthful vigour, but it will not preserve him from lying in the dust of death. Wickedness may be pleasant to him and hidden under his hypocritical tongue; he may spare himself the pain of forsaking it, and he may retain it in his mouth; yet, by it his bread is turned into bitterness, and the poison as of the deadly viper is in his belly. The wealth that he has unjustly absorbed God will cause him to vomit and to cast away. He may imbibe the poisonous flattery of the asp-like deceiver, but the viperous tongue of the slanderer will slay him. Though dwelling amidst the sources of plenty, yet the streams of honey and butter promised to God's people he will be unable to see for his profit. That for which he has wrongly laboured he shall restore, without enjoying the fruits of his evil toil, and his misdirected commerce shall be profitless as the sand; he shall not exult in it, because he has oppressed and neglected the poor, and unlawfully seized houses which he has not built. Because he felt no quiet contentment in his heart, he shall not preserve that in which he delights. Then shall nothing remain of his substance, so that at his death no man will wait for his possessions. In the fulness of his sufficiency he shall be distressed, so that every kind of toil will come upon him. When he is filling his belly with food, God will send against him the fury of His anger. He shall flee from the iron weapon, and the bow of brass shall cause him to glide away into the hand of death, when the arrow is drawn out from his body, and its glittering point comes out of his gall. The terrors of death will come upon him, and the darkness of the pit conceal his hidden treasures. A fire not kindled by man shall devour him, and feed on whatever survives in his tent. The heavens shall reveal his iniquity, and the earth will raise herself up against him. The produce of his house shall roll down and trickle slowly away in the day of God's anger." From such allegations, unsupported by any proof of their truth, did Zophar draw the sweeping conclusion, that "they represent the portion and heritage appointed by God for the wicked man."

The language of Zophar is equivalent to a definite charge of conscious iniquity against Job. It is a charge which, in his reply to Bildad, he had distinctly repudiated, when he affirmed that his sufferings must be attributed to the direct action of God, who refused to hear his cry for justice by being informed of the cause for which they had been sent. He had moreover appealed to his friends to take pity on him since God had so touched him, and to abstain from persecuting him by mistaken imputations of evil doing. He had confessed his faith in the coming advent of his Divine Redeemer, who in the latter days would appear on earth at his resurrection from the grave, and from whom, in his reanimated flesh, he expected to receive the full vindication of his earthly conduct. To meet such deeply-seated convictions the superficial statement, that worldly suffering is invariably due to the commission of sin, is valueless to give relief, and its credibility is disproved by the general experience of mankind. No thoughtful mind denies that a vast amount of misery in this life is due to the act of personal sin, but the afflictions to which the godly are frequently exposed must be traced to other sources, and one of the objects for which this inspired history was written is to reveal that at times their origin belongs to a higher sphere than that of earth. This is a Divine truth, which the shallow-minded man of the world, of whom Zophar is the representative, is either unable or unwilling to believe. "The natural man receiveth not the things of the Spirit of God, for they are foolishness to him, neither can he know them, because they are spiritually discerned."

CHAPTER XIX

JOB'S SECOND REPLY TO ZOPHAR

(CHAP. xxi.)

Problem—" Why do the wicked prosper ?"

JOB commences his reply to Zophar by a request in his turn for a hearing: " Hear what I have to say, and let my words take the place of your consolations; treat them with impartiality, and after I have spoken you may mock on if you will." Then he adds, "My complaint is not to man. My cry for justice is to God, and even if it were to man, there is no reason why my spirit should not be overwhelmed. Turn your faces towards me, and be astonished at my miserable condition, and then put your hand upon your mouths and cease from your unjust accusations; for when I remember and contemplate the inequality which is the general accompaniment of earthly prosperity and adversity, I become troubled, and terrors seize my flesh."

The main object of the speech of Zophar was to show that punishment for their sins was the earthly portion of the wicked, whereby indirectly he accused Job himself of the commission of evil. The inconsistency of this statement with the generally recognised fact that the wicked frequently passed their lives in prosperity, and that in this world they often escaped the retribution which was justly due to their bad conduct, caused the mind of Job to become exercised by a fresh problem. He asks, "Why do the wicked live and become old and mighty in their wealth?" To show the reasonableness of his question he adduces many examples of the prosperity that may be witnessed in the current lives of evil persons.

They are often happy in their family and social surroundings: "Their seed and their offspring is established in their sight before they die. Their houses are peaceful and free from terror, and yet the rod or sceptre of God is not raised against them. Their cattle are prolific. They send out their young ones as a flock of sheep, and their children joyfully dance around them. They take up timbrel and harp, and make merry at the sound of the organ. They pass the whole of their days in happiness, and are only reduced to a state of dismay by the summons to depart to Sheol in the very midst of their enjoyment of good. Therefore they say unto God, Turn from us, for we delight not in Thy ways. They ask who is Shaddai, or the Almighty, that we should serve Him, and what profit is there when we intercede with Him." Thus their conduct is marked by a twofold form of ungodliness, in wilfully rejecting the counsel of God and in a contemptuous refusal to recognise His omnipotence.

Well may Job comment upon their reckless unwisdom and unbelieving folly and say, "Lo, their good is not in their own hand. Of themselves they have no power to retain possession of any of the blessings which they have hitherto enjoyed. Promotion cometh not from the east, not from the west, nor yet from the south. God is the judge. He putteth down one and setteth up another. Far from me therefore be this error of self-confidence, and this suicidal counsel of the ungodly." Man cannot defy his Maker with impunity. His longsuffering forbearance may endure for a time to lead men to repentance, but to those who despise His goodness there is no escape from the judgment of God, who will render to every man according to his works; to those who do not obey the truth, indignation and wrath, tribulation and anguish upon every soul that doeth evil. "Sooner or later the candle of the wicked will be put out, and their destruction will come on them, when God sends upon them their death-throes in His anger. They are then as straw before the wind, and chaff which the storm carries away. God will lay up the punishment of his iniquity for his children. He will requite him, and in his inner consciousness the wicked man knows it. His eyes will see his destruction, and he shall drink of the wrath of the Almighty. What delight has he then in his house which survives him on the earth, when the number of his months are cut in twain?" Thus his earthly prosperity passes away, and his place knows him no more. In kindred terms does Job describe the final fate of the wicked; but still it offers no solution to his question, why their prosperity should have been so long tolerated on earth.

Yet none can presume to deny that God was cognisant of their preservation: "Will any teach God knowledge? He even judges those who are the high ones." Omniscience, equally with omnipotence, is an attribute of God. They are also both displayed with an inequality that accompanies the different deaths to which men succumb, as well as the lives which they have enjoyed. Man may be ignorant of the causes of such inequality, yet not so an omniscient Creator. He, without whose knowledge not a sparrow falleth to the ground, cannot fail to know the reasons "why one man dies in his full strength, being wholly at ease and prosperous, his breasts full of milk and the marrow moistening his bones, and why another dies in bitterness of soul and never eateth in comfort. But in death the inequality ceases, for they both lie down together in the dust, and the worm covereth them."

The statement of Zophar, that retribution in this life is invariably visited upon the wicked, is disproved by the general experience of humanity, and the injustice of his inference, that Job's sufferings are due to the commission of sin, is clearly manifested. The recognition of this imputation of wrong-doing by Job himself is visible when he adds, "I know your thoughts and devices for which ye so violently condemn me, when ye ask what is become of the house of the whilom noble? where is the dwelling of the wicked man? Is it not vanished, and in its stead a mere tent is seen, like the tabernacles of the wicked?" The more forcibly to show the fallacy of their opinions, Job refers them to the knowledge which has been acquired by those who have travelled over the face of the earth. "If you will not accept my views," he says, "compare them with the experience of the men who have passed their lives in visiting distant countries, and you may perhaps recognise the signs they give of having seen the wicked preserved for the day of destruction, to be brought forth in the day of wrath, when death will remove all visible signs of the inequalities of existence. What man would dare to tell the proud despot during his life of the danger of his evil conduct, or to requite him for the misery that he has inflicted on others? Yet sooner or later he is brought to the place of burial, and often by a violent death, and men will in vain watch over his sepulchral mound for his return to life. But there is no escape from the power of the grave, neither will the funeral pomp restore him to life. The very clods of the valley among which he is buried appear to be sweet to one who, forgetful of a future existence, believes only in the dissolution of the body. He knows how all men will follow after him in death, and how innumerable has been the number that have succumbed to its power." The perfect and the wicked alike have perished and been gathered to their dust. This is the universal experience of man, and from this warfare there is no escape. All alike die, whether it be the innocent babe or the long-lived, hardened sinner.

Having thus exposed the fallacy of their statements, he asks, "How then can your vain words bring me comfort, since in your answers there remaineth transgression against the truth?" The solution of his problem remains unanswered, and his mind continues disturbed at the thought that no answer has been given to the question, "Why God often without discrimination appears to grant prosperity to the wicked?"

CHAPTER XX

ELIPHAZ'S THIRD REPLY TO JOB

(CHAP. xxii.)

THE conclusion of Job's reply to Zophar, in which he pointed out the unsuitableness of the words spoken by the three friends to give him comfort and support, owing to their inherent disagreement with the general experience of mankind, and to the falsity of their insinuations of his personal sinfulness, excited the angry feelings of Eliphaz. In his two former replies he had vainly endeavoured to prove that suffering should invariably be traced to the commission of personal sin, supporting this theory by statements derived from his own experience, and by inferences based on the general depravity of the human race. In the present instance, he proceeds to accuse Job of actual offences against the laws of God, but without giving any corroborative proof of the correctness of such accusations.

Possibly in allusion to Job's question, why God allows the wicked to prosper, he commences his reply by first asking " how a man can be supposed to carry out the purposes of God in the same way as a wise man acts in his own affairs? How can the righteousness or integrity of a man's life be regarded as a matter of either delight, or of gain to the Almighty? He then asks, whether it is possible to conceive that the fear of man causes God to reprove him, or to bring him to judgment?" Such sarcastic remarks, when tested by the word of God, are shown to be without point. Scripture reveals that suffering is inflicted, not from fear of man, but for the promotion of man's happiness, either in the way of correction, when he has transgressed the Divine laws, or for the purpose of perfectioning his character. In later days the Divine Son condescended to learn obedience by the things which He suffered, and having been made perfect, He became the author of eternal salvation to all that obey Him. Thus the words of Eliphaz are confuted by the recognised action of God.

Having thus opened this attack, Eliphaz no longer hesitates to directly charge Job with the wilful commission of sin: "Is not thy wickedness manifold, and is there any end to thine iniquities? For without sufficient cause thou hast made thy brethren naked by taking their clothing as a pledge. Thou hast not supplied the needs of the hungry and thirsty. When thou wast a man, strong in the arm, and regarded with partial favour by other men, thou lookedst at the earth as thine own possession, and regardedst it as thy settled home; thou sentest widows away empty, and crushedst the arms of the orphans when they cried to thee for help. Therefore now snares are around thee, and sudden fear troubles thee. Darkness encloses thee so that thou canst not see thy way, and the outbreaks of popular fury, like the bursting out of waters, overwhelm thee."

Eliphaz proceeds to accuse him of denying the omniscience of God. Thou sayest, "Is not God in the heaven, and thou lookest at the height of the stars, how exalted they are, and thou askest, Can God who is infinitely higher know what is done on earth? Can He judge what is done by its inhabitants through the gloom that surrounds it? The clouds conceal Him so that He cannot see, and He is far off, walking on the very circuit of the heavens. Hast thou not kept in the paths of the antediluvian age which men of iniquity have trodden, who thus became wrinkled before their time, and who, when the flood was poured out over the foundation of their houses, said unto God, Depart from us, and what can the Almighty do to injure us?" In such arrogant terms does the self-complacent, prosperous man of the world reproach, for his alleged selfishness and impiety, the holy sufferer, whom the Almighty, before the assembled hosts in the heavenlies, had commended as "perfect and upright, fearing God and turning from evil."

Permanent earthly prosperity and high social position have a tendency to render their possessors uncharitable in their judgment of others, upon whom the hand of affliction has heavily fallen, and whose lowly position exposes them to the scorn of the powerful and wealthy.

Eliphaz now exchanges his rôle of the judge for that of the moralist. He had denounced what he considered to be the iniquity of Job, and compared his character before his reduction to poverty with that of the prosperous, wicked man. He draws attention to the ingratitude of the ungodly, for the mercies with which they had been blessed. "God filled their houses with good, yet they recognised neither the Giver, nor the obligations under which He had laid them. Forgetfulness of God, and impatience of control, formed the foundation on which their evil lives were built up. In a spirit of Pharisaic self-righteousness he now declares that the counsel of the wicked was far from himself, and that he neither approved its principles nor regulated his life by its maxims. But he added, we the righteous see their career and are glad, and the innocent laugh them to scorn, for whilst our adversaries are destroyed, the fire also devoureth their remnant."

In a similar self-righteous spirit he proceeds to address himself personally to Job, presumptuously advising him "to acquaint himself with God by placing his tabernacle under His protection, whereby peace will be assured to him and the increase of his goods." He appeals to him "to receive the law from his mouth, and to lay up his words in his heart; for if he returns to the Almighty, and puts away iniquity from his tents, he then assures him that he shall be again built up. He goes on to speak of the necessity of almsgiving. Cast thy vintage to those who dwell upon the dust of the earth, and the gold of Ophir to those sitting in the rocks of the valleys, for then the Almighty will be thy defence and quickly cause silver to come to thee. Then thou shalt delight thyself in the Almighty, and lift up thy face to God. Then thou shalt entreat Him, and He will hear thee, and thou wilt thus repay thy vows. Thou shalt determine to do a thing, and it shall be established, and light will shine on thy ways. When men would try to abase thee, thou shalt say, God will magnify me; He will save and lift up the lowly eyes; He shall deliver the habitation of the innocent, and thou shalt be delivered by the purity of thy hands." The whole passage is a groundless insinuation of selfishness in the most generous of men.

The reply of Eliphaz entirely evades Job's question, why the wicked are often allowed to continue in prosperity during their earthly lives. The purport of his words is directed to show that suffering must necessarily be traced to personal transgression of God's law, and that the only mode of relief is to be found in a return to right conduct. The prosperous man of position in the world, of whom Eliphaz is the representative, realises that his earthly success has been mainly dependent on the steady and industrious use of his mental faculties and bodily powers. He observes that inattention to health is destructive of force of body, and that the neglect of study is injurious to the development of the mind. Observation shows that a vast amount of the misery of life is due to self-indulgence and idleness, and thus a hasty conclusion is drawn that in all cases suffering must be the result of conscious and personal wrong-doing. Insufficient attention is given to the fact that the effect of sin is not confined to the person that commits it. The sin of Adam in partaking of the forbidden fruit subjected every member of the human race to the penalty of natural death; but no one believes that the new-born babe, unconscious of good and evil, succumbs to death in consequence of his own actual transgression. So with Job. His misery was the result of sin; the sin, however, that caused it, was not due to any evil which he himself had done, but to the sin of Satan, who was endeavouring to tempt him to reproach God for having allowed him to be reduced to penury and bodily torment. The man of worldly prosperity confines his thoughts to earthly considerations, with little or no regard to the higher motives which govern the actions of the Almighty. Hence the judgment of Eliphaz, that the suffering by which Job was visited was sent as the punishment for his personal iniquity, failed to commend itself to one who was utterly unconscious of the commission of any wilful transgression of duty, and gave no reply to his question, "Why does God allow the wicked to prosper in this life?"

CHAPTER XXI

JOB'S THIRD REPLY TO ELIPHAZ

(CHAPS. xxiii., xxiv.)

Problem—" Why do not the perfect witness the punishment of the wicked ? "

IN continuing the discussion, Job takes little notice of the speech of Eliphaz. He at once proceeds to give utterance to his earnest desire to be admitted into the presence of God to plead his cause before Him ; and as a reason he adds, that " To-day my meditation is very bitter, for God's hand is too heavy to allow the suffering to be alleviated by mere sighs. Oh that I knew where I should find Him, and I would at once go to His established place of audience. I would set in order my plea before Him, and fill my mouth with arguments to convince Him of my innocence. Then I should be able to know the words with which He would answer me, and I should understand what He would say to me. I cannot believe that He would multiply His power so as to contend more forcibly with me, but on the contrary He would feel more inclined to increase my power to plead with Him. Then a righteous man might be able to convince Him, and I should be permanently delivered from my Judge."

In such a sorrowful and despairing tone does Job make known the earnestness of his desire to plead his own cause with God. He feels himself beyond the help of man, and he sees only one remaining resource in directly appealing to God. Yet all seems to be in vain, for he adds, " Behold, I go forward in the path of the ordinary duties of life, but He is not there causing me to realise His assisting presence. If I look back and contemplate the events that may have led up to my present condition, I cannot perceive any reasons for His toleration of my misery; whichever way I turn I cannot perceive Him. I do not realise the motives that regulate His actions. The wicked prosper, and the godly suffer. I have tried to do my duty, and leprosy has been permitted to seize me in its loathsome embrace. Yet God knows the way that I take, the way which I believe to be in accordance with His will."

A new idea presents itself to his mind. Is God tempting me and testing my obedience ? " If so, I shall come forth out of the trial as pure gold out of the crucible, for my foot has held fast to His way. I have kept it and I have not declined from it. I have not gone from the commandments of His lips. I have hid the words of His mouth within my heart more than the wishes and decrees of my own mind." In these expressions Job reveals that he was not far from discovering the cause of his sufferings. Could he have grasped the full truth, that the trial had not been laid upon him for sin, but had only been permitted to be inflicted by the Satan for the manifestation of his perfected endurance, his sorrows would have been marvellously alleviated. This revelation could not then be made, for Job himself had been divinely selected as the channel through whom it was to be given to mankind. Thus therefore for a short period the darkness still must rest upon him, and God must still appear to him as deaf to all his cries. This he feelingly expresses when he adds, " Yet still God remains in one mind to afflict me, and whatever His soul desires that He does, for He is completely fulfilling the afflictions that are decreed for me, and with Him there yet remain many other such like sorrowful things to be accomplished through my continuous misery."

With these words his complaint closes, and turning to his friends he tells them that such are the reasons " why he is troubled at the thought of God, and why when he contemplates all that has happened to him he is filled with awe at His presence. It is because God has made his heart soft, and the Almighty Himself has troubled him, because he was not cut off before the darkness of sorrow had come upon him, and because He had not covered him with the darkness of the grave, so that this

L

darkness of sorrow might have been removed from his face."

In this address Job is represented at one moment earnestly desiring the presence of God that He might vindicate his integrity before man, and yet at another moment the presence of God fills his mind with awe, in consequence of the darkness of sorrow by which his soul was overwhelmed. To reconcile these discordant feelings, attention should be given to the nature of his soul's darkness. It was the result not so much of the misery to which he was subjected, as the sense of being forsaken by God, who remained deaf to his prayers to be instructed in the reasons for which it had been sent. The three friends, from different standpoints, had strenuously asserted that suffering was invariably the result of sin. The fallacy of such statements was fully patent to Job's mind, and the consciousness of his integrity remained unshaken. Yet the reiteration of their mistaken theory was productive of mental disturbance, whereby Job was led at moments to doubt the justice of God. This is naturally followed by a general weakening of faith in God's love as well as in His justice, owing to the inequalities in the earthly conditions of the good and the evil, which, without faith, are difficult to be understood. "He that cometh to God must believe not only that He is, but also that He is a rewarder of those who diligently seek Him." Suffering, therefore, by the believer, is recognised as one of the steps whereby he is advancing on the road that leads to the Beatific Vision. Job's desire for God's presence was therefore proportioned by his faith. When faith became dim the dread of God's presence troubled his mind, whereas whenever his faith became stronger, the greater became his desire to appear in the presence of God for the vindication of his integrity. After a momentary eclipse of faith the holy patriarch recovered his sense of reliance on God's mercy, feeling assured that finally he would come out of the fiery ordeal purified as gold refined in the furnace. The conviction of his uprightness, notwithstanding his impatient words extorted by pain, strengthened his assurance.

He now proceeds to review the statements of Eliphaz concerning the invariable punishment of the wicked in this life. He observes the inconsistency of his remarks with the indisputable fact that evil-doers are frequently prosperous until the very moment of their deaths, and a fresh problem presents itself to his mind. He asks himself, "why believers in God are not permitted to witness their punishment?" He bases his inquiry on the doctrine that the regulation of all things, both in the present and in the future, is in the hands of God: "Since the knowledge of the proper seasons for their punishment is not hidden from the Almighty, why do not those who know and realise Him to be the Moral Governor of the world have a clear vision revealed to them when these days of chastisement are to arrive?" When looking at God's omniscience, Job fails to understand the equity of His allowing the wicked to continue in prosperity, without some period being made known when their retribution shall commence before the close of their earthly lives.

He cites several examples of their immunity from punishment taken from different classes of society. He first adduces some cases of tyrannical treatment to which the poor and helpless are exposed: "The landmarks of family properties are removed. The droves of cattle are violently driven away and consumed by the spoilers. The needy are turned out of the ways whereby they have been enabled to support life, and the poor are obliged through fear to hide themselves. Like the impetuous wild asses of the desert, these tyrants hasten forth in the morning to carry out their work of spoliation. Their victims have to seek food for themselves and their children in the barren wilderness. They are used as slaves to reap the corn and to gather in the vintage of the wicked, by whom they are reduced to a state of nakedness, and exposed to cold and tempest with only the bare rock for their shelter. These ruthless robbers pluck the orphans from their mothers' breasts, using them as hostages to retain their parents in slavery, at the same time causing them to remain without clothing, and even depriving them of the scanty sheafs, which they may have gleaned in the intervals of their labour in the oil-vats and wine-presses from which they dare not even quench their burning thirst." These oppressions he shows are not confined to those living in the open fields: "Men groan within the city, so that the souls of the wounded cry out under the lash of the brutal taskmaster." The contemplation of such frightful atrocities excites the wonder of Job, that they should be tolerated by an All-wise God: "Yet God imputeth not turpitude to them." He apparently permits them to carry out their iniquity without interference, and to end their days undisturbed by the dread of evil.

He then proceeds to deal with another class of evil-doers; they are those "who rebel against the light of conscience" without any recognition of God's ways, or without any attempt to be guided by His direction. The former class was composed of those who sinned habitually with callous indifference to the feelings of others. These are sinners against light, fully recognising their responsibility, yet hardening themselves in guilt. Job classes together the murderer, the adulterer, and the robber, those who carry out their wicked devices in the darkness of the night, forgetful that with the Almighty there is no darkness at all, and that to Him the night is as clear as the day. No disguise can remain impenetrable to His all-seeing eye. He reminds himself, however, that the punishment of these sinners commences even in this life. Inattention to the calls of conscience is destructive of the power to appreciate earthly blessings. "The morning which to the godly brings increased joy becomes to them more terrible than the darkness of the night. It unites them with terrors which are the precursors of the shadow of death, owing to dread of God's anger through the conviction of their sin, impressed upon them by the reproaches of a guilty conscience. The punishment of God comes swiftly. Like the rapid and never-ceasing waters of a mighty river the retribution of their crimes is realised as inevitable. Their earthly portion is cursed with failure, and they are unable to enter into the happy and peaceful joys of the vineyard."

He proceeds to describe the certainty of their punishment "under the emblem of the melting of the snow, and the evaporation of its water, by the heat of the summer sun. No less surely does Sheol absorb the souls of those who sin, while the worm feeds sweetly on their decaying bodies. While the memory of the perfect remains after death, that of the wicked passes out of remembrance. Even the womb that bore them, or the love of the mother, is quenched and extinguished. Nothing remains except the decaying carcass, on which the putrefying worm feeds sweetly. So surely does such wilful wickedness become shattered by the blast of God's anger like the tree broken by the tempest. Such is the final fate of those who evilly entreat the barren, who bear no children to increase the number of their slaves, and who do no good to the unprotected widow, for God can draw down even the mighty by His power, and when He rises up in anger no evil-doer is sure of life. For a time it may be given him to be in safety, and to rely upon the power of his wealth, but the eye of God is upon all his ways. For a little while the wicked may be lifted up, and then in a moment they no longer exist, they wax poor, and as all others they become contracted in the agonies of death, and are suddenly cut off as the head of a growing ear of corn."

Job closes his discussion with Eliphaz by challenging him to disprove his statements: " If things are not as I have said, who then will prove me to be a liar, and will show that my utterances are of no value ? " He thus silences Eliphaz, the representative of the successful man of the world, who has established his position by his own prudence, industry, and attention to the right principles of mere earthly conduct, as he had before silenced the shallow-minded man of society in the person of Zophar. He shows that the theory, that suffering must be invariably attributed to the commission of personal sin, is not consistent with the events of human existence. The experience of the prosperous man as to the causes of human suffering is circumscribed by the character of his wealthy associates as well as by his limited acquaintance with the poorer classes, vast numbers of whom are by philanthropists known to be endeavouring to rightly perform the duties of life amid much unmerited hardship and misery. The second argument with which Eliphaz supported his theory, based on the general experience of mankind of the prevalent depravity of the human race, is equally fallacious, for while the existence of such depravity may be admitted, he adduces no valid reasons to account for the inequality of the sufferings with which it is attended. When, therefore, he finally refers the cause of Job's suffering to the commission of personal sin, without stating the actual offence for which it has been inflicted, Eliphaz entirely fails to prove his case. Thus Job's appeal that his error may be clearly declared remains undecided, and his claim to integrity is not shown to be without foundation, and his words remain unanswered. Yet this does not solve the fresh problem which he had propounded, "Why believers in God are not permitted while on earth to witness the punishment of the wicked?"

CHAPTER XXII

BILDAD'S THIRD REPLY TO JOB

(CHAP. XXV.)

FROM the closing speech of Bildad he appears to have taken umbrage at the words of Job in which he asserted the integrity of his life: "God knows the way I take; when He has tried me I shall come forth as gold. My foot has held to His directions. His ways I have kept, and from them I have not declined, neither have I gone back from the commandment of His lips. The words of His mouth I have hid in my heart more than my own determined wishes" (xxiii. 10). Bildad therefore proceeds to show the impossibility of any mortal man appearing righteous in the eye of the Almighty Ruler of the Universe.

As the representative of the deep thinkers of the age, he bases his argument on God's overruling providence, and on the inherent failure of even the material universe to be free from imperfect action. He first affirms the absolute sovereignty of the Almighty with the necessary accompaniment of a feeling of solemn awe in all those who witness the display of His Divine power: "Dominion and awe are with Him." The same feelings were realised by the holy Psalmist: "Clouds and darkness are round about Him; righteousness and judgment are the habitation of His throne." Even the material mountains are said to melt before the presence of the Lord of the whole earth. The stronger the recognition of the presence of the Absolute, the deeper is the feeling of awe which seizes on the mind of the worshipper. When Moses, to whom alone of all mortal men it was permitted to speak with God face to face, was summoned into the Divine presence on the heights of Sinai, he became so overwhelmed by the fear-inspiring sight as to be obliged to give utterance to the words, "I exceedingly quake and fear." When God appeared to man under the lowly guise of the whilom Galilean carpenter, the deeper recognition of His Divine nature caused the humble apostle to kneel before Him with the reverential prayer: "Depart from me, for I am a sinful man, O Lord." The awe-inspiring realisation of God's presence is revealed in the worship of the sacred Seraphim in the heavens above. With twain of their wings they covered their faces, and with twain they covered their feet. Satan alone in the heavenlies dares to approach God with the proud refusal to recognise His essential majesty, and with the arrogant assertion of a claim to impugn the truth of a Divine utterance.

But such reverential awe is not intended to be provocative of terror. In those who are rightly exercised by this holy feeling it becomes productive of peace, such as Bildad correctly declares when he adds, " God maketh peace in the heavenlies." Peace comes home to all who, being purified from evil by union with the Divine Son of Man, are being delivered from the temptation to sin through the attacks of the personal Satan and of his attendant hosts of evil angels. While in the flesh men are exposed to their malign influence, yet for their support Bildad was inspired to reveal the existence of antagonistic forces, similar to those which were witnessed when at Dothan, in answer to the prophet's prayer, the eyes of his servant were opened to see that the number of those who were sent to protect God's people was greater than that of those who were contending against them. Bildad asks, " Is there any numbering of God's troops of guardian spirits ? and upon whom throughout the whole universe does He not cause His light to arise ? "

This contemplation of the omnipotence and omniscience of the Almighty leads the calm philosopher to further inquire, " How then can mortal man be justified or be reckoned righteous with God, and who that is born of woman can be accounted pure ? " In support of his contention he directs Job's attention to the contemplation of the heavenly orbs : " Look even to the moon, and God praises not its unsullied clearness, and the stars are not held as pure in His eyes." If these natural objects, which more than all others are regarded by man as manifestations of spotless purity, appear in the sight of God to be tainted with blemish, how is it possible, he asks, that "mortal man, who is only a worm crawling upon earth, and the son of Adam, who is only a worm liable to the corruption of death, should be ought else but impure?" Mortal man is by nature carnal and grovelling, and the sons of Adam are by heredity subjected to mental as well as bodily corruption.

Bildad's arguments, however, utterly fail to satisfy Job's requirements, or to solve his questions. Job does not for a moment deny the essential impurity of man. Bildad's question, "How can man born of woman be pure?" is only an echo of the words of Job spoken at an earlier period of the discussion, "that no one can bring a clean thing out of an unclean." Job's contention is confined to the feeling that his suffering is disproportionate to any actual offence against the will of God, of the commission of which he is utterly unconscious.

CHAPTER XXIII

JOB'S THIRD REPLY TO BILDAD

(CHAP. xxvi. 1-4)

THE unsuitableness of Bildad's words to give him support under his sufferings appears to have excited the anger of Job. The contemplation of God's omnipotence is ill-calculated to give comfort under trial, without also some revelation of His mercy in making all things work together for good to those who love Him. The forces of nature only inspire terror in the mind of the observer, unless he realises that they are regulated by the determining will of an All-merciful personal Ruler. The destruction of his family and that of his flocks by the fire from heaven, thereby bereaving him of his home and wealth, were submitted to by Job without a murmur, because he remembered that the disaster was permitted by the same loving hand from which he had received all his former blessings: "The Lord gave, and the Lord hath taken away, blessed be the name of the Lord." So also the reiteration of man's hereditary impurity, without showing how it may be counteracted, is of little avail to solve the problem why suffering should be permitted without a revelation of the causes which had led to its infliction. The tendency of the philosophic mind is to deal with acknowledged facts, without giving sufficient attention to their hidden causes and their complex developments. Evolution is realised as being one of the ordinary processes of material growth; but the origin of the primeval atom is passed by with but little investigation as to its origination, and the change of its nature from its simple character into the composite molecule cell remains unaccounted for. Two unigenous atoms may by accretion increase in bulk, but their nature remains unchanged. The formation of the cell demands the union of some extraneous substance, which, by chemical affinity or otherwise, may alter the character of the united unigenous atoms. God's omnipotence may account for the existence of phenomena, but it gives no reason for the inequality which pervades the sufferings of the human race. Man's inherent impurity may account for the existence of suffering, but it gives no reason for the inequity which appears to accompany the treatment of the perfect and the wicked.

The failure of the three friends to give comfort to Job may be traced to their fixing their attention on the apparent causes to which in ordinary cases suffering may be traced, neglectful, however, of the numerous instances for which no moral reason can be adduced for its infliction. The new-born infants, unconscious of right and wrong, are incapable of actual transgression, yet, like the babes in Bethlehem, they suffer and they perish under the sword of the tyrant. The bold statement, that this evil is due to the omnipotent hand of God, would not have calmed the minds of the mothers in Ramah. Rachel weeping for her children would not be comforted because they are not. She needed the reminder that, though no longer on earth, yet they had by death been translated to a state in which earthly pain is compensated by eternal bliss. In suffering, the victim's mind should be directed to the love of God, who by it is leading him to greater perfection of character and increased capabilities of enjoyment, through gradual purification from the hereditary liability to evil to which the human race has by altruistic sin become subject.

The sufferings of Job are by the history shown to originate with the sin of the Satan, parallel in a higher degree with the visible manifestations of demoniacal possession in the days of our Lord's earthly life, and with those more secret demoniacal influences to which there is every reason to believe, under a less accentuated form, the members of the human race are still unceasingly exposed. Had his three friends been better acquainted with the esoteric causes of human misery, instead of continuously attributing his misery to personal guilt, they might not only have strengthened him under his spiritual temptation to accuse God of a disregard for his plaintive cries, but have also freed themselves from his well-merited reproaches when he asked them, "How have ye helped a man without strength, or given power to an arm which has been deprived of force?" Had they rightly realised the truth of the doctrine of vicarious suffering, a form of suffering no less frequent than that which is caused by personal sin, and one so clearly witnessed in the pain and trouble borne by parents in the support and education of their children, they would not have exposed themselves to Job's bitter taunt, that while accusing him of hereditary impurity they had given no corrective counsel to one whom they considered was destitute of wisdom, and that they had not caused one whom they regarded as contending with God, to understand what were the true conditions of existence. Had they been able to show to Job that the object of his trial was to reveal to the heavenly hosts, as well as to the human race, that notwithstanding the hereditary taint of sin, man was possessed of power of will sufficient to resist the temptation to apostatise, and to preserve his faith in the love of God under the extremes of pain and penury, he would have derived strength to bear his terrible misery with greater fortitude and patience, by being enabled to look forward to the recompense of the reward, as in later days his Redeemer was enabled, for the joy set before Him, to endure the cross, and to despise the shame, so as to become fitted to sit down at the right hand of the throne of God. Well might the holy sufferer conclude his reproaches by asking them to contrast their feeble knowledge with the deeper inspiration of God's breath possessed by himself, "To whom hast thou uttered words? and whose spirit came forth from thy lips?"

With these words Job appears to have closed the discussion which he had been holding with his three friends. His words, which immediately follow, down to the intervention of Elihu, assume the character of a soliloquy, in which Job gives utterance to the thoughts which are engendered in his mind by the contemplation of God's nature and the events of his own life.

CHAPTER XXIV

JOB'S PARABLE

(CHAPTERS xxvi. 5—xxxi.)

At the close of the discussion which had taken place between Job and his three friends, a period of silence appears to have intervened before any fresh utterances proceeded from his lips. This is apparent from the difficulty of discovering any connection between Job's reproaches on account of the want of consideration shown by his friends for his intellectual capacity, as well as for his spiritual endowment, and the way in which he abruptly commences that which in the history is called his parable. It is a collection of proverbial statements which contains the doctrines and principles by which his life has hitherto been regulated.

The character of his opponents' arguments had excited his astonishment, upon which he asked them whether they realised the position of the man whom they were thus addressing: "To whom hast thou uttered these words? and by whose inspiration have thy words been caused to go forth?" No answer was given to this interpellation, and in a most disconnected manner Job is represented as briefly describing the condition of the dwellers in Sheol, and the original formation of the mundane system, and other kindred mysterious subjects which have no direct bearing upon the matter of the discussion. This parable will therefore represent the subsequent difficulties by which his intellect became disturbed. None of the problems to which he had given utterance had received their solution, and the contents of the parable may be regarded as the inner workings of his mind, endeavouring to arrive at some definite conclusion, " why the perfect man was exposed to suffering, for the infliction of which no adequate reason could be assigned ? "

The parable takes the form of a soliloquy.

It has three divisions marked by the twice recorded expression, " Job continued his parable."

1. The first division treats of the hidden workings of the Almighty in the governance of the souls in Sheol, and in the formation of the universe (xxvi. 5).

2. The second division treats of the earthly portion of the wicked, and their sudden destruction, witnessing to the superiority of Divine wisdom over human knowledge (xxvii., xxviii.).

3. The third division gives a retrospect of his past life as contrasted with his present condition, and concludes with a strong affirmation of his own integrity (xxix.- xxxi.).

These utterances represent the character of the thoughts which, with greater or less distinctness, pervade the minds of afflicted persons in their endeavours to discover the reasons for which God has permitted them to suffer.

CHAPTER XXV

JOB'S REFLECTIONS ON SHEOL AND CREATION

(CHAP. xxvi. 5.)

JOB commences his parable by giving utterance to the thoughts that arose in his mind on the contemplation of God's omnipotence. It is the natural feeling that is common to all who suffer extreme pain or endure great sorrow, to apply to God for assistance in consequence of their recognition of His Almighty power. Where man fails, they realise that God can give them support. This was the feeling of the leper who came to our Lord with the sincere prayer, "Lord, if Thou wilt, Thou canst make me clean." For the strengthening of their reliance on God they meditate on the wondrous workings of His power. So was it with Job. On the failure of his friends to give him help, he supports himself by the contemplation of God's eternal power.

His thoughts are first directed to the state of man after death: " He realises the condition of the shades of the departed travailing in continued existence under the waters of the abyss, and of their inhabitants. He recognises that Sheol is naked before Him, and that no covering can conceal Abaddon, the place of final dissolution, from His sight." All is naked before the eyes of Him with whom man has to do. These shades are possibly those of the apostate angels, who are revealed by St. Jude as being reserved in everlasting chains under darkness unto the judgment of the great day. Their condemnation to confinement under the waters of the mighty abyss, the abode of the rebel hosts of the Satanic demons, is one of the greatest displays of God's irresistible omnipotence. These two states present themselves to his imagination as two localities to which the dead are sent after the dissolution of their bodies by the hand of death, the one being the Sheol of rest, reserved for the departed saints in the intermediate state, and the other the Abaddon, or the place of destruction, in the lake burning with fire and brimstone, to which the wicked are consigned after the final judgment. The contemplation of the state of rest was calculated to support him to endure with resignation his earthly sufferings, in the assured hope of the vindication of his integrity and of his final acceptance by God; whilst the contemplation of the Abaddon, or fiery retribution, was calculated to allay his doubts of the perfected justice of God in the earthly toleration of the evil conduct of sinners, which, unless repented of and forsaken, will necessarily be followed by their destruction.

Job then proceeds to contemplate the omnipotence of God, realised in the creation of the mundane system, from which the invisible things of His nature are clearly seen, even His eternal power and divinity: "He perceives how God has stretched out the ceiling of the firmament over the chaotic waters of the primordial abyss, and caused the earth itself to be suspended on nothing beyond its inherent obedience to the laws of gravitation. He has enclosed the waters above the firmament in dense masses of fluid evaporation, and has not permitted the underlying cloud to be cleft asunder by their weight. He has mercifully caused the unapproachable glory of His heavenly Throne to be concealed by spreading over it the veil of His cloud. He has, in condescension to man's requirement, decreed a circuit of the solar light to pass upon the face of the aerial waters until the final termination of light and darkness. The pillars which sustain the atmospheric heavens become weak and are astonished at His rebuke," in allusion to the volcanic action by which the mountain ranges were projected and depressed, in the original cleavage of the crust of the earth for the formation of the dry land, suddenly emerging out of the terrestrial as well as the aerial waters by which it was at first covered, so that man might be provided with the means, whereby through the cultivation of his talents he might be able to subdue the earth, and to elaborate its production for the support and enjoyment of life. The contemplation of God's work of creation gives support under affliction, as being a revelation not only of His omnipotence, but also of His love. Thereby the thoughts of the sufferers are directed to the original blessing given to Adam, and through him transmitted to every child of man: "God blessed them, and said to them, Be fruitful and multiply, and replenish the earth and subdue it, and have dominion over everything that moveth upon the earth. Behold I have given you every green herb, and every tree, which is on the face of the earth; to you it shall be for meat."

Though man through sin incurred the forfeiture of the blessing, and perished under the waters of the flood, yet to the saved remnant God's love was again revealed in the renovated and enlarged blessing given to Noah: "I will not again curse the ground any more for man's sake; while earth remaineth, seed time and harvest, day and night, shall not cease. Be fruitful and replenish the earth, and the fear of you shall be upon everything that moveth upon the earth; into your hands are they delivered, and they shall be meat for you." Up to the period of the deluge the Divine grant of food was restricted to vegetation, but on Noah's coming out of the ark it was extended to the flesh of animals. By the contemplation of such displays of power and love, those suffering under affliction may without fear cast themselves upon God's mercy, being fully assured that His ability is equalled by His love to grant their petitions whenever the proper moment shall arrive to give them relief.

But Job realised that these mighty manifestations of God's power are not confined to the earthly sphere. He recognises that they are extended to that of the heavenlies: "By His understanding He woundeth Rahab, the proud Satanic opponent of the Divine will. By His spirit He hath garnished the heavens with the homes of the elect. His hand has pierced the fleeing serpent." Rahab was an ancient name for Egypt, possibly descriptive of the hostile character of the Satanically possessed Pharaoh, who perished in the Red Sea when fighting against the chosen people of God; and the fleeing serpent was the idolatrous emblem of the Satanic Dragon, who, under the form of a crocodile, had become one of the objects of Egyptian devil-worship. (Isa. xxvii.; Ezek. xxxii.) The power of Satan, when directed against the people of God, is exposed to continuous defeat in accordance with the terms of the primeval curse pronounced over him at the fall: "I will put emnity between thee and the woman, and between thy seed and her seed. He shall bruise thy head, and thou shalt bruise his heel." The truth of these words of God is individually realised by all undergoing suffering which is the result of the hereditary taint of sin in the human race. In proportion to his faith in God's promises, witnessed by persistent refusal to yield to the temptation of Satan, man is supported under his trials by being reminded of the action and character of the fleeing serpent, in accordance with the Divine assurance, that if "he resists the devil he will flee from him."

Job's knowledge of the garniture of the heavens, of which the stars as the homes of the elect are a visible emblem, may be traced to the remembrance of the faith of the patriarchs, who at the call of God went forth from their earthly dwellings, not knowing whither they went, but looking forward in full assurance that there was provided for them a city that hath foundations, eternal in the heavens, whose maker and builder is God. As the patriarchs were thus supported by their faith to bear the trials of their earthly pilgrimage, so Job endeavoured to support his fainting spirit by the same thoughts, which are here revealed as a solace to all others similarly afflicted.

By the contemplation of God's power to enable them to resist the temptations of Satan, and to cast out the unclean spirit from the hearts of those demoniacally possessed, as well as by the consideration of His love in giving them the promise of the heavenly home, those suffering under trial are supported by the full conviction that what He has promised He is not only able, but also determined to fulfil in behalf of all who submit themselves to His all-wise guidance and protection.

Yet in concluding this division of his parable Job adds, "Lo these are only the extreme outskirts of His ways; but how little a whisper is heard concerning Him, and the thunder of His power who can understand?"

The infinitude of the Almighty Jehovah is beyond the power of man to comprehend.

CHAPTER XXVI

JOB'S REFLECTION ON THE SUPERIORITY OF DIVINE WISDOM OVER HUMAN KNOWLEDGE

(CHAPS. xxvii., xxviii.)

In the second division of his parable, which is marked by the expression "Job continued his parable," he first attempts to derive comfort from the contemplation and affirmation of the integrity of his past life. The consciousness of innocence is at all times a solace to the afflicted, provided its consideration is accompanied with humility of mind. Sooner or later an answer of peace will come to the sufferer who, like Hezekiah, is able to plead that he has "walked before the Lord in truth, and with a perfect heart, and done that which is right in His sight." The spirit of Job had been greatly irritated by the mistaken accusations made by his friends as to his commission of wilful sin. Against this he rebels, and in strong language repudiates the charge: "As God lives, who has turned aside my sentence of right judgment; and as the Almighty lives, who has embittered my life, so long as the breath remains in my body, and the spirit of God remains in my soul,

I will give good heed that my lips shall speak no iniquity, or my tongue give utterance to words of deceit, in admitting that I have wilfully done wrong of which I am perfectly unconscious. God forbid that I should admit your false accusations to be true. Until I expire I will not repudiate the sense of my own integrity, of which in motive and act I am fully persuaded. I therefore hold fast to the assertion of my righteousness, and will not allow my heart to reproach me for any evil which I have not committed. If he so desires it, my enemy may act as a wicked man, and he who rises up against me as an unrighteous one by falsely accusing me of evil, but to the admission of the truth of their words I will be no party. In so doing I should act the part of the hypocrite; and what is the hope of such an one even if he gain the false praise for which he seeks, when God casts away his soul? Will God hear the cry of such an one in his distress? or will he be able to take delight in the thought that God will hear him at any time? Will he not even lose the power and the desire to give utterance of prayer to God. Far better is it for me to teach you how the hand of God works, and the secrets of the Almighty which I will not conceal. But lo, you yourselves have seen the truth of what I am telling you. How then comes it that ye are altogether vain enough to rely on your mistaken opinions?"

These words of Job represent the feelings of persons who, though they have passed their lives in the conscientious performance of duty, yet from some unknown cause have become exposed to afflictions which their friends erroneously persist in attributing to the commission of some personal act of sin. They seek solace in affirming their integrity, and rightly refuse to imagine that God will be pleased with any hypocritical admission of guilt of which they are unconscious. The incongruity of such apparently unmerited suffering, when compared with the frequent instances in which the wicked enjoy prosperity and sin with seeming impunity, leads them to question whether such prosperity will continue permanent, and to inquire what will be the future portion of the wicked, so as to be strengthened by the assurance that in God's good time their own integrity will be vindicated, and the wisdom of their choice of the righteous life made fully manifest.

These considerations appear to have prompted Job in his endeavours to strengthen his powers of suffering by the contemplation of the final fate of the wicked. He proceeds to describe the future "portion to which the wicked must look forward as decreed by God, and the inheritance which the terror-causing oppressors of their fellow-men will receive at the hand of the Almighty. He perceives that when their children are multiplied they become victims to the sword, and exposed to the dangers of famine. Those who survive them are quickly buried in consequence of their unexpected deaths, and their wives do not weep on the removal of their harsh husbands. Though they may have heaped together silver and changes of raiment, yet at their death these pass into the hands of the righteous and innocent. There is no stability in their houses, which are like the frail webs of a moth, and the leafy hut of the vineyard guardian. The rich man may lie down in death, but his soul is not gathered to those of his predeceased and righteous forefathers. He opens his eyes in Sheol, but he is not with them, for the impassible gulf divides them. Terrors overwhelm him as a flood of waters, and a sudden tempest of indignation carries him away in the night of death. Some forgotten impulse of past hatred seizes the mind of his enemy, and he hurries him out of life, and a storm of anger hurls him from his place on earth, for God will cast upon him wrath, and will not spare him, notwithstanding all his efforts to escape from His hands. Men will clap their hands with joy at his decease, and hiss him with disdain out of his place in the world." By such considerations does Job strengthen himself in his firm determination to remain faithful in his allegiance to God in the midst of all his suffering, whilst he contemplates the dangers of the impending ruin to which the wicked, though for a time prospering, expose themselves at last by their evil conduct.

These thoughts are equally helpful to sustain those who, like Job, are undergoing apparently unmerited sufferings. The experience of life, and the revealed knowledge handed down through tradition from the commencement of man's existence, testify to the truth of the prophecy of Enoch, that "the Lord cometh with ten thousands of His saints to execute judgment upon all, and to convince all that are ungodly of all their ungodly deeds which they have committed." This doctrine strengthens faith in the Divine assurance, that if a man fears God and works righteousness he will be accepted of God.

But the causes why undeserved suffering is tolerated still remains concealed. Job feels that some wise reason must exist for this apparent miscarriage of the Divine justice, and he looks around for the source whence wisdom can be obtained for the solving of the question. He recognises the power of man to arrive at the possession of human knowledge for the support and amelioration of his earthly life. He exemplifies this by the mode in which man has discovered the hidden treasures which they have obtained from the bowels of the earth. He displays the growth of scientific invention, witnessed in the working of mines: "The lode of silver is traced. The mode of refining the golden ore has been discovered. Iron is extracted from its embodiment of dust. Copper is melted out of stone. Man has put an end to darkness in the recesses of the mine by the introduction of artificial light. He searches the farthest points whence the veins of metal originate, in spots where all is gloom and shadow like the darkness of death. He comes across subterranean torrents, never before seen by man, nor touched by his foot; and he causes them to pass away into the deeper hollows of the earthly sphere. Whilst the surface of the earth supplies man with bread, from the deeper excavations of its crust exudes the volcanic fire. The sapphire, the lead, and the gold are found amidst its stones. Its hidden paths are unknown to the wing of fowl, and unseen by the vulture's eye. The lion and his whelps have never traversed them. Man alone has put his hand upon the rock, and in his search for wealth has overturned mountains, pierced channels through the granitic ranges for setting free the hidden stream, and then dammed up the overwhelming flood until the precious ore has been laid bare before the miner's eye."

Such mighty results have attended man's search after secular knowledge, but "where," asks Job, "is wisdom to be found, and where is the place of understanding?" Secular knowledge may be discovered sufficient to supply man's bodily wants, but it is insufficient to solve the deeper problems which present themselves before the human soul, or to support the spirit of man under the constantly recurring trials of life, or to enable him to meet the approach of death, and to enter into Sheol with calm resignation and assured hope of acceptance in the presence of the Almighty Ruler of the Universe.

Job realises that Divine Wisdom alone is capable of imparting these blessings; that wisdom, which is from above, pure, peaceable, gentle, full of mercy and good fruits; that wisdom, which was fully manifested in the earthly life of the Incarnate Word, full of grace and truth. Job recognises the failure of all earthly knowledge to give peace, and therefore directs his thoughts to the discovery of the source whence Divine Wisdom may be obtained. "Where," he asks, "is Wisdom to be found, and where is the place of understanding?" "Man knows not its orderly arrangement; it is not found in the land of the living. The abyss saith, It is not in me; and the sea saith, It is not with me. Man cannot give merchandise instead of it, and the trader can produce nothing to supply its place. Silver cannot be weighed as its price." The products of the mine, the working of which he regards as one of the strongest evidences of the force of the human intellect, are discerned as valueless in comparison with the possession of wisdom. "Neither the gold nor the crystal can equal it in inherent worth or transcendent purity." The attaining of wisdom exceeds the value of every precious stone. "Whence, then," he repeats, "cometh wisdom, and where is the place of understanding?" It is veiled from the eyes of every living man, and secreted from the vision of the angelic denizens of the heavens. The Abaddon of the fiery lake and the valley of relentless Death profess to have heard the fame of its existence for the destruction of evil and the renewal of life. But God, he continues, understands its ways and its methods of action, and knoweth the place of its inception in the bosom of the Almighty. He looks to the extreme parts of the earth, and He beholdeth all that exists beneath the heavens. When He gave creative force to the wind, and equalised by measure the waters over the face of the earth; when He made a decree for the primeval rain mist and provided a way for the lightnings of His thunder voices, then He looked and declared the perfection of His creative wisdom. He then established its eternal continuance, and unceasingly persists in searching into its interminable operations. But to the Adam He said, "Lo, the fear of Adonai, the Supreme Lord, this is wisdom; and the turning from evil, this is understanding."

This definition of wisdom, from the precision with which it is introduced, should be regarded as a direct revelation given by God to Adam, which had not then hitherto been recorded in any extant written document, but which had been handed down to Job by oral tradition. It is similar in character with the saying of our Lord, "It is more blessed to give than to receive," which was only recorded by St. Paul at Miletus many years after our Lord's ascension. Nothing can be conceived more capable of affording consolation to the afflicted than the realisation that the conscientious life has been revealed as the truest wisdom. The sense of his integrity was the great support of Job in his resistance to the temptation of losing faith in God's wisdom: "Though He slay me, yet will I trust Him," was the principle by which he was enabled to endure his aggravated misery, being fully convinced that no revelation of an All-wise God would fail in its fulfilment, and that at the proper moment the uprightness of his conduct would be vindicated and the sufferings of the perfect man would be compensated. Such thoughts represent the feelings of all undergoing apparently unmerited sufferings when exposed to the mistaken reproaches of man, or when labouring under a sense of injustice on witnessing the prosperity of the wicked, or when realising the failure of secular knowledge to give solace to the soul in her resistance to the temptation of losing faith in God's wisdom and love. To all such the assurance has been given that "Wisdom shall be justified of her children, and that their affliction, which is but for a moment, shall work out for them a far more exceeding and eternal weight of glory."

CHAPTER XXVII

JOB'S RETROSPECT OF HIS PAST LIFE

(CHAPS. xxix., xxx., xxxi.)

AFTER a period of silence Job again continues his parable, in which he endeavours to console himself by a review of his past prosperity and honourable position. He then proceeds to contrast this with the miserable condition to which he had been reduced so as to become an object of scorn to the most abject of men. He finally concludes by a solemn protestation of the due performance of his individual and social duties. The apparent tendency of his words is to extract support from the consideration that his sufferings are apparently unmerited, with the underlying hope that sooner or later God would have mercy upon him in vindicating his uprightness and restoring him to happiness. As the representative of those undergoing suffering for the infliction of which they can discover no adequate reason, the words of Job express the feelings of persons so afflicted, and offer modes of consolation for their support.

He commences with a wish "that his position

was the same which he had enjoyed in past months, in the days when God visibly protected him from harm. He recalls to remembrance how God had plentifully bestowed upon him His spiritual and intellectual blessings, when the rays of His directing word shone upon his mind, and under the guidance of its light he walked through the darkness and ignorance of the age. He recalls periods in which, when reproached for error, the secret counsel of God rested on his home, and when the realised presence of God was still with him. He carries back his thoughts to his family joys when his children were still around him. He alludes to the material prosperity which he had enjoyed when he washed his footsteps in the milk of his numerous herds, and was able to extract rivers of oil from the countless olive-trees growing on the rocks around his dwelling. He then refers to the high social position which he held when he sat as a magistrate on the judgment-seat of the city, and when princes and nobles held their peace to listen to his wise decisions, productive of happiness to those who heard, and causing the eye of the seers to testify to their correctness, because he delivered the poor, the fatherless, and the helpless. Thus the blessings of the perishing were invoked upon his head when he caused the heart of the widow to rejoice. He clothed himself with righteousness as a garment, and with impartial justice as a diadem and robe.

He restored the erring to the right path, and strengthened the weak on the road of life; he was a father to the poor, whilst he diligently investigated the truth of their statements. Thus he was enabled to shatter the devices of the wicked and to deliver the spoiled from their hands."

Comforting indeed was the retrospect of his past days, of which the conscientious performance of duty was the guiding principle. Yet, like Hezekiah in later days, Job appears to have forgotten the transitoriness of all earthly employments. In their absorption in carrying out their godly work, they had lost sight of the nearness of affliction and of sickness and of death. The leprous boil reminded the king of the uncertainty of life. "Set thine house in order, for thou shalt die but not live," was the message of God conveyed to him by the prophet. Job in the zenith of his prosperity was reduced in a moment to penury, and in a few months cast out as an excommunicate leper. Until that moment he had been fully convinced that "he would die in his nest amid the comforts of his genial home, and that his days of earthly happiness would be multiplied as the sand of the sea. He had believed that the root or source of his earthly prosperity would be productive of continuous growth from his commerce with the currents of popular life, whilst he had expected that the dew of God's blessing would unceasingly rest upon his harvest. He had confided in the ever-increasing estimation in which he was held by his friends, and the perpetual renewal of the promise of strength to his hands of which the bow in the clouds was an emblem. He had imagined that the attentive ear of mankind, and their reverential silence on hearing his counsels, would continue without intermission whilst they waited for his words, which proceeded from his mouth, with the thirsty eagerness of the parched soil looking to receive the genial rain. He had witnessed their utter discomfiture when he laughed at their inchoate proposals and their refusal to accept dismissal from his presence. He relied on his having been elected to direct their policy, to sit as their chief, and to dwell among them as the king over their separated clans, out of consideration for his vast capabilities to counsel them in all times of difficulty and distress."

From these expressions of his inner thoughts, it would appear that Job's long-continued success in life had made him over-confident in the expectation of its perpetuity. He would probably have been less impatient under his trial had he been acquainted with the history of Joseph, from whose unmerited consignment to the desert pit, and slavery in the prison, he might have discovered that at times suffering should be regarded under a disciplinary aspect, as being intended to train its victims for higher positions of authority in this world or the next. Affliction was the means by which Joseph was being fitted to become the Vizier of Egypt, so that having himself suffered he might be the better able to succour those who were to be afterwards tried by poverty and famine. So also the Divine Son is revealed as having, under His earthly condition, been made perfect through suffering in learning implicit obedience to the will of the Father. Thus, as the Christ He was raised to the right hand of the throne of God, whereby He became the Author of eternal salvation to all those who obey Him. The knowledge of these examples would have given to Job one solution of his problem, as to the reason why the perfect are exposed to suffering, and have tended to give him consolation under his bitter trials, in their being sent for the perfecting of man's character, so as to render him capable of more extended work for God in the future state.

Job next proceeds to compare his past happy life with the miserable condition to which he has been reduced, and the insolent manner in which he was treated by the very scum of the earth, on their perceiving his present inability to supply their wants, and to restrain their evil conduct. He deals first with the most abject classes of mankind. "He shows how the sons of those, whose fathers he would have rejected as unfit to care for his sheep-dogs, now make sport of his wretched appearance, men whose strength of hand has perished before coming to maturity, rendering them incapable of work for their own support. Hence their solitary lives are exposed to want and famine. They flee into the waterless waste to feed on the scanty herbage of the desert, because they have been driven as thieves from among men to dwell as troglodytes in the ravines of the dried-up winter torrents, and in holes of the dust and rocks. They yell among the bushes, and herd together amidst the nettles. They are sons of the vilest, of men without character, who are the refuse of the earth." And now, continues Job, "I am become to them as a song and a byword. Even these abhor me, and flee far off from me to escape the infection of my disease; they spare not to spit at me; because God has opened my cord, or relaxed the thread of my life, and has afflicted me, so that they let loose the bridle of their tongues in their insolence before me. Upon my right hand the rabble of their offspring rise up, they trip up my feet, and raise up obstacles against me for my destruction. They spoil my plans so as to profit by my calamity, and yet they themselves are helpless against a foe. They come against me like the mighty breakers of the sea, and roll themselves under its desolating fury. Therefore renewed terrors return on me, and my free action is overthrown as by an irresistible impulse. Thus my safety passes away as a thick cloud."

These feelings of Job are prophetically revealed by the Psalmist as being realised by his great antitype, the Lord Jesus: "Those for whom when they were sick He fasted, and went heavily as one that mourneth for his mother, rejoiced in His adversity; yea, the very abjects gathered themselves together, they tore at Him and ceased not, they gnashed upon Him with their teeth, and gaped upon Him with their mouth, saying, Fie on Thee, fie on Thee." But how different was the result of the contemplation of such ignominious treatment on the mind of our Lord from that which appeared in the mind of Job. Perfected submission to the will of God marks the character of His petitions for relief: "Lord, how long wilt Thou look upon this; deliver My soul from their destructions, and Thy beloved from the lions." No word of self-justification escapes His lips, and no charge of cruelty is made against His Divine Father. Even when the prayer seemed to be unheard the lowly confession comes from His mouth, "But Thou continuest holy, O Thou praise of Israel." The remembrance of insult under injury can only be calmly borne, when the thought which pervaded the mind of the suffering Christ is engendered in those, who are realising the wretchedness of man's unkind reproaches. "Father, forgive them, for they know not what they do," was His loving prayer. So love for man, and the recognition of the Fatherhood of God, will equally support all others who are exposed to man's persecution.

Unhappily for himself, Job's remembrance of the injurious treatment he had received from men on being reduced to penury and exposed to disease had a different effect. It made him hard in his feelings to man and impatient towards God. He continues his parable—" But now my soul is perturbed within me; days of affliction have seized me. By night God pierces my bones with unrest, and gnawing pains prevent my lying down. By the force of my disease my clothing bursts itself open, and then binds me as the collar of a coat. God hast cast me into the mire, and I am become like dust and ashes. I cry to Thee and Thou dost not answer me; I stand still and Thou regardest me not. Thou art cruelly turned against me. Thou hast exposed me to the storm and causest me to be driven by it. Thou dissolvest all my substance. For I know that Thou wilt turn me over unto the hand of death, the house of meeting for all flesh."

But a gleam of hope again presents itself to his mind: "Surely He will not send forth His hand against the mere wreck of a man, though men cry for his destruction. Did not I weep for any whose days were hard to endure, and did not my soul grieve for the poor? Yet when I looked for good, then evil came; and when I waited for light, then gloom arose. My bowels worked within me from pain, and were never still. Days of affliction anticipated all my hopes. I walked mournfully and obtained no warmth. I rose up in the congregation and cried for misery. I am become like a brother to the dragons, or like those demoniacally possessed, crying amid the tombs and cutting themselves with stones. I am become a companion to the sons of affliction; my skin is become black through the inflammation of my disease, and my bones are parched with drought. Instruments of music, which should promote joy, serve only to accompany my voice of mourning and the sound of my weeping."

In such despairing terms did Job describe his physical sufferings, which had become intensified by the feeling that God had forsaken him and no longer regarded him with favour. No hope appeared to remain for him on this side of the grave; all was darkness, impenetrable even to a ray of hope. Such an one needs to consider the impossibility of a loving Creator ever willingly afflicting or destroying the children of men. The cause of the trial may for a time remain concealed. Like the three hours' darkness which preceded our Lord's deliverance from the agonies of death, its moments should be passed in the contemplation of God's past fidelity to His promise to save all those who call upon His name. It was this perfected reliance on God's word that in the darkest hour of our Lord's humiliation led Him to exclaim: "My God, My God, why hast Thou forsaken Me?" with the happy result that His human spirit was almost immediately after received into the hands of His Divine Father. Firm faith in God's love and truth is the great preservative against imagining that God will ever forsake those who love Him.

After another short pause it would appear that Job realised a feeling of unrest in consequence of the heat of his language towards God, which led him to see the necessity of justifying his statements to his own mind. This prompted him to review his past life, and to examine into its accordance with the will of God. "He first directs his thoughts to the chastity which had distinguished his inner nature, in restraining the wandering of his eyes as well as his secret desires. He recognises how impurity deprives a man of his share in the portion of spiritual blessing which comes from God, and imperils the earthly inheritance which he has received from the Almighty, in being productive of danger to life and alienation from home. He next appeals to the all-seeing eye of God to vindicate his avoidance of falsehood and deceit. He asserts his willingness to be weighed in the balances of a righteous God to prove the integrity of his commerce with man. If he is proved guilty of having wandered from the pathway of uprightness, or of having allowed his heart to be allured by the desire of his eyes, or of having permitted the action of his hands to be blemished with evil, he admits the justice of being visited by the retributive failure of earthly success through the advantage that may accrue to others by his mistaken conduct, as well as of being farther punished by the degradation of his children. He proceeds to admit that if he had been unfaithful to his marriage vow, he might be justly visited with the misery of seeing his wife reduced to slavery and exposed to pollution; for adultery he declares to be, not only a heinous crime punishable by the civil judge, but also an inward fire destructive alike to the moral sense and intellectual progress. He shows the justice he had displayed in his treatment of his household, admitting that the rejection of their equitable complaints would have deprived him of any hope in being able to justify his conduct before Him, by whom they as well as he himself had all been created and fashioned in the womb. He recalls to mind his generosity to the poor in his protection of the widow, and in his feeding of the fatherless, of whom he constituted himself the parent in their moment of need. He summons the perishing and the naked to testify to his supply of their wants, and declares his readiness to submit to legal retaliation if he has raised his hand against the orphan in the perversion of his cause at the seat of justice. He gives also his reason; for there was an awe over me at the thought of destruction from God, and on account of His majesty I could not endure to act unkindly to the needy. He proceeds to show his allegiance to Almighty God by his refusal to rely upon gold for his support, and upon his wealth for happiness, and still more by his rejection of the material light and of the moon as objects of secret veneration and of public worship, an iniquity, he adds, which is punishable by the civil judges." Thus does he testify to faith in God alone as the source of light and life, and as the Almighty cause of the continuous monthly succession of the times and seasons. The recognition of the heavenly orbs as objects of worship was a denial of God as the Creator, and in the ancient Sabean or fire worship was accompanied by throwing a kiss from the hand towards the rising sun.

"He manifests the kindliness of his disposition in the absence of joy on the destruction of his enemies, in refusing to excite himself against them when misfortune was upon them, and in allowing no word of execration against them to escape his lips. He reminds himself that none of the men of his tribe had cried out for better wages or had been dissatisfied with his treatment; that strangers were always welcomed to his house instead of being obliged to lodge in the streets. He fails to convict himself of making excuses for any wrong-doings, or for hiding them like Adam in his own bosom instead of openly confessing them to God. He finally asks himself whether he ever allowed the fear of the masses, or the contempt of the better instructed classes, to terrify him into silence or to drive him away without boldly giving expression to the true convictions of his mind?" This consideration of his past life was calculated to give Job great comfort under his trial, and the more so that it was not uttered from any self-righteous adulation of what had formed the ordinary character of his daily habits. In this portion of his soliloquy there is no trace of self-laudation. He merely gives a sketch of the actions which marked his usual life, together with the principles and reasons which led to their performance. He regards them as the necessary duties which are incumbent upon every God-fearing man, and in proportion to their right fulfilment he realised the amount of comfort which would be granted to those whose consciences were, therefore, in a state of peace.

Job's failure to obtain the fulness of consolation was due to his refusal to submit his will to the will of God, and in his forgetfulness that the thing formed has no ground for saying to him who formed it, Why dost thou treat me thus? But his words gave no solution to his question, Why do the perfect suffer? His views as to the cause of this differed from those of his three friends. They held that suffering was invariably the result of personal sin. Job appears to have thought that, where personal sin had not been committed, it was an act of injustice on the part of God to allow the perfect to suffer. Hence through the whole discussion he endeavoured to vindicate his integrity, and exposed himself to the charge of self-justification. He had not realised the force of the lesson afterwards taught by the Divine

Sufferer in Gethsemane, that when pleading for a removal of affliction the prayer must be qualified by perfect submission to the will of God: "Father, if Thou be willing, remove this cup from Me; nevertheless not My will but Thine be done." Job consequently forfeited the blessing of receiving spiritual strength sent down from above through angelic ministrations to support him in the conflict.

It was this spirit of self-justification that "led him to desire that one of the angelic ministrants around the heavenly throne should be appointed to hear his defence; and that as he bore the mark of the sacred Thau, as the branded slave of Jehovah he intimated his strong entreaty that the Almighty should reply by a decisive judgment of his case. He felt so confident of his own position as to desire that his opponent, unknown to him as he was, should have written a book with a full description of his impeachment, that he might bear it on his shoulder before the heavenly judgment-seat, being fully assured that by his acquittal he would be able to bind it as a crown of honour upon his head; then as the Nagid, or chief ruler over God's people, he feels that he would come near to his Divine Judge to declare the number and character of all his steps in the performing the duties of his high office" (xxxi. 35).

He finally concludes the discussion with the forcible imprecation, "If my land has cried out against me, or its furrows have wept together for my ill-treatment; if I have eaten its strength without payment, or have caused its owners to breathe out their lives, then let the thorn grow forth instead of wheat, and the noisome weed instead of barley."

The words of Job are ended.

CHAPTER XXVIII

THE INTERMEDIATE STATE

Sheol—Hades

Job's sufferings appear to have been greatly aggravated by the imperfect knowledge which in his days prevailed as to the nature of the Sheol, or Intermediate State. He was a firm believer in the continuity of life after death, although he repeatedly gives utterance to prayers that "it would please God to destroy him." But his faith in a future resurrection is clearly manifested in his assured hope that "from his reanimated flesh he shall see God." His desire for death arises from the certainty that it is necessarily attended with the cessation of bodily suffering. Of his final acceptance by the Almighty at the general resurrection he has little doubt, for "he has not concealed the words of the Holy One." Like St. Paul, he has lived in all good conscience before God, and he therefore "holds fast to his righteousness, and will not let go the sense of his conscientiousness so as to allow his heart to reproach him with falsehood before God" (xxvii. 6).

Thus the approach of death, as the end of bodily pain, was welcomed by him.

Job's troubles, however, were not produced solely by bodily suffering. They were increased by mental disturbance, from his inability to solve many metaphysical problems, which presented themselves to his mind. Of these the most prominent was that which originated from his ignorance of any definite doctrines respecting the condition of the soul in Sheol, or the Intermediate State, on its separation by death from its earthly environment. The Hebrew word Sheol is derived from the root "to ask," descriptive of its insatiable nature (Prov. xxvii. 20; xxx. 16). It is usually rendered by the word "hell," but often mistakenly by "the grave."

The principal idea which pervaded Job's mind as to its character is that of gloom and isolation. He describes it as "a land of darkness and of the shadow of death, a darkness productive of weariness by its monotonous unchangeability, similar to the palpable darkness which for three days covered the land of Egypt, rendering movement impossible, so that life resembled a state of death, reducing natural order into chaos, in comparison with which the ordinary nocturnal darkness became as light (x. 21). Not a voice was to be heard. From it there was no return to earth. The eye of man who had entered its gloomy portal would see man again no more (vii. 8, 10). The shades of the departed were its only occupants (xxvi. 5). In such despairing terms does Job describe the abode of the soul in Sheol, until at times his hope of deliverance becomes so faint as to raise a question in his mind, whether, if a man die, he will again live" (xiv. 14).

The old patriarchal faith, however, took a less gloomy view. On the approach of death the patriarchs realised that they were being gathered to their predeceased fathers (Gen. xv. 15). In later days a revelation was given to the prophet Isaiah (xiv.), wherein he is shown the mighty kings of old lying in their glory, each one in his own house awaiting the advent of their faithful successors, or witnessing the casting down of the arrogant tyrants into the stones of the pit as despised carcases to be trodden under foot.

Personal recognition and intellectual inter-communion by its denizens are suggested by the prophet, similar to those which were afterwards more clearly revealed by our Lord and His apostles.

Far different is the character of Hades, or the Intermediate State, as revealed by our Lord.[1] In the

---

[1] Much confusion has arisen from the use of the English "hell" as a translation for Hades and Gehenna. In the New Testament Hades, or "the unseen place," describes the Intermediate State (Matt. xi. 23; xvi. 18; Luke x. 15; xvi. 23; Acts ii. 27, 31; 1 Cor. xv. 55; Rev. i. 18; vi. 8; xx. 13, 14). With this Gehenna has no connection. It literally means "The valley of Hinnom," the place of secular capital punishment (Matt. v. 22, 29, 30; x. 28; Luke xii. 5), or else the apocalyptic lake of fire, as in Matt. xviii. 9; xxiii. 15, 33; Mark ix. 43, 45, 47; James iii. 6, to which the wicked will be consigned at the final judgment (Rev. xxi. 8).

history of Dives and Lazarus, in a very condensed form its prominent features are depicted (Luke xvi. 19). To regard this as a parable is detrimental to its intrinsic value; our Lord describes the event as an historic fact, apparently revealing what had been and still was happening to two known men. He gives the name of one and clearly affirms the existence of the other: "There was a certain rich man, and there was a certain beggar named Lazarus." He relates certain events in their lives, the fact of their deaths, and the localities to which they were consigned at death, together with the causes whereby their respective conditions in the Intermediate State had been determined.

He describes the Intermediate State under the general name of Hades, or "the unseen place," descriptive of some invisible locality to which the soul departs at the moment of death. Our Lord's human soul went to Hades, as did that of the rich man (Acts ii. 27). It comprises two divisions, one of bliss and the other of torment. Its unseen character is shown by our Lord when foretelling the fate of Capernaum, at one time exalted to heaven, or lifted up high in the atmosphere of a lofty mountain, and then to be thrust down to Hades, or some unseen cavity, by a volcanic disturbance, so that its site still remains unknown (Matt. xi. 23). He elsewhere declares that the gates of Hades shall not prevail against His Church, intimating the continuity of her work and worship in the Intermediate State, witnessed in His preaching to the spirits in prison, and the intercession of her holy martyrs in behalf of the conversion of their persecutors revealed by St. John (1 Pet. iii. 19; iv. 6; Rev. vi. 9). Power of admission and of deliverance from Hades is possessed by our Lord, under the symbols of the keys of Death and of Hades, causing St. Paul to give utterance to the joyful assurance of the resurrection in the exultant cry, "O Hades, where is thy victory" (1 Cor. xv. 55). In all these passages Hades is descriptive of the locality to which the soul goes at death, invisible to the eye of man, until he is freed from the fleshly body.

Hades is composed of two parts, separated by an impassible gulf, the respective occupants of which can see and converse with one another without power of contact. The rich man in the penal division saw Lazarus in the state of happiness, and conversed with Abraham, who showed him the causes of his suffering. The occupants of Hades, for purposes of recognition, are revealed as necessarily being in possession of some kind of form. They cannot be merely disembodied spirits, for pure spirit, as far as man can discover, is incapable of being seen. Thus God in His plenary infinitude is Spirit, "Whom no man hath seen at any time, but who has been declared by the only begotten Son who is in the bosom of the Father" (John i. 18). Form is essential to visibility, and in its essential nature is only attenuated corporeity. Formlessness is destructive of individuality; or, according to the Buddhist philosophy, the absorption of the individual into the concrete Nirvana.

St. Paul, in the second epistle to the Corinthians (v. 2), appears to allude to this soul-body, or form, saying, " In this our earthly body we groan, earnestly desiring to be clothed upon with our little house, which is from heaven." The original term for the little house is used by St. Jude (6), to express the habitation forsaken by the apostate angels when they intermarried with the daughters of men (Gen. vi.). It appears to be the integument of the souls, but not their fleshly bodies or their lost heavenly homes. Similar is the soul-body with which believers desire to be clothed upon.

Some form of soul-body is clearly referred to by our Lord, as without it there would have been no inter-recognition of Abraham, Lazarus, and the rich man. Its form is apparently similar to that of the human body, being in the image of God, in which man was originally created. The history refers to several members of the body, the bosom, the finger, and the tongue, similar to those revealed in angelic appearances, and in the visions of predeceased saints, as Elijah and Moses, who have been permitted to reappear in their soul-bodies on earth. Without such forms recognition amongst the departed would become impossible in the Intermediate State. The individual would be absorbed in the concrete spiritual condition, or, in Buddhist phraseology, in the concrete Nirvana. The existence of this soul-body is not only emphasised, but manifestly revealed by our Lord's work in Hades. In His human soul He went and preached to the spirits in prison. The Preacher could only be distinguished from His hearers by the possession of a soul-body, separated from each of those of His hearers, existing under similar conditions as spirits, quickened in their separated soul-bodies. The preachment of our Lord, quickened by His spirit in His human soul, becomes a revelation that the spirits of the departed are also quickened on union with their respective soul-bodies as the environment of their respective spirits.

The soul-body as the organ of individual life, through the inbreathing of the spirit of lives (Gen. ii. 7), is necessarily possessed of intellectual faculties, whereby it becomes capable of work in the Intermediate State. This is revealed by our Lord in the preaching of Abraham to the rich man, and his intercessory prayer for his brethren. The existence of work in Hades is also revealed in the character of the names, by which the abodes of the saints, or the happy ones, are distinguished. Abraham's bosom, to which Lazarus was carried by the angels, is descriptive of the enjoyments and duties of social life, realised in the name borne by St. John as the disciple who leaned on Jesus' bosom at the last supper. Our Lord's preachment to the spirits in prison, the subsequent evangelisation of the dead, the intercession of the martyrs for their persecutors, are all characteristic of intellectual Hadean work. The Paradise, entrance to which was promised to the penitent thief, and its realised existence revealed to St. Paul (2 Cor. xii.), is clearly descriptive of some definite locality to which the souls of the good have access at their deaths. The name given to it by our Lord is manifestly significant of work under some form not purely intellectual, and possibly under changed conditions similar in kind to that appointed for man in Eden. The torments of thirst and heat, to which the rich man was exposed, reveal forms of suffering conditioned by substantial agencies, which are utterly invisible to those who are still abiding in the flesh.

Sheol, or Hades, appears therefore to be not only a definite locality, but also a locality conditioned by substantial as well as intellectual employment. The nature of such conditions is not as yet fully disclosed. Their existence, however, is manifestly revealed. When angels are described as ministering spirits, the possession of a body as the organ of life is not only not precluded, but has been evidently verified by actual experience on their intercommunion with mankind (Heb. i. 7, 14). The possession of a soul-body as the organ of life by those who have ended their earthly existence, though such body may be invisible to man while resident on earth, is therefore not only not improbable, but appears to be supported by arguments to which it is difficult to refuse acceptance.

If there be any force in these remarks, the Intermediate State for the good is not, as Job mistakenly assumed, a land of darkness and of the shadow of death, but on the contrary, under changed conditions of life at present unintelligible to man, a place of restful enjoyment, of happy work, of ministerial employment in evangelising the impenitent deceased, united to gladsome praise and reverential worship of the Almighty. The blessed dead are represented as resting from their labours, but they are also followed by their works, just as in the highest degree God rested from His Creative work. Experience and revelation witness to the perpetuity of His Providential work, as shown by our Lord: "My Father worketh hitherto, and I work." The happy work of the Intermediate State is equally unceasing; for wherever there is life, there is development or growth, which is the result of work. Its character may be of substantial production, or intellectual and spiritual progression. Beyond this man knows little, as both the locality of Hades and its esoteric character are still unrevealed.

The development of the deceased saints is now universally admitted, both in character, knowledge, and power. This appears to be taught in the parable of the ten virgins. While intermittently sleeping, yet the wise were careful to keep their lamps trimmed. The partial rest of Hades is accompanied by the cultivation of the human faculties, whereby the saints become continuously better prepared for entrance into the heavenly city.

But while the development in sanctification, and consequent purification from their earthly defects in those who have obtained an entrance into Paradise and its blissful environment, is fully granted, yet it is not only gravely questioned, but also strongly denied, that any hope of purification, or of development in goodness, can be conceded to those who have died impenitent. Many of our most learned divines dogmatically affirm that no second test, no opportunity of retrieving the past, no second probation is possible in Hades, because the door of repentance has been irrevocably closed against the man who dies in a state of wilful impenitence. Such dogmatic affirmations are only warrantable by the production of definite texts from Scripture, which is the alone court of appeal in matters beyond the grave, and the correctness of the interpretation of these texts must also be fully established.

The doctrine of punishment of a non-reformative character, which is the generally accepted view of the punishment of the wicked in Hades, is apparently opposed to the essential nature of God as Love. God is revealed as not willingly afflicting the children of men, and as chastening those whom He loves. Retributive punishment without a reformative motive appears to militate against such statements. The doctrine of everlasting torment, which is only another form of non-reformative punishment for sin committed during a man's earthly existence, whether such torment commences in Hades or at the final judgment, appears to be equally inconsistent with the loving nature of God, and it is questionable whether it can be supported by Scripture proof. It is universally agreed that man's condition in Hades is determined by his life on earth, the good entering into happiness and the evil into misery proportioned to their conscientious or unconscientious conduct; but whether such condition is finally determined at the moment of death, so as to admit of no change in the coming or Hadean age, is open to grave doubts. The supposed condemnation of those dying impenitent to a state of torment in Hades, from which it is alleged there is no escape except by their subsequent consignment to accentuated misery in the raised body at the final judgment, has appeared to be so opposed to the Divine nature of Love, as to have led men to the enunciation of the two antagonistic theories of Universal Restitution and Final Annihilation at the Last Judgment. Both of these theories necessarily involve the acceptance of the doctrines of the existence of probation in Hades, and of the capability of the evil to repent, and to become possessed of powers of development in good during their abode in the Intermediate State.

The restriction of the claim to development in goodness, and to purification from earthly defects in those dying in a state of sanctification, and the denial of such claims to those dying in a state of impenitence, appear equally to preclude the possibility of development in goodness in those dying in a state of penitence. In either case purification for the enjoyment of the Beatific Vision is admitted to be needed, and the question resolves itself into one of degree, opportunity, or character. The moment of death causes no break in the continuity of life. It is only the migration of the soul and spirit to a fresh sphere of conscious existence. The principles which govern their continuous existence remain unchanged. The body alone ceases to exist. Conversion and purification are not confined to the action of the body. They pertain in a much higher degree to the action of the soul and spirit. Therefore, without express revelation to the contrary, there appears reason for believing that conversion and purification are equally capabilities which appertain to the soul and spirit in the Intermediate State. Consequently the doctrine of the capability of conversion in the case of the impenitent appears to be supported with equal authority as that for the purification of the penitent; and for the determination of the result probation in Hades is in both cases equally requisite.

This doctrine of development in grace even in those dying in a state of impenitence, and that also of the existence of probation in Hades, is witnessed in the history of the rich man. He had died a selfish man. Under the teaching of Abraham he became a converted soul anxious for his brethren's welfare. Admission to the society of the blest might still be denied to him in Hades, but at the general judgment, when Hades ceases to exist, the impediment of the impassable gulf will be removed, and his position in the new heaven and the new earth will be determined out of that which is written in the books by which he will be judged. The gospel has been preached to him when dead by Abraham. The opportunity for its reception has rendered him capable of being judged as if he had heard it in the flesh, while his obedience to its injunctions as to love of his brethren has witnessed to its power of enabling him to live according to God in his renovated spirit. His abode in Hades has evidently been to him not only a period of reformative punishment, but also one of probation, by which he has given proof of sincere if not perfected conversion.

Had Job enjoyed the knowledge granted to St. Paul in his vision of Paradise, or had he heard of the promise of admission to its happy scenes accorded by our Lord to the penitent thief, much of his mental disturbance would have been calmed. Paul's earnest desire to depart and to be with Christ witnesses to the happiness of this restful abode of the saints, whilst the names given to it by our Lord are expressive of their mutual recognition and social lives, as well as of the character of their peaceful activities of mind and soul in the cultivation of the yet unrevealed conditions of their new sphere of existence.

Had Job, again, survived till the days of St. Peter, he would have been comforted under the mental disturbance engendered by his unsolved metaphysical problems as to the fate of the perfect and of the wicked, by the assurance that consignment to an unconscious existence in Sheol forms no part of the Divine purposes. He would have recognised that the preaching of our Lord to the typical disobedient antediluvian spirits, followed by the further preaching of the Gospel to the dead, naturally involved a condition of intellectual activity, the results of which are dependent on the doctrine that life in Hades is a state of probation giving promise of increased spiritual knowledge to the good, and of a fresh opportunity for conversion to the impenitent. The Intermediate State thus becomes a sphere of hopeful expectation of the final acceptance of all submissive hearers, and a further revelation that the love of God will be eternally manifested to His

P

obedient servants whatever be the sphere of their existence.

Thus Job would have realised that problems insoluble to man on earth will then receive their full explanation, and that the promised blessing of perfect peace would be attained by all those whose minds, like his own, are stayed upon the Lord Jehovah.

CHAPTER XXIX

THE INTERVENTION OF ELIHU

(CHAP. xxxii.)

A LENGTHENED silence appears to have followed the conclusion of Job's soliloquy, for the three friends declined to reply, on the alleged reason that they regarded his utterances as those of a self-righteous man. Their action led to the intervention of a fourth person, whose presence had not before been recorded, though the tenor of his words shows that he had heard the whole discussion, a corroborative proof of the correctness of the theory that it had been the event of a single day.

His name was Elihu, the son of Barachel, of the family of Ram. From his description as the Buzite, he was evidently a personage of importance, notwithstanding his youth. His name and descent are typical as well as historical. As Elihu, "He is my God," he represents the inspired prophet in the sense that Moses was Divinely appointed to be to Aaron instead of God, in the fulfilment of their mission to the Egyptian king. He traces his descent from Barachel, "the blessing of God," illustrative of the doctrine that the gift of inspiration is derived from the outpouring of the Spirit upon the prophet. He belongs to the family of Ram, "the Exalted one," representative of the prophet's relationship to "the exalted and lofty One that inhabiteth time." As the Buzite, "the despised one," he is typical of Him who was divinely sent to Nazareth, that He might be called the Nazarene, in its true sense of the Nazarite or "the afflicted one," or one separated from His brethren to undergo contempt and death, in order that, by His preaching and subsequent unjust condemnation to the cross as a blasphemer, He might become the Author of eternal salvation to all those who obey Him.

While listening to the discussion, Elihu's anger had been aroused, "because Job had justified himself rather than God, whom he had accused of tearing him in His wrath, and of hating him, and yet not for any violence which was found in his hands, while at the same time he alleged that his prayer was pure." Elihu was equally incensed against the three friends because they had accused Job of sin, but had failed to give any proof of the truth of their accusation. He appears to have delayed a short time before speaking, to give them a further opportunity of replying to Job's parable, out of consideration for their age; but on their continued silence his wrath was rekindled, and he forced himself to give utterance to his own opinions. He first shows that his hesitation in speaking arose from the consideration of his own age as compared with themselves. He expected to find their wisdom commensurate with the number of their years. He felt, however, that the sense of the indwelling of God's Spirit within him, and the realisation of a Divine inspiration from the Almighty, had given him a deeper understanding than that which accompanied either their position or their age, and thus he felt impelled to address them. Therefore I said: "Hearken unto me; I will also show my opinion. Behold I have waited for your words, I have given ear to your reasons, whilst ye searched out what to say. Yea, I have attended unto you, but there was none of you which convinced Job or answered his words. He then gives a reason for their failure, showing that it was Divinely ordered, lest they should attribute their success in convincing Job to the force of their own arguments, and imagine that they therefore had found out the secrets of wisdom. He then solemnly pronounces, that God has cast him down and not man. You have attributed his misery to earthly causes, whereas its origin must be traced to the direct instrumentality of Almighty God. He therefore states his determination to adopt a different line of argument, for Job, he says, has not directed his word against me, and consequently I shall not answer him with your speeches."

The force of Elihu's words, and the sudden conviction of their truth, utterly confounded the minds of the three friends, and deprived them of all power of reply, so that after a short delay Elihu again declared his intention to take his share in the discussion, and to declare what he knew about the matter; for, says he, " I am full of the subject, and the Spirit within me constrains me to speak, for my inner mind is as a vessel in which wine ferments, where there is no vent, and which is ready to burst asunder as a new skin bottle. I will therefore speak that I may relieve myself—I will open my lips and answer; but while doing so, I will show partiality to no one, nor give flattering surnames to any, since for so doing my Maker would soon take me away."

CHAPTER XXX

ELIHU'S INDICTMENT OF JOB'S SELF-RIGHTEOUSNESS

(CHAP. xxxiii.)

ELIHU now addresses himself directly to Job, claiming to speak from God, and to give him the opportunity which he had desired of having some one to plead for man with God, as a man pleadeth for his neighbour: "Wherefore, Job, I pray thee, hearken to my utterances, for I have opened my mouth to speak words proceeding from uprightness of heart, as well as to impart knowledge which cometh from purity of lip." In support of his claim, Elihu—in allusion to his inspiration—refers "to the Spirit of God by whom he was made, and to the quickening of his mouth by the breath of the Almighty. If then thou art able to return to me an answer, set thy words in order before me, and stand forth, for according to thy request, I, who am also a man like thyself, formed out of clay, am standing before thy face in God's stead. Lo, my terror will not therefore frighten thee, nor will my hand be heavy upon thee."

Having thus declared his office, Elihu proceeds with his indictment against Job. "I have heard thy voice saying, I am pure and am free from transgression. I am innocent, and there is no iniquity in me; but God finds causes of alienation from me; He counts me as an enemy; He has put my feet in the stocks so as to prevent my success in life. He observes all my steps, so as to detect my sins." Such is the indictment that Elihu lays against Job. It is one in which he not only charges him with self-righteousness, but also with accusing God of a deliberate intention to treat him unjustly, in seeking for reasons to deprive him of the blessing of His presence. He then goes on to establish its truth, "Lo, in this thou art not righteous." Thy claim to self-righteousness is suicidal to itself. It is an act of sin; for when a man has done all that is commanded, he must still admit himself to be an unprofitable servant, he has only done that which it was his duty to do.

Elihu then adduces another argument in support of his indictment. He draws it from the fact of God's omnipotence: "God is greater than man." How great, then, is the presumption of man in contending with God, and in challenging Him to give reasons for the commands He utters. The servant does not strive with his master; he simply does what he is told to perform. Much more so, then, does it befit man to yield himself implicitly to the will of God, and with Samuel to say, "Speak, Lord, for Thy servant heareth."

Elihu then proceeds to show how inattentive men are to the ordinary calls of God, thereby implying the need of suffering as an agency to cause them to listen to His voice. This is a knocking at the door of the heart, not necessarily for the conviction of sin, but also to prepare men for the reception of greater blessings, or to summon them to higher duties. "God," he says, "speaks in one way, and then in a second manner when men regard Him not, in a dream, in a night vision, in the falling trance, in slumberings on the bed. Then He opens their ears and impresses His instruction on their minds, that He may turn man from his purposes and hide pride from him. Thus He keeps back his soul from becoming corrupt, and his life from passing away by the sword-thrust." Such is the action of the Word of God, which is a discerner of the thoughts and intents of the heart. By such warnings man is protected from unseen dangers, and occult mental impressions become promoters of his happiness. He goes on to explain the function of pain, and the method of its interpretation. It is for man's deliverance from corruption, and for advancing his enjoyment of the light that belongs to eternal life. Like the leprous boil of Hezekiah, it is sent to convince a man of the transitory character of life, and to give him the hope of renovation. "Man is chastened with pain on his bed, and has continual irritation in his bones. So that his life abhors his bread and his soul its desired food. His flesh is consumed and passes out of sight, and men see not his wasting bones, because his soul draws near to corruption and his life to the place of the dead." The last verse contains the reason for which the pain was sent, as being intended to counteract the forgetfulness that the present life is not eternal, a forgetfulness to which even the perfect are exposed through their absorption in the performance of the duties of their several callings.

Elihu proceeds to show "how gracious God is to him if He sends an invisible angel as an interpreter of His Divine purposes in thus sending affliction, or even one of the learned, to make known to him what is right for him to do. In his ministerial character such an one will intercede for him to be ransomed from going down to the pit of corruption, since he is able to give him the consoling assurance that one has been found through whom reconciliation has been made. Thus the freshness of his flesh, more even than that of a young man, will be restored to him according to the days of his youth, in accordance with the prophetic promise, that they who wait upon Jehovah shall renew their strength, and mount up with wings as eagles. He will entreat for him to God, who will accept him and cause him to see His face with the shout of joy, and will render to him the reward of his righteous conduct."

He reveals how anxious God is to welcome even the repentant sinner, for "He looks upon man, and if any one confesses his fault and says, I have sinned and perverted what is right, and yet He has not requited me as I deserved, then God will ransom his soul from passing away in corruption, and his life shall see the light." Thus did Elihu reveal to Job one of the functions of pain as amongst the things wherewith God works oftentimes to preserve man's soul from the corruption of the pit, so that it may be enlightened with the light of the living. He thus declares that suffering is not only punitive in respect of the past, and preservative in respect of the present, but also protective against future errors and faults.

Elihu then closes this portion of his address by a solemn admonition to Job to give heed to what he has said: "Mark well therefore, and hearken unto me; if thou hast anything to say, answer me, and speak, for I shall delight in thy justification; but if not, hearken to me, hold thy peace, and I will cause thee to learn wisdom."

This first portion of Elihu's message from God contains several lessons in connection with the subject of affliction. It reveals that in some cases, as in that of Job, it originates with God and not with man. Therefore any attempt at self-justification, in imputing injustice to God, is inconsistent with the relationship which exists between an omnipotent and omniscient God and the creatures which He has made. Elihu shows that beneficence to man is at all times the object of affliction, in delivering man through chastening influences from concealed dangers, which may become his ruin unless some interpreter of the Divine Will were sent to make known to him, that a propitiation had been provided for his atonement, through whose intercession a favourable answer may be expected to his prayer, that he may enjoy the light of the living.

CHAPTER XXXI

ELIHU CONVICTS JOB OF IMPUTING INJUSTICE TO GOD

(CHAP. xxxiv.)

APPARENTLY after a short pause Elihu resumed his address, directing his words especially to the three friends: " Hear my words, ye wise men; and give ear to me, ye knowing ones: for the ear trieth words as the palate tasteth food. Let us therefore make choice of correct judgment, so that we may know between us what is truly good; for Job has said, I am righteous, and God has turned away the judgment that should have been pronounced over me. Being convinced of mine innocency, can I lie concerning the sentence that ought to have been spoken about me? The wound wherewith God has stricken me is mortal, although there has been no transgression of His law." Elihu then draws attention to the character of Job's words: " What man is like Job, who thus indulges in scornful expressions as easily as a man drinks water? He travels in the company of the workers of iniquity, and he goes in the way with wicked men; for he has said, Man is not cherished as a friend by God, although he endeavours to make himself acceptable to Him." Thus he shows how those who allow themselves to use unguarded language in accusing God of injustice in His dealings with man, and of the perversion of right judgment, tend to place themselves on a level with the wicked. True faith leads to a distrust of one's own judgment, and to a patient submission to the Divine Will from a full consciousness that God can never be false to His promise, "to fulfil the desire of those that fear Him, and to preserve all those that love Him."

Elihu then sets himself to affirm the justice of God, notwithstanding Job's exposure to suffering, and the impossibility of His rejection of any with whom He has declared Himself well pleased, as in the case of Job, of whom God said, There is none like him on earth, perfect, upright, fearing God, and turning from evil. "Therefore, hearken to me, ye men of heart. Far be it from God to cause evil, and the Almighty to cause iniquity; for the work of man He will requite to him, and according to his way of life He will cause him to find his recompense. Truly, indeed, God will not cause a man to become wicked, and the Almighty will not pervert judgment." When, therefore, God permits the perfect to be exposed to suffering, its infliction must be attributed to some concealed cause, the knowledge of which is necessary to be obtained before a person is in a position to charge God with injustice for its toleration.

Freedom from suffering has nowhere in Revelation been promised to man on earth, either before or since the fall, of which the punishment is natural death, which is often unattended by either physical or mental suffering, and through heredity becomes the lot of all born into the world, be they perfect or wicked. The cultivation of the soil in Eden involved labour. This is only a modified form of suffering, through the exercise of self-denial, without which no one can do good to man, or render acceptable worship to God. Exposure to self-denial, and consequent suffering in abstention from what is forbidden, has at all times been, and still continues to be, one of the essential conditions of human existence, so that to charge God with injustice in the toleration of suffering in even the perfect man, is not only inconsistent with true righteousness, but also with accurate reasoning.

Ehihu adduces a fresh argument to prove the sin of imputing injustice to God. He asks, "Who has power to claim an oversight in respect of God's governance of the earth, or who has placed the whole world under His control?" If God set His heart upon man to gather back to Himself his spirit and his breath, all flesh would expire together, and man would return to the dust out of which he was formed. If, therefore, thou hast understanding, hear this, and give ear to the voice of my words." God is admittedly the moral Governor and loving

Creator. "How then can one who hates right judgment, govern and bind all together in loving concord? or how canst thou call Him wicked who is the most righteous? Will any call a king a man of Belial, or say to self-sacrificing nobles, ye are wicked? Will any call Him unjust who shows no partiality for princes, and makes no difference between the full and needy, for all of them are the work of His hands? In a moment men die, and at midnight the people are shaken and pass out of life, and the mighty are turned aside without any visible cause, for His eyes are upon the ways of each, and He sees all their steps. There is no darkness, nor the shadow of death, where the doers of iniquity may hide, so that He needeth not again to consider his case. He will not continuously put affliction upon him, to cause man to go to God for judgment."

The drift of these words of Elihu is to show that the omniscience of God is so infinite as to exclude the necessity of any second examination into a man's conduct, so as to lead to a revision of the Divine sentence. "Thus, without any ostensible investigation, He breaks in pieces mighty men, and causes others to stand in their stead, for He has discerned the character of their works, and overturns them in a night and crushes them. He striketh them down publicly under the hands of the wicked, in the place where men behold them, because they turned away from following Him, and did not consider any of His ways, so that they caused the cry of the poor to come to Him, and He heard the mourning of the afflicted."

These considerations lead Elihu to point out, not only the impropriety but also the utter uselessness of any resistance to the Divine Will. He shows that perfect submission is the only true attitude of the believer, united to the humble prayer that God would reveal to the sufferer any unrecognised sin which he may have unconsciously committed. He accentuates the importance of following this advice, by reminding his hearers that the recompense which is the result of conduct is entirely dependent on the decision of the Almighty, for he adds, "When He causes men to be quiet, who will pronounce a sentence of condemnation? When He hides His face who then can behold Him? No one knows the cause of His hiding. It may be for events affecting a nation in preventing a hypocrite from reigning, or for matters pertaining to man in causing the people to be freed from his evil devices."

Happy is it when a man returns and says to God: "I have been lifted up with pride, but I will not offend again; that which I see not, do Thou teach me; if I have done iniquity I will do so no more." Yet the answer to the prayer, as well as the time when it is granted, must be left in His hands, for he asks: "Do you think that God will requite thee according to thy expectations? Thou hast rejected His judgment, therefore thou must choose whose judgment thou wilt accept; I cannot do this for thee, therefore speak what thou dost know."

Apparently after a short pause to allow of a reply from Job, Elihu appeals to the bystanders, saying: "Let men of understanding hearts speak to me, and let a wise man hear me. Job has spoken without knowledge, and his words have been destitute of prudence. My desire, therefore, is that Job should be tried to the uttermost because of his answers among men, whom, in allusion to the harsh accusations of the three friends, he calls men of iniquity. He has added transgression to sin; he clappeth his hands among us as if he were victorious, and he multiplieth his words against God." In such solemn terms does Elihu at the same time reprove the hasty and scornful words in which Job had ventured to reproach the Almighty, and the harsh accusations made against him by the three friends.

The second portion of Elihu's address is to show the impiety of imputing injustice to God in the toleration of affliction, even when its cause has been concealed from the sufferer. This he proves by the consideration that exposure to suffering is the necessary accompaniment of right service both to God and to man, in its disciplinary character of perfectioning man for the performance of his duty. He proceeds to declare how the sin becomes aggravated by the certainty that an omniscient moral Ruler is enabled in all cases to form a right judg-

JOB'S IMPUTATION OF GOD'S INJUSTICE 243

ment of what is required by the sufferer, whose ignorance of the Divine purpose of the suffering, as well as of its particular object, renders him incapable of sufficient knowledge to entitle him to charge God with arbitrary treatment of any who may be exposed to its action. Hence he concludes that perfect submission to the Divine Will is the necessary qualification to render any one acceptable for the service of God.

CHAPTER XXXII

ELIHU AFFIRMS GOD'S INDEPENDENCE OF MAN'S HELP

(CHAP. XXXV.)

AFTER again awaiting a reply from Job, who still remained silent, Elihu proceeded to make another indictment against him, illustrative of another characteristic which accompanies the feeling of self-righteousness. It manifests itself in a mistaken idea as to the mode in which the righteousness of man is productive of advantage to God, and in the thought that deliverance from sin is not necessarily attended with profit to man. He asks Job, "Dost thou think this to be in accordance with right judgment when thou sayest I am more righteous than God, and when thou also askest how will my being free from sin help forward the administration of the Divine purposes, and how shall I be profited thereby?" Although the actual words of the utterance of which Job is here accused are not actually recorded in the history, yet their admission into the record pre-supposes that they were spoken by him, whilst the tone of the reproaches which Job addressed to God in His toleration of his suffering testifies to their accordance with the self-righteous spirit of the words. They are painfully illustrative of the true nature of self-righteousness, which shows itself in the assertion of man's judgment in opposition to that of God, whereby in its connection with any definite subject of which man affirms that God has acted unjustly, he proclaims himself to be more capable of right action than God Himself. Man consequently pronounces himself to be more righteous than his Maker.

Such opinion is shown to originate from one or other of two causes. Man loses sight of the object of his formation in his obligation to do the will of God, whereby in a certain sense he may be said to be of advantage to God in carrying out the purposes of the Divine administration in the sphere in which he has been placed; and by neglect in the performance of this duty he incurs the guilt which accompanies the refusal to promote the glory of God. Secondly, in assuming that freedom from sin is unprofitable to man, he forgets the fundamental law by which human existence is conditioned, that the indulgence in what is forbidden, which is the outward manifestation of sin, is fatal to life. Elihu sets himself to controvert these statements of Job: "I will return an answer to thee and thy companions. He appeals to the infinite omnipotence of God. Look to the heavens and see; view the skies how high they are above thee. If thou sinnest, or if thy transgressions are multiplied, what dost thou do to Him? If thou art righteous, what dost thou give to Him, or what does He receive from thy hand? Thy wickedness may be a matter of danger to a man like thyself, and thy righteousness productive of blessing to a son of man, when men cry out for safety from the multitude of the oppressors and from the arms of the mighty; but how can they affect the unchangeable character of the omniscient Judge, by whom the evil are punished and the good rewarded? Yet man in his self-sufficiency does not ask, Where is God my Maker, who giveth psalms of joy in the night, who teaches us more than He does the cattle of the earth, and maketh us wiser than the fowls of the heavens?" Thus man, by the neglect of prayer to God, and having recourse to man for help in trouble, gives evidence of self-righteousness in refusing to submit his will to that of God, who has appointed prayer to Himself as the right channel through which to obtain relief under suffering. When, however, under stress of affliction, prayer is at length offered, and it is not at once answered, the cause must be referred to the arrogance of the wicked in their resistance to the revealed laws which regulate the use of prayer; for "surely God will not hear vain words, nor will He regard them. Even if thou sayest that thou canst not see Him, and that therefore prayer cannot reach Him, yet still it cannot be denied that the case has been laid before Him. Therefore thou must wait for His decision."

Elihu applies these principles to the case of Job. He shows how the long-suffering of God had been manifested in tolerating Job's impatience: "Now because God has not visited upon him His anger, and has taken no recognition how much he has been at variance with the Divine Will, yet His very abstention from proceeding to extremes in its display should be regarded as the witness of His merciful treatment of his sin. Therefore Job has opened his mouth, and strung together words without knowledge."

The third portion of Elihu's message is directed to prove the sinful character of self-righteousness, by the falsity of imagining that a man's righteousness is productive of advantage to God, without regard to the fact that righteousness has been defined and commanded to be practised solely with a view to the profit accruing thereby to the man himself, in order that he may attain to higher degrees of happiness. In support of this view he makes an appeal to the omnipotence of God, which makes him utterly independent of man's help in carrying out His Divine purposes, and shows that without submission to the will of God, witnessed in sincere prayer for His assistance and strict obedience to His commands, man is utterly incapable to perform his duty in a right manner, and thus loses his claim to be regarded as a perfect man.

CHAPTER XXXIII

ELIHU'S REVELATION OF GOD'S JUSTICE AS THE MORAL GOVERNOR OF THE WORLD

(CHAP. xxxvi.)

In the next portion of his address Elihu sets himself to prove the justice and the righteousness of God, from the revelation of His character recognised in His ordinary dealings with the human race. He introduces the subject by asking his hearers to come around him, while he again spake to them words illustrative of God's nature. "He traces the origin of his knowledge to far-off sources, giving them an assurance that in thus attributing righteousness to God, his words shall be free from falsehood, inasmuch as he has claimed for himself inspiration from God to enable him to become possessed of perfect knowledge of the subject of the discussion."

He therefore commences by showing that "though God is mighty in physical strength and in wisdom of heart, yet that He rejects none who come to Him in sincerity and truth, and that although He will not ultimately preserve the existence of the wicked, yet He will pronounce right judgment for the poor.

Therefore He does not withdraw His eyes from the righteous, whom He regards with equal favour as with kings upon their thrones, in giving them a permanent settlement and promotion to honour. But if at any time they are condemned to bondage in chains, or are caught by the cords of affliction, He then reveals to them the causes of their troubles by a review of their past work, and of their transgressions when they have lifted themselves up in opposition to the Divine law. Thus He opens their ears by chastisement, and commands them to return from their iniquity. If they will listen and serve Him, He will enable them to pass their days in good and their years in pleasantness; but if they refuse to hear, they will perish under the stroke of the weapon, and expire through lack of knowledge. He shows how the hypocrites in heart excite against themselves God's anger, in refusing to cry to Him for help when He bindeth them in restrictions which cannot be broken. Thus they cause their souls to perish in early youth, and live amidst those excommunicated from the communion of the saints. But on the other hand, He delivers the afflicted by means of their affliction, and opens their ears to instruction through the oppressions to which they are exposed."

In such language Elihu describes the disciplinary character of suffering, in its being sent by an All-righteous and All-wise God to correct the evils that arise not only from moral wrong-doing, but also from involuntary ignorance, and in its being sent to lead men to amendment of life, and to search after deeper knowledge of God's dealings with man. These reasons are respectively illustrated in the repentance of the Prodigal, and the conversion of St. Paul. In the case of the former, the affliction was sent as a punitive correction, whereas in the latter its object was to remove the scales of ignorance with which the eyes of the conscientious believer had by his hereditary training been blinded. Elihu goes on to show where Job had failed to derive the blessing which his misfortunes were calculated to convey. Like St. Paul, no fault could be alleged against the integrity of his past life or the conscientiousness of his conduct. Job's error had consisted in his forgetfulness or ignorance that one of God's methods to exalt a man is by teaching him through the display of His Almighty power, even when such manifestation was attended with loss or misery.

The truth of this doctrine was wonderfully displayed in the reduplicated prosperity which attended Job's restoration to happiness, and the beneficial effect of his moral training was realised in his recognition of his ignorance of the concealed operations of the Divine purposes. Such inherent ignorance is the natural result of the fall, when man became deprived not only of bodily power, but also of mental vigour and spiritual self-control. The restoration of these was one of the objects of our Lord's incarnation, when in His perfect humanity the restraint of His childhood, the education of His youth, and the practical application of knowledge in His manhood, were shown to be conditions of discipline necessary for the obtaining intellectual vigour for the due performance of His work of man's salvation. Thereby He obtained the fulness of success in the glorification of His threefold humanity, in body, soul, and spirit, when exalted to the right hand of the throne in heaven, through the perfected submission of His own will to that of the Divine Father. The remembrance that the character of His temptation was common to all men, and that the faithfulness of God is pledged to permit no suffering beyond the capability of man to endure it, or to give a way of escape to enable him to bear it, would have preserved Job from the fault of charging God with unrighteousness in the toleration of his apparently unmerited misery.

Having shown the causes of Job's failure to preserve calmness of mind under the pressure of his affliction, Elihu proceeds with a warning of the danger of indulgence in anger manifested against God's dealings. "He assures him that in accordance with the working of the Divine principles, if he had abstained from such manifestations of impatience, in due time God would have stirred him up to greater reliance on God's love, and would have enabled him to resist with greater patience the power of his unknown Satanic oppressor, by directing his thoughts to the existence of a place where there was no anguish, and where the quietness of his table would have been accompanied with richness of blessings. He shows how he had for a time forfeited this blessing of calmness under affliction, when, through the impetuosity of his temper, he had exposed himself to the doom of the wicked, and made himself liable to the pains of retributive judgment. Where anger exists, he points out that care should be taken lest it excite him to clapping of hands or scorning of God's will, or to thinking that a great atonement will enable him to recover his lost position of favour with Him." Elihu then asks, "Dost thou think that thy cry for help will be of any avail as a defence, or even a display of thy physical force? Pant not for the night as if thou wert sure of acquittal, so as to ascend into heaven, whilst many peoples are still remaining on the earth beneath. Be guarded, therefore; turn not thy face to iniquity, for even this thou hast preferred to bearing affliction, as witnessed by thy reproaches against God's righteousness." In such forcible language does Elihu point out to Job the dangers to which his impatience had exposed him. He reveals that the true attitude of man towards God consists not only in the endurance of whatever He may be pleased to place upon him, but also in submission to this with patience and resignation.

Grave objections have been raised against the character of Job owing to a mistaken rendering of the passage in St. James's Epistle: "Ye have heard of the patience of Job," whereas in the history he is revealed as giving way to great impatience of spirit and of utterance. The passage according to the true rendering of the Greek would be better translated, "Ye have heard of the endurance of Job." The object of his suffering was to test man's power of endurance of evils resulting from reduction to penury, pain, and sorrow, without unfaithfulness in his allegiance to God. In such endurance no sign of failure can be discovered in Job. His conduct was open to blame in the impatience of his language towards God. It was this which distinguished his conduct from that of our Lord. They were both exposed to the endurance of poverty and suffering. Both endured what God was pleased to allow to be inflicted upon them. But while Job failed in patience under the trial, our Lord was never betrayed into the utterance of an impatient expression. The nearest approach to a feeling of remonstrance is seen in His patient resignation witnessed by His words upon the cross, "My God, My God, why hast Thou forsaken Me?" If Job had been actuated by the spirit which led the aged Eli to say, "It is the Lord, let Him do what seemeth Him good," on the receipt of God's message as to the impending fate of his family, he would have been spared the censure which Elihu was Divinely commissioned to convey to him.

Elihu then proceeds to corroborate the truth of his words by appealing to the infinite manifestation of God's omnipotence in the regulation of all that goes on in the universe. "Lo, God exalteth by His power. Who can teach as He does? Consider the irresponsible character of His government, for who can exercise any control over His ways, or who can say to Him, Thou hast wrought iniquity. Hence arises the inherent necessity that man should magnify His work, about which men sing praises, so that every one may see it, even from afar."

The last clause may possibly have been added by Elihu on his pointing out the signs of the distant whirlwind, which from the context would appear to have begun to manifest themselves. Such corroborative signs appearing in the heavenly or atmospheric sphere in support of Divine messages sent through inspired ministers are not infrequent in Scripture. The thunderstorm in the days of the wheat harvest attested the truth of Samuel's warning of the sinful character of the desire of the Israelites to take to themselves a king. The storm which caused the shipwreck at Melita also attested the truth of Paul's warning to the Roman centurion of danger in leaving the Fair Havens near to the city Lasea. The statements of scientists, that the processes of nature are determined by the unalterable action of natural law, exclusive of any possible intervention of the Divine will, is opposed to the teaching of Scripture. The law of gravitation was suspended when the human body of our Lord ascended into the heavens, and when He walked on the waters of the Sea of Galilee. The principles by which natural laws are governed may be immutable, but the details of their action are recognised as capable of change to render them adapted to the general requirements of successive ages.

In this fourth section of Elihu's address he proves the justice and righteousness of God from the revelation of His character in His ordinary dealings with man. He shows how both the perfect and the wicked are placed under the discipline of suffering for their deliverance from mistaken courses and for their instruction in right conduct. He then concludes with a grave warning that impatience under affliction exposes a man to the loss of that calmness of mind and resignation of spirit which is productive of inward peace and future blessing.

CHAPTER XXXIV

ELIHU'S REVELATION OF GOD'S OMNIPOTENCE

(CHAPS. xxxvi. 26; xxxvii.)

In the concluding portion of Elihu's speech, he appears to address himself to show that the omnipotence and the infinity of God are reasons for implicit faith in His righteousness productive of perfect submission to His will. This is implied when he reminds Job that it is through the action of His Almighty power that man is raised to an exalted position, and that no one else can efficiently teach the means whereby this is to be attained. The Psalmist bears witness to the same truth: " Promotion cometh neither from the east, nor from the west, nor yet from the south; God is the judge. He putteth down one and setteth up another." No simple self-effort, no mere admixture of secular knowledge, no real separation from the doctrine of the Divine Word will enable a man to become permanently exalted above his fellow-men. An elevated position attained only under these conditions may endure for a brief period of earthly existence, but the hand of death changes it altogether: " Then the wise alone will be seen to shine as bright examples of the true life, and they that turn many to righteousness as stars, or evangelists, in the renovated world." Of their fitness God is the alone Judge; by Him alone, one is abased to the lake of fire, and another is raised to one of the heavenly thrones. This is further corroborated by our Lord when addressing His apostles as His successors in His prophetic mission. He tells them "that separated from Him they can do nothing."

The approaching whirlwind, of which the signs were becoming apparent, appears to have been appealed to by Elihu in support of the doctrine which he had been enunciating. The writer of the Epistle to the Hebrews witnesses to the truth of the fact, that on important occasions the Almighty gives visible signs of His approval of the words of His messengers. He tells them that "the great salvation, which at the first began to be spoken by the Lord, was confirmed to them by those that heard Him, God also bearing witness both with signs and wonders, and with divers miracles and gifts of the Holy Ghost," whereby they were testified to be true preachers of the Word. St. John in the Apocalypse reveals, under symbolical language, that the Divine purposes are accredited to man by many visible signs. The prophetic voices are attested by the flashing lightnings of spiritual conviction, and the warning thunders of physical disturbance and of social disorder accompanying the development of the Divine purposes throughout the universe. Even our Lord's announcement of His approaching glorification, on the visit of Greek proselytes desirous to see Him, was verified by a voice from heaven which to the hearers assumed the sound of thunder. He Himself teaches that the working of miracles was one of the principal means by which He was to be recognised as the Coming One, or the promised Messiah, when for a resolution of their doubts He referred certain disciples of the Baptist to the miracles which they had seen Him performing.

Elihu, therefore, directs the attention of his hearers to the approaching tempest as a manifestation of God's almighty power. "Lo, God is exalted far over all, and yet we know not the number of His years, nor can man search Him out." Even the shallow-minded Zophar had recognised the unsearchable nature of God: "Canst thou by searching find out God, or wilt thou find out any limit to the infinite power of the Almighty?" The truth of his words are here corroborated by the inspired Elihu, not as a bar to seeking after the knowledge of God, but as a stimulant to never-ceasing search. It is only the unbelieving Agnostic who, because he finds himself unable to penetrate into the fulness of the Divine nature, considers this as a valid reason to remain in ignorance of that, which may be learnt of the knowledge of Him, who is able to make man wise unto salvation in accordance with His promise: "Seek ye the Lord, and ye shall live."

In support of his argument, Elihu calls their attention to "the evaporation by which the drops of water are drawn out of the primeval deep, and condensed into the mist, which the skies distil and drop upon man abundantly. He then asks whether man understands how the cloud is spread abroad, or how the thunder crash is formed which accompanies the vapoury coverings by which God is hidden, or how He spreads the flashing lightning above it, with which also He covers the sea, the root-source of the watery particles from which the clouds originate. By withholding these He judges the people in producing drought, and then He giveth food by means of the fertilising rain. He covers the lofty palms with the lightning gleams, and directs their flashes as one shooting at a mark. His thunder gives notice of God's presence announcing the jealousy of His anger against sin." He then adds: "Surely at this my heart is troubled, and leaps out of its place on hearing the raging of its voice and the threatenings that go out of His mouth. He directeth it under all the heavens, and His lightning appears over the extreme parts of the earth. After it a voice roars. He thunders with a voice of majesty, yet displaces them not by whom His voice is heard or obeyed. God thundereth with His voice, doing marvellous and great things which are unknown to man, for He saith to the snow, Fall thou on the earth ; and so He commandeth to the gentle shower and the rain of His great force. He sealeth up the hand of every man by the wintry cold, to cause all mortal beings to know His work. The wild beasts retire in winter to their lairs, and dwell in their dens to obtain warmth. The whirlwind cometh from its secret chamber, and frost from before the scattering blizzards. From the breath of God is given ice, and the breadth of the waters is made rigid by the frost. Surely by deluges of rain He exhausts the thick clouds, and His sunlight scatters the atmospheric vapours. They are turned round about under His direction to do all that He commands them over the face of all the habitable earth. He findeth them, and uses them as instruments whereby to govern the world, or to punish sinners, or to show mercy upon all who love Him, whithersoever He sends them." In such expressive language did Elihu describe how the operations of the Divine purposes throughout the universe are manifestations of His almighty power when God visits the earth with awe-inspiring storms, which, though developed under the laws of natural order, are also regulated by the determining will of an all-wise personal God, revealing Himself not only in the formation of these mighty works, but also in the motive for which they have been sent.

He again makes a fresh call upon Job's attention :

"Hearken, Job; stand still, and consider the marvels which God does. Dost thou know the period when He placed them in their due order, and when He first caused the lightning of His cloud to shine forth? Dost thou know how the thick clouds are balanced in space, and the other marvellous works of Him who is perfect in knowledge? Dost thou understand how the summer heat is to thee as a robe when He quiets the earth with the balmy south wind? Hast thou with Him spread out the expanse of the skies, and made it strong as a molten mirror?"

Apparently after another short pause, intended the more to emphasise his words, Elihu abruptly addresses Job: "Thou hast professed to know the ways of God, for thou hast charged Him with the perversion of right; cause us, therefore, to know what we shall say to Him touching these things, for we cannot order our speech aright on account of our dark ignorance. Will any one tell Him when I speak? or if a man says anything wrong will he be swallowed up by God's anger?" By such questions he appears to be endeavouring to convince Job of the unreasonableness of his prayer, to be allowed an opportunity to plead his cause before God, instead of patiently submitting to any suffering it may please Him to impose. Finite reason is incapable of understanding the full meaning of the purposes of the Infinite. They are beyond man's power to grasp, and the only true attitude of the believer is to remember the promise, "that he which endureth or patiently submits to the action of the Divine will, even to the end, the same shall be saved." This is the main doctrine revealed in the history. The endurance of Job was rewarded by restored prosperity, notwithstanding his impatience under the suffering, whilst happily it was sufficiently controlled to prevent his yielding to the temptation of apostatising from his allegiance to, and from his faith in God.

The Approaching Storm.

To show that at times the face of the Almighty appears hidden from man, when faith weakens and joy diminishes, Elihu points to the increasing darkness of the approaching tempest, while at the same time, to sustain his courage, he also reminds him that such gloomy moments are, in the providence of God, succeeded by brighter gleams, when peace and comfort are restored to the sufferer. "Even now men see not the bright light in the skies, but let a wind pass over them and they will be cleansed from the gloom; for the golden sunlight will again come from the hidden regions of the heavens." These interchanges of darkness and light, of sorrow and joy, convey a solemn warning of the awe-inspiring majesty that belongs to God: "As for the Almighty, who can find the limit and excellence of His strength, of His judgment, and of the fulness of His righteousness? Surely He will not continuously afflict the children of men. For this, therefore, men look up to Him in reverential fear; but He regardeth not with His favour those who are wise in the conceit of their own hearts."

With this warning Elihu concluded his address, the contents of which were stamped with the Divine approval, testified by the appearance of Jehovah when He answered Job out of the whirlwind.

The reality of the Theophany is witnessed by the words which Job uttered at the moment of his deepest humiliation: "I have heard of Thee by the hearing of the ear, and now mine eye seeth Thee" (xlii. 5). There was evidently vouchsafed to him an appearance of the Divine Personality, from whom the voice proceeded, such as was realised by Isaiah and Ezekiel on their respective calls to the prophetic office. To deny the reality of the Theophany in submission to the opinions of modern criticism, exposes the dissentient to the peril of unbelief in any other revelation, in which a visible manifestation of the Deity is recorded, and the promoters of such unbelief, in the words of Scripture, are unconscious imitators of the personal Satan, who approached Eve in the garden with the doubt-inspiring words, "Yea, hath God said?" Far different was the conduct of the Son of God, when, in His human nature, He silenced the Satanic tempter by a quotation from Scripture, prefaced by the words, "It is written, Thou shalt worship the Lord thy God, and Him only shalt thou serve." He who came to be man's example by act and word, thereby proclaimed the Divine authority of the written Word, as the final court of appeal, to enable him to become wise unto salvation through faith in Himself.

The drift of Elihu's words, in his rebukes of Job and his three friends for the character of their utterances, evoked by the misery of the suffering patriarch, and causing Job to give way to impatient language addressed to God, when aggravated by their fallacious reasoning due to their mistaken views of the true causes of affliction, divides itself into five heads.

Elihu reveals—

I. The sin of self-justification from its inconsistency in imputing injustice to God, owing to the relative positions of an omnipotent Creator, and of the creatures which He had made.

II. The impiety of such an imputation of injustice in God, from the consideration that affliction is the necessary discipline requisite to fit man for the due performance of his duties to God and to man.

III. The fallacy of imagining that an omnipotent God is dependent on man's assistance in carrying out His Divine purposes.

IV. The manifestation of God's justice and righteousness realised in His ordinary dealings with the human race.

V. The display of the omnipotence and omniscience of God, witnessed by His control of natural order universally observed in the processes of the mundane system.

From such considerations Elihu reveals the necessity of implicit submission to the will of God, subsequently illustrated by the all-perfect example of the Divine Son of Man, during the whole period of His earthly existence, whereby He was enabled to become the Author of eternal salvation to all who believe in Him, and to enter upon His glorious inheritance through His elevation to the right hand of the throne of God.

CHAPTER XXXV

THE THEOPHANY

(CHAP. xxxviii.)

ELIHU's address appears to have been somewhat abruptly cut off by the outburst of the whirlwind, to the approach of which he had been directing Job's attention. It was accompanied by a Theophany in which the Almighty revealed Himself under some mysterious but undescribed manifestation, and in which Jehovah proclaimed His presence by an audible voice. To this Job bears witness when, at the close of the history, he is shown to have made a humble confession of his sin in his impatient resistance to the Divine Will, pleading ignorance of things too wonderful for his understanding, which by the direct teaching of Jehovah had then been removed: "I have heard of Thee by the hearing of the ear, and now mine eyes seeth Thee" (xlii. 5).

The doubts which have been cast upon the objective reality of this Theophany lose force, when proper attention is given to the frequent accounts of these mysterious manifestations in the Sacred Scriptures, in which the visible appearance of Jehovah to man is revealed in unmistakable terms. The Lord God is recorded as walking in the garden of Eden, causing His voice to be heard by Adam, and accusing him of his sin in yielding to the temptation of eating from the forbidden tree. Before the Exodus in Egypt, God spake to Moses proclaiming that as El Shaddai, or God Almighty, He had appeared to the fathers, Abraham, Isaac, and Jacob, although He had not been known to them by the name Jehovah (vi. 3). The first recorded appearance of Jehovah to Abraham took place at Sichem, when the promise of the land into which he had come was then definitely given to him: "Jehovah appeared unto Abram, and said: Unto thy seed I will give this land." On his return from the exile, to which Jacob was condemned for his sin against his brother Esau, it is revealed that God appeared unto him a second time at Bethel, when he came out of Padan-Aram, and blessed him, when the new name of Israel, which he had received at Penuel, was confirmed to him. Both these appearances of God were followed by the erection of altars in commemoration of these mysterious occurrences (Gen. xii. 7 ; xxxv. 7). The visible manifestation of God to Moses is revealed in the marvellous manner by which he is distinguished from any other prophet, when "Jehovah declared that while to other prophets He would make Himself known by a vision and speak in a dream, with Moses it should not be so, for with him I will speak face to face and not in enigmas, and that the similitude of Jehovah he should see" (Num. xii. 7). A Theophany was vouchsafed to the child Samuel, when Jehovah came and stood and announced to him the fate of Eli's house (1 Sam. iii. 10). Isaiah (vi.) saw Adonai, the Supreme Ruler, sitting on the throne high and lifted up in the heavenly temple, and Ezekiel (i. 26) beheld the similitude of a human form seated on the throne, supported by the Cherubim, on the banks of the river Chebar, at their respective consecration to the prophetic office. In the Apocalypse (iv., v.) a kindred vision of the Divine Personality was revealed to St. John, when "on the throne laid in the heaven one sat in sight like to a diamond and ruby." His description, as holding upon His right hand the book of the world's prophetic history from the Incarnation to the Consummation of the age, is suggestive of the human form.

These and other records of Theophanies must, in consequence of the terms in which they are described, be accepted as having been actually witnessed by the persons to whom they were vouchsafed, or else a doubt is thrown on the veracity of the writings in which they are recorded. Inasmuch as these records constitute a very large portion of the Sacred Scriptures, it also follows that if the rationalistic view is to be accepted, that they are mere psychological intuitions, or impalpable visions of a subjective nature and divested of all objective reality, then the doubt in their veracity must be extended to the principal part of the written Word of God. The inconsistency of such a conclusion is evidenced in the origin, growth, and continuous existence of the Jewish Church, and its fulfilment in the Christian Church, to whose care the custody of the sacred writings was Divinely entrusted. The former traces its origin to the command given from God at Sinai: "Let them make Me a sanctuary, that I may dwell among them" (Exod. xxv. 8), and the latter to the Theophany on the mountain in Galilee, when our Lord appeared to His eleven apostles, saying, "All power has been given to Me in heaven and on earth. Go disciple all nations, baptizing them into the name of the Father, and of the Son, and of the Holy Spirit, teaching them to observe all things whatsoever I have commanded you, and lo, I am with you all the days of your existence, even unto the consummation of the age. Amen" (Matt. xxviii. 16).

The law given to Moses was by him committed to writing, and entrusted to the keeping of the Levites, who bare the ark of the covenant of Jehovah (Deut. xxxi. 24, 25). The Divine revelations, which were afterwards continuously received, were preserved by similar written records, whose veracity was recognised by a chain of inspired prophets. Thus our Lord witnesses to their inspired character, when, quoting from the CX. Psalm, He challenges the

Pharisees to prove the correctness of their statement, that Christ was the Son of David, by asking them, "How then doth David in spirit call Him Lord?" (Matt. xxii. 42). It is beyond belief that when our Lord inculcated the importance of searching the Scriptures, He would not have cautioned His disciples against basing their knowledge upon writings whose claims to be inspired, He in the plenitude of His wisdom must have known to have been fallacious, if the views of modern critics are to be accepted (John v. 39). So in referring His disciples to the books of the Jewish Canon under their recognised title of the Law of Moses, the Prophets and the Psalms, as the source whence they were to derive their knowledge of His Messianic work in the salvation of man, our Lord stamps their contents with the seal of veracity, and testifies to the fidelity with which the Jewish Church had performed her sacred function in the guardianship of her canonical books (Luke xxiv. 44).

The reception of the Book of Job into the Jewish Canon before the advent of Christ, and our Lord's acceptance of the Canon as it then subsisted and in which it found a place, testifies to its Divine inspiration, and its historic accuracy as a revelation of heavenly mysteries, which are only capable of being made known to man objectively by the utterance of the Divine word, and subjectively by knowledge imparted directly by the Holy Spirit, or indirectly through the instrumentality of angels or prophets, whose inspiration has been accredited by visible signs. The reality of the Theophany in the whirlwind, recorded in this history, appears therefore to be fully established, and the modern pronouncement, that "there was no Theophany," and that the voice from the storm was only a subjective revelation, capable of being received by any one who contemplates the works of nature, not only contradicts the express words of the record, but is also inconsistent with the ordinary interpretation of the sacred writings. The same sceptical explanation might be given of the descent of the Spirit coming down upon our Lord at the Jordanic baptism, under the bodily form of a heavenly dove, and also of the voice of the Father out of heaven, recognising His Divine Sonship. Such crude interpretations may be acceptable to the materialistic mind, but they fail to give spiritual satisfaction to those who have committed their salvation into the hands of "Him who came down from heaven, even the Son of Man, the ever existing One in heaven."

CHAPTER XXXVI

THE FIRST VOICE

JEHOVAH'S REVELATION OF HIS OMNISCENCE

(CHAPS. xxxviii., xxxix.)

THE Divine voice issuing from the whirlwind is revealed as demanding, "Who is the man who is darkening counsel by utterances destitute of knowledge? and then calling upon Job to gird up his loins like a mighty man, whilst Jehovah asked him certain questions to which He also summoned him to reply." It was the Divine method by which the Almighty excited the attention of Job. Whilst the vision of the whirlwind and the sound of the voice were calculated to alarm his physical susceptibilities, the character of the questions tended to quicken his mental faculties, whereby he became reduced to a state of fear, which is the precursor of real submission to the Divine Will: "The fear of Jehovah is the beginning of wisdom." It is the condition in which a sense of danger is aroused in man, accompanied by a recognition of his natural impotence, of his intellectual ignorance, and of his spiritual alienation from restful reliance on God's love and mercy. The terrors of Sinai were sent "to prove the people, so that the fear of God should be before their faces, that they should not sin against Him." In a similar way the fear, engendered by the sound and matter of the words of Jehovah, appears to have been intended to lead Job to realise the greatness of his error in the language into which his intense sufferings had betrayed him, so that by repentance and resignation he might be restored to his accustomed serenity of mind and control of spirit. For this purpose the sense of the omnipotence of Jehovah is realised in the contemplation of the works of nature, productive of a feeling of the infinitesimal littleness of man when contrasted with the infinite nature of the Almighty, seen in His purposes and operations. Murmuring against the current events of life is, in its intrinsic character, an act of rebellion against the Creator, so that the only consistent position of the true believer in God's providential oversight is for him to lay his hand upon his mouth, and to silence any outward expression of discontent, whilst he submits his will to that of the Almighty, in full assurance that whatever God orders is intended for the promotion of the well-being of all that He has created.

THE CREATION.

The voice of Jehovah proceeds to direct Job's attention to the utter inconsistency of questioning the Divine operations, by reminding him of his extreme ignorance, in the fact of his non-existence at the period of the creation of the earth and its atmospheric environment: " Where wast thou when I laid the foundations of the earth ? Tell me if thou knowest, so as to show thyself capable of understanding ought that was antecedent to thy birth, and if so, say; Who laid down the admeasurements of the earth, or stretched out the line of the builder over the matter of which it is composed ? In what are embedded the sockets upon which her supporting pillars stand, or who cast her corner-stone into its allotted position ? Wert thou one of the Morning Stars who then sang together their alleluias, or of the Sons of God who then shouted their praises, as the marvellous framework of the earth became consolidated before the entranced vision of these two celestial orders of intellectual pre-existences ? " None but those who have seen the primeval atoms, and witnessed the action of their inherent forces by which they became consolidated, so that cosmic order evolved out of the chaotic fire-mist, can venture to arraign the Divine Architect in the development of His designs, and in the creation of the majestic deep, beneath whose glassy surface the protoplasmic matter, of which the earth was formed, lay hidden in the opaque darkness which concealed it even from the eyes of the angelic choirs, whose voices were hymning the praises of Him whose voice was then pronouncing the Creative fiat.

Jehovah proceeds to question Job's knowledge as to the formation of the sea and of light, as well as its moral action in the control of the wicked: "Canst thou tell who fenced in the sea with its granitic doors, when on its pushing forth it issued from the womb of the unfathomable abyss; when I placed the thick cloud of the ascending vapour to be its covering, and swaddled it with the darkness which lay upon the face of the deep; when I broke up its expansive bosom by the volcanic eruption, and set the plutonic rocks to act as bars and doors against its encroaching waves, and said, Hitherto shalt thou come, and no farther, and here shall thy rolling breakers be stayed in their proud resistance? Dost thou know the agencies whereby the waters of the mighty ocean have been restricted to their allotted place? Hast thou commanded thy days to be one continuous bright morning, as the days of Him with whom there is no darkness at all? Hast thou caused the dayspring to know its place, or the period when its light shall take hold of the ends of the earth, so that the wicked may be shaken out of it? For the dayspring giveth a new impression to the surface of the earth, as one sealing a document does to the wax on which the seal is impressed. It causes all things to stand out visibly as a garment. But from the wicked it withholdeth their light or means of subsistence, whereby they may exalt themselves; and by it the arm of the crafty is shattered, for the light of the dawn is fatal to the concealment of wickedness. Hast thou reached to the springs of the sea, or hast thou walked in search of the origin of the untrodden abyss? Have the gates of death been rolled back for thee to enter them, and hast thou seen the gates of Sheol, or of the shadow of death? Hast thou realised how far the width of the earth extends itself? Declare if thou knowest all these things," before thou presumest to question the rectitude of Mine action. Again, "Which is the way to the place where light tabernacles, and where is the abode of darkness, that thou mightest betake thyself to its border, and know the paths that lead to its house? Dost thou know any of these things in consequence of having been born when they were formed, or because the number of thy days is great? Hast thou entered into the treasures of the snow and hail, or understood their beneficial use in the restraint of distress and war, for winter is prejudicial to the progress of infectious disease and of military operations? Dost thou know how the light is distributed, or the primeval winds dispersed over the surface of the earth? or who has divided a channel for the rain-floods, or a way for the swift flashes of the lightning to cause it to rain on the desert where no man dwells, and to fill with moisture the desolate waste so that its vegetation may bud forth? Canst thou tell if the rain has a father, or who has begotten the drops of dew? From whose womb went out the frost, and who has begotten the hoar-frost, when the waters are hidden as by a stone, and the face of the deep is hardened by the ice? Canst thou bind the stars into their summer constellations, or loose them when bound in their wintry occultation? Canst thou cause the signs of the Zodiac to go forth in their season, and guide Arcturus, or the constellation of the Great Bear, and his attendant stars in their circuit round the Pole Star? Dost thou know the decrees by which the heavens are governed, or canst thou limit their influences on the earth? Art thou able to lift up thy voice to the thick cloud, and to command an abundance of water to fall upon thee? Wilt thou send forth lightnings, so that they shall go forth and shall say to thee, Behold us? Who has placed wisdom in the cloud forms, and given understanding to the atmospheric phenomena to perform their allotted operations? Who by his wisdom can count the cloud courses of the skies, and cause to lie down the waterspouts of the heavens as they empty themselves, so as to enable the dust to be poured into the mould, and to cause the clods of the earth to cleave together?"

Thus did Jehovah call upon Job to contemplate the evolutionary operations of created matter, and the developing processes by which the atmospheric environment of the mundane system was rendered energetic for the production of vegetation to supply the requirements of the living creatures by which the surface of the earth was to become inhabited. Inductive science may be marvellously potential in discovering the laws by which existing phenomena may be governed, but is it equally potential in discovering the primordial matter out of which such phenomena were evolved, and the forces by which activity was given to the inert atoms, so that light supplanted the darkness, and empty space became the sphere of cosmic organisation? Some creative energy is required to account for the presence of phenomenal existences, so that man may understand the everlasting power and Divine nature of the all-determining Will of God.

The Adaptation of Animals to their Environment.

Having thus called Job's attention to his utter inability to understand the Divine methods whereby the light is diffused over the world, and the movements of the atmospheric phenomena is regulated, and the processes whereby the watery covering of the earth is restricted within fixed limits for the formation of land, serviceable for its occupation by sentient beings, Jehovah proceeds to question his knowledge of the means, whereby its teeming population of animal and bird life has been endowed with special powers to sustain their individual lives, and to preserve the existence of the respective families to which they belong.

Selecting certain typical specimens, He asks Job whether he understands the principles that govern the peculiar modes of their formation and their instinctive habits of life. Commencing with the carnivorous feline races he inquires, "whether he understands the instinct which directs the lionesses in the hunting of their prey, and in securing its capture for their young lions, by stealthy approach and concealed ambushment in their leafy coverts; or how the carrion-feeding raven soars on high, as it searches the surface of the earth for the dead carcases on which to feed their deserted young ones, crying to God for food from their solitary nests?"

In the selection of the carnivora, to give the first illustration of His infinite power in the regulation of their instinctive rapacity, it is possible that God desired to impress Job with the feeling of his ignorance of the causes, why animals should have been created, whose sole work in life was devoted to the destruction of other living creatures, witnessing to the truth of the scientific fact, that altruistic death is essential to the preservation of individual life, whereby the necessary food supply is provided for the survivor. This doctrine receives its highest fulfilment in our Lord's warning, "Except ye eat the flesh of the Son of Man, and drink His blood, ye have no life in you."

From the savage bloodthirsty animals, Jehovah next directs the contemplation of Job to the gentler races of untamed animals, witnessing to the correlation prevailing between the two kingdoms of animal and vegetable existence in the mutual adaptation of their respective production. He asks, "Dost thou know the appointed period of the year, and the number of the months of their parturition, when the graminivorous races produce their offspring, so that birth should coincide with the season when vegetation puts forth its vernal energy, in the plenteous sprouting of the green herbage on which the typical chamois and deer tribes feed, so that their young ones escape a death to which their birth in winter would have exposed them, and thus they are enabled to keep pace with the growth of the corn crops, until able to go forth by themselves and return no more to the protection of their dams?"

Jehovah next proceeds to inquire whether Job can assign a cause why animals, suited by their speed and power to perform the varied work for which man desires their assistance, should, however, at their creation be endued with such untameable wildness of character, and fierceness of disposition, as to render them valueless as beasts of burden or of tillage, so that their lives are devoted only to the enjoyment of freedom and of food.

"Hast thou sent forth the untamed denizens of the desert steppes, escaping from the shoutings of the pursuing multitudes and the voices of the harsh drivers, preferring, like the wild ass, to dwell in the arid waste, and to feed on the scanty herbage of the mountain range, whilst its timid congener, the domestic ass, submits its shoulder to the burden in return for its plentiful supply of stalled provender? Will the mighty rhinoceros and other pachyderms be willing to till thy land, and to abide in thy stable; or canst thou trust their fierce tempers that thou shouldst harness them to thy cart when thou gatherest in thy harvest?"

In contrasting the habits of the ostrich, in the care of its eggs, with those of the stork, whose domestic love for its young ones has acquired for itself the epithet of "pious," from whence it derives its Hebrew name, Jehovah appears to ask whether Job can account for the vast dissimilarity of disposition which prevails amongst the fowls of the heavens? "The wing of the ostrich waves exultingly over her back; but has it the pinion or feather of the pious stork, when it forsakes its eggs and allows them to remain warm in the sun-dried dust, forgetful that the foot may scatter them, or the wild beast crush them? Is she hardened against her young ones as if they belonged not to her, or does she labour in vain when, without fear, she absents herself for a while from her unconcealed nest on the open surface of the earth? Has God given her no instinctive knowledge, and has He not imparted to her understanding, when she raises herself on high as a palm tree, and laughs at the speed of the horse and his rider?"

Turning Job's attention to the character of the horse, Jehovah appears to ask how the apparent paradox is to be explained, that the God of peace should have formed an animal, which alone of all others is noted, not only for its fitness, but also for its delight in the prosecution of that which is abhorrent in the eye of God, the pursuit of human warfare, where men, instead of endeavouring to promote the prosperity of their brethren, are devoting their energies to their destruction. Can Job explain why God has endued the horse with the love of battle? " Hast thou given the horse his warlike might, and clothed his neck with the quivering mane? Canst thou cause him to flutter about as the locust? The grandeur of his snort is terrible to witness. He paweth in the vale, he rejoices in his strength, and is ready to rush upon the weapons of war. He laugheth at fear: nothing dismays him; he turneth not back from the face of the sword. The quiver rattleth against him, together with the glittering dart and spear. With trembling and rage he swallows up the earth in his hasty progress; he is not discomfited at the voice of the trumpet, for at its sound he gives a neigh of joy; he scents the battle from far; he listens to the thunder voices and shouts of the princes." In such expressions God reveals that the horse stands alone in his excited joy at the sound of human warfare.

From the warlike delight of the horse Jehovah

directs Job's thoughts to the keen-sighted energy with which the hawk and eagle tribes prosecute their eager pursuit after the living prey on which to feed their young ones with its blood: "Does the hawk fly by thy wisdom, as she spreads out her wings in the refulgent daylight? Does the eagle soar aloft at thy voice, to make her nest on the edge of the precipice where she lodges in her hunting eyry, to espy the place where the wounded are, so that she may feast on their remains?" Thus Jehovah calls on Job to explain why the keenest vision and the swiftest flight should be granted to the ravenous birds who prey on the defenceless animals or the wounded victims of the desert robbers, who have been left to linger in the agonies of death, powerless to protect themselves from the vulture's beak.

In directing Job's attention to the habits of these animal and bird tribes, he causes him to realise, that although man was acquainted with the wonderful diversity that was apparent in their natures, yet of its causes he was in a state of the densest ignorance. The study of phenomena may show the laws whereby they are governed, but the primordial principles on which they are based can only be discovered by a revelation of the will of Him from whom they emanate.

By such illustrations, drawn from the facts and principles of creation and providence, did Jehovah reveal to Job the infinitude of His omniscience and consequently the wickedness of attempting to impute to Him unrighteousness in the development of the Divine operations: " Shall he that contendeth with the Almighty turn Him from His purposes ?" Can man hinder the work of God, or prevent His performance of that which He has designed to do ? Can the thing formed say to Him that formed it, Why hast Thou made me thus ? Does man know why the inception of life is attended with the agonies of parturition, or why the preservation of the individual is accompanied with the destruction of the concrete, or why the overwhelming flood is fatal alike to mature manhood and helpless infancy ? Why the tender lamb is permitted to become the prey of the ravening wolf, or the poisonous berry to be productive of torment to the unconscious babe ? Hence he that is ignorant of such elemental principles, and attempts to convict God of incompetency in His designs, must sooner or later answer for his presumption. He thereby imperils his own existence by contravening the laws of the Absolute. Man may reproach his Maker for separating continents by the impassible ocean, but he who, unbidden by Him, attempts to tread upon its surface is quickly submerged beneath its waves. He who tries, unsummoned by the Most High, to ascend into the heavens is soon exposed to sudden destruction by the collapsing balloon. One only by His inherent omniscience—the Lord Jesus Christ—was able to walk upon the sea, and to resist the force of gravitation, when in His resurrected body He passed through the clouds of heaven. The man who would avert the sorrows of life by the destruction of his body, finds that the punishment of suicide must be endured in the belly of Sheol; whereas He who submitted to the pains of death in obedience to the revealed will of the Father, was quickened in the spirit with renewed powers for the promotion of God's glory, in preaching to the dead that gospel whereby they were enabled to live according to God in their regenerated spirits.

In subsequent years, during His earthly ministry, our Lord, as the Word Incarnate, revealed the eternal force of these principles of law when He showed the danger of non-compliance with the Divine Will, which, if persisted in, would terminate in the destruction of the offender. Under the form of a parable He showed how, in the building up of the Divine purposes, the rejected stone is perilous to those, who fall against it in their resistance to the laws, which govern its appointment to be the head of the corner, but that it is fatal to those upon whom it falls as the penalty of their insensate rejection of its office, as the connecting link between the heavenly and the earthly, ever growing upwards as the apex of the pyramidal temple, whilst extending itself from underneath in gathering together the living stones of which it is composed from the earthly quarry of concrete humanity, out of which they have been hewn (Zech. vi. 12). Unconditional submission to the will of God, evidenced by faithful obedience to the laws which regulate natural existence, is the one revealed method whereby the trials of life can be sustained, and the soul supported under the sorrows to which it is exposed from the assaults of Satan.

Job's Recognition of his Ignorance.

The vision of the Almighty, the voice from the whirlwind, and the words of Jehovah, calling Job's attention to the contemplation of the works of God in creation and providence, revealed to his mind the extent of his ignorance of the hidden principles which regulate the operations by which organic nature has been evolved out of chaos, and all sentient beings are endowed with faculties and knowledge, rendering them capable of the performance of the duties for which, by an all-determining Will, they have been called into existence. In contrite terms he makes his humble confession: "Lo, I am vile. What answer can I return to Thy questions? I can only lay my hand upon my mouth, to prevent further utterance of refusal to place implicit reliance on Thine absolute wisdom and infinite love in the regulation of all the events of my life. Once I have spoken impugning Thy righteousness in the toleration of my sufferings. Shall I speak a second time? I dare not repeat my offence, for I recognise how deeply-seated is mine ignorance of the secret causes of all cosmic existences. No, I will add no more; I must resign myself entirely into Thine hands."

Happy is it when a sufferer is thus brought, like the holy patriarch, to the recognition of his ignorance of the laws which govern his existence and those of his earthly environment. Such a feeling is provocative of a desire for true knowledge, the attaining of which is promised to all those who are willing to do the will of the Father. Our Lord's condescension in veiling, by some ineffable energy, the manifestation of His Divine omniscience until the moment when, at the Jordanic baptism, the fulness of the Holy Spirit, under a visible form, descended and permanently abode upon Him, appears to have been Divinely ordered to lead Him in the perfection of His humanity to the use of the Sacramental means of prayer, instruction, and baptism, as an example to show how man is enabled to grow in wisdom. Thereby He was prepared for the period when, in the development of the Divine purposes, He became fitted to be endowed with that measure of the Holy Spirit, which rendered Him capable to receive from the Divine Father the commission to enter upon the ministry of the Word, through the preaching of which repentance and remission of sin is granted to all true believers, so as to enable them to become partakers of eternal life.

CHAPTER XXXVII

THE SECOND VOICE

JEHOVAH'S REVELATION OF HIS OMNIPOTENCE

(CHAPS. xl., xli.)

On the conclusion of Job's humble confession of his sin in impugning the righteousness of God in the toleration of his misery, for which he had been unable to discover an adequate reason, together with his sincere admission of his profound ignorance of the principles of the laws whereby the Almighty manifested His omnipotence in the works of nature and in the regulation of animal life, the voice was heard proceeding a second time out of the whirlwind, calling upon Job "to gird up his loins like a man of might, and to cause Jehovah to know the purport of the further inquiries that He was about to ask." This second interpellation from God appears to have been intended to reduce Job to a state of perfect submission to the Divine Will, in showing the utter impossibility of successful resistance to what God was pleased to do, and the essential weakness of all human effort to fully control the conduct of mankind: "Hast thou power to frustrate My decisions?

Canst thou cause Me to be condemned as evil in order that thou mayest appear to be righteous? Can the axe boast itself against him that heweth therewith, or can man, formed to be the servant of God, refuse with impunity to obey the word of his Maker? Hast thou an arm like that of God to shield thyself from His vengeance? Canst thou send forth thy warnings of the danger of resistance to His commands with the voice of thunder such as God utters? Canst thou adorn thyself with the pomp and dignity that attend the possession of supreme authority? or canst thou clothe thyself with the glory and majesty which are the attributes of universal dominion? Send forth the fulness of thy wrath against the opponents of the Divine laws, and then cast thy regards upon the arrogant impugners of His will; wilt thou thereby be able to humble them to the dust? or look upon every one that is haughty, canst thou cause him to bend his knees in lowly submission, and thus crush the wicked under the burden of their own devices? Canst thou hide them together in the dust of the grave, or bind their faces in the hidden recesses of Sheol? If thou canst thus reduce man to submission to the Divine will, so that he ceases to exalt himself against the Most High, then will I also confess thee before them as one possessed of powers sufficient to save himself by his own right hand."

By such additional utterances, in relation to the

governance of man, did Jehovah proceed to convince Job of his extreme impotence and of his failure in submission to the Divine will. Job had boasted of the high position which he had once enjoyed in the presence of his fellow-citizens, and of the high estimation in which he had been held by his brother Sheiks. By his reduction to penury and exposure to disease these had been forfeited, and even his closest friends had ventured to accuse him of wilful sin. Reliance on bodily strength, or intellectual vigour, is thereby shown to be insufficient to enable man to retain his influence over the minds and conduct of his fellow-men. Something far more potential is required to enable man to control the social evils to which humanity is exposed. One of the objects of the Incarnation was to reveal how such absolute authority over the human will was to be attained, even by an unconditional surrender of self to the will of God. For this purpose the Word became flesh, and in the womb of the Virgin the perfect Man was conceived of the Holy Spirit, coming into the world as a helpless infant, exposed to the trials of an indigent condition, subjected to the necessity of manual labour, and Divinely constrained to attain the fulness of human wisdom by the ordinary channels of instruction and study. Thus our Lord as man became capable to receive the fulness of the Spirit, whereby He was trained to submit Himself implicitly to the will of the

Divine Father, so that from the moment of birth to the death upon the cross, the guiding principle of His life, in His perfected self-surrender, might be manifested in accordance with the prophetic utterance, "I come to do Thy will, O God." To promote such submission to the Divine will in the mind of Job, in proportion to his human capabilities, appears to have been the object for which the voice of Jehovah was heard the second time issuing out of the whirlwind.

BEHEMOTH AND LEVIATHAN.

To still more forcibly accentuate the importance of this doctrine of implicit submission to the Divine will, Jehovah proceeded to direct Job's contemplation to two typical animals, whose untameable nature had hitherto defied the power of man to control them. They were the Behemoth, or African river-horse, and the Leviathan, or Egyptian crocodile, apparently cognate with the prehistoric terrestrial megalotherium and the oceanic ichthyosaurus, respectively emblems of the carnal and intellectual, or the physical and psychological, natures of the human race. They represent two developments of the Satanic opponent of Almighty God. As an animal, the serpent, incarnated in a fleshly body, approached Eve to tempt her to eat of the forbidden fruit. As the most subtle or intellectual of living beasts of the field, the same draconic spirit exerted its demoniacal craftiness to beguile Eve to seek for the acquirement of wisdom by means forbidden by the Creator.

BEHEMOTH.

The description of the Behemoth, or the hippopotamus, is characterised by bodily force, conditioned by a sluggishness of disposition due to its graminivorous food in "eating grass as a bullock." Sensuality and voracity are the marks of its carnal propensities, realised in the power of its loins and of the muscles of its belly. He delighteth in the strength of its tail, or vertebral column, rigid as the cedar, in its resistance to external force. The interweaving of its muscles renders its bodily strength to be provocative of terror. Its bones are as strong as bars of copper or iron, incapable of fracture by those who oppose its progress. It is called "the principal of the ways of God," expressive of its gigantic size, and its endowment with huge incisive tusks, with which, as with a scythe, it provides itself with the vegetation on which it feeds and protects itself from its human and animal foes. Its natural inactivity is depicted by its concealment under the shady trees and in the deep morasses, whilst its amphibious nature is shown by the fearlessness it displays when the rushing floods press against its flanks, or the descending rapids rush against its mouth. The difficulty of its capture, either in the open field or by the hidden snare, is revealed by the question, "Will a man take him when he presents himself visibly before his eyes and the concealed traps he pierces through with his nose?" Thus the Behemoth is typical of the carnal nature of man, reliant on his inherent power to gratify the selfish propensities and sensual indulgences in which he wallows, whilst when aroused he gives way to the extremes of cruel resentment against those which disturb his natural sloth or vicious practices. The control of the flesh, which is beyond the power of man to obtain, is however revealed as being open to destruction from the sword-thrust of the Word of God, dividing asunder the soul and the spirit or the joints and the marrow, of man's corrupted animal nature.

LEVIATHAN.

Whilst the character of the Behemoth is distinguished for its inactivity, that of the Leviathan, or crocodile, is marked by fierce aggressiveness. Its capture by the hook, or cord, is impossible from the bony nature of its jaws. Its ferocity is shown by its utter fearlessness on being attacked: "Will he make supplication to thee, or speak soft words to avert thy assault?" Its untameable nature renders it useless for work or amusement: "Wilt thou take him for a servant, or play with him as a bird?" Its body is unfit for food or commerce: "Shall thy companions make a banquet of him, or divide his parts amongst the merchants?" "Its scaly skin cannot be pierced by spear or dart. The hand that touches it is in danger of immediate death. Its capture alive is hopeless, for its very appearance provoketh fear, so that no one dares to rouse it out of its sleep."

But what is impossible to man is possible with God, for Jehovah asks, "Who is able to present himself before Me, and to stand unsummoned in the unapproachable light in which the Almighty has enshrouded Himself for the hiding of His face, which none can see and live? Who has anticipated My purposes in the causation of existent phenomena, that I should be called upon to render a reason for the things that I have done, since whatsoever is under the whole heavens is Mine by creation and possession?" By such unanswerable arguments does Jehovah reveal the consummate presumption of those who presume to question His decrees, or to assert their arrogant claim to dispute His doings, or to arraign Him for the toleration of their personal misery, for which they can assign no adequate cause.

The Leviathan appears to be the emblem of the intellectual pride and spiritual alienation of the human heart, which was engendered in the mind of man by the successful attack of the serpent in Eden. It is the name given by the prophets to the fleeing and perverted serpent, the dragon in the sea, descriptive of the Satanic spirit by which Pharaoh, the proud Egyptian opponent of God's will, was possessed, witnessed by his arrogant denial of the sovereignty of Jehovah in his utterance to Moses, "Who is Jehovah, that I should obey His voice? I know not Jehovah, neither will I let Israel go." Thus in greater or less degree does man manifest the pride of his heart in his intellectual opposition to obey the commands of God. The irreclaimable nature of human pride is revealed under the character of the Leviathan in its resistance to all restraint, its fearlessness of all who oppose its progress, its inaptitude for service, its unfitness for social life, its imperviousness to reproach, and its invincible cruelty to all who attempt its destruction.

The more fully to illustrate the formidable character of the Leviathan as the emblem of the arrogant self-assertion of intellectual pride, in its stubborn insubmission to the will of God, Jehovah proceeds with a more detailed description of the nature and habits by which it is distinguished: "I will not be silent as to the members of its body, its aggressive might, and the grace of its equipment. Who can roll back the face of its scaly integument, or come within the range of its double retaining jaws? Who can open the doors of its face and their terrible encircling teeth? The furrows of its scales are its pride, shut as by a rocky seal, each one so closely united to the next that not a breath of wind can come between them, rendering them incapable of being severed asunder. Its sneezings flash forth light, and its eyes twinkle as the stars of the morn. Burning lamps seem to issue from its mouth like sparks of fire. A vaporous smoke goes forth from its nostrils as from a boiling pot or steaming geyser. Its living breath is like the flame of burning coals bursting from its mouth. Force lodges in its neck and terror springs up before it. The flakes of its flesh cleave together so firmly compressed as to be immovable. Its heart is firm as a stone and hard as a nether millstone. The mighty fear when it raises itself, and miss their aim through the shattering of their weapons. The sword of the hunter cannot arouse it, nor the spear or dart or sharpened shaft, for it esteems iron as straw and copper as rotten wood. The arrow will not make it flee, and the sling stone drops from its scaly back into the surrounding reeds; clubs are counted as stubble, and it laughs at the quivering spear. Sharp-pointed potsherds, like the iron teeth of a harrow, form its couch. When rushing through the deep it makes it boil like a pot, and it lashes the sea into foam like the compound of the apothecary. No one dwelling on the dust of the earth is its master, for it is made devoid of fear. It looks with contempt on every high thing, and dominates as an invincible king over the whelps of the fiercest lion."

This detailed description of the Leviathan appears

to symbolise the nature and methods by which the pride of the human heart manifests itself in the life of man. It is revealed as a concentration of the will upon the one object of self-exaltation, originating from one principle of action, energising through a multiplicity of motives so beautifully adjusted in their respective influences, as to be in perfect subordination to the primary principle of self-will. The intensity of its self-love renders it dead to any feeling for others. Its cruelty is witnessed by the tenacity with which it holds all those who come within its grasp. Its defensive plans are so firmly adjusted as to exclude all possibility of the admission of any opposing influence. Its snorting nostrils, its flashing eyes, its seething breath, are the outward manifestation of its internal fury, its sarcastic disdain, and its contemptuous opinion of those with whom it comes in contact. Its relentless stubbornness is marked by the sorrow which it produces. Its stern repression of all passion and affection renders facile the prosecution of its selfish aims. Its fierce excitement terrifies its opponents, and its callousness to attack is fatal to the success of their reproaches. Its superciliousness enables it to rest undisturbed by the sharpest invectives, whilst the impetuosity of its attack causes confusion to its environment. It acknowledges no one as its master. It is incapable of fear, and it regards itself as higher than the highest.

This detailed account of the Leviathan describes

symbolically the characteristics of the pride of the human heart in its determined insubmission to the will of God. Originating in a self-sufficient reliance on its own powers of mind and body, it persistently abandons itself to the relentless pursuit of its own selfish views and aims, utterly regardless of the evils which may result to others. It is governed by no principle but that of self-will. It recognises no master beside itself, and remains equally deaf to the entreaties of man and to the commands of God. Its intellectual power is so adroitly energised as to cause its malignant nature to be concealed under a veil of illusive wisdom. One only has power to control its action and to shatter its design. The Almighty, by whose word the soul of man became first endued with intellectual life, has power to confound the wisdom of the wise and to bring to nothing the understanding of the prudent, whereby insubmission to the will of God is revealed, not only as being inconsistent with true wisdom, but also destructive to the continuity of human existence.

Job's Recognition of his Impotence.

The enunciation of this doctrine appears to have been the object of the second voice of Jehovah issuing from the whirlwind. By it Job was caused to recognise the utter futility of man's resistance to the Divine will, and the limited knowledge possessed by man in respect of the Divine purposes. Omnipotence and omniscience are revealed as the essential attributes of the Almighty, from the operation of which there is no escape. In lowly repentance Job therefore makes his humble confession of sin, in having so impatiently inveighed against God's dealings with him: "I know that Thou canst do everything, and that no evil thought can be concealed from Thee, or its utterance defended. Who am I, that I should have attempted to veil the counsels of God under words, which were uttered by one without any knowledge of the Divine purposes? Hence it is that I have spoken of things which I did not understand, things far too marvellous to be apprehended by my highest thoughts, and concerning which I knew nothing. Hear me, therefore, when I speak and confess mine ignorance, and when I ask Thee, do thou cause me to know what is necessary for me to understand? Formerly I heard Thee by the hearing of the ear, but now mine eye has seen Thee. For this, my presumption, therefore, I despise myself, and repent in dust and ashes."

These words of Job reveal the nature of the voice from the whirlwind. It was the audible utterance of words actually spoken by Jehovah. Job not only declares that he heard them by the hearing of the ear, but he also adds that a vision of the form of the Speaker had been vouchsafed to him: "Now mine eye seeth Thee." To deny the fact of a Theophany impugns the veracity of Job and of the writer of the record, and invalidates its claim to be a faithful revelation of hidden mysteries otherwise incapable of solution by the mind of man.

The words uttered by the Almighty in respect of His governance of the universe convinced Job of His omnipotence, and consequently of the folly of insubmission to His will. He attributes his impatience to its true cause, to his intense ignorance of the purposes of God, although he had attempted to conceal it under a veil of assumed acquaintance with the Divine counsels. Hence his impatient utterance in respect of problems of which he had no knowledge. The vision of Jehovah convicted him of his transgression, and caused him to repudiate his self-assurance, and to abase himself in the penitential garb of dust and ashes.

In lowly terms Job thus testified to his perfected submission to the will of God.

These utterances of Job reveal also the true character of perfect submission to the Divine will. It is witnessed in the full recognition of the omniscience and omnipotence of Jehovah, rendering any resistance permanently impossible. All resistance betrays man's ignorance in imagining that his will can override that of God. Its duration is, moreover, limited by the Divine will, and it is simply tolerated by the goodness of God to afford him an opportunity to repent. Thus, the primary function of the Holy

Spirit is to convince man of sin in his unbelief in God's wisdom revealed in Christ. This is succeeded by the conviction similarly impressed on the conscience by the same Holy Spirit, that righteousness is the alone method whereby deliverance from sin, witnessed in sorrow, disease, and death, can be attained by the full imitation of the example of Him, who in His human nature has gone to the Father, and is no longer seen by man's bodily eye. The road trodden by our Lord of perfect submission, still remains the only way whereby access can be attained to the eternal city. It is the way of holiness in the right performance of duty, in the patient endurance of affliction, and implicit obedience to the commands of God.

CHAPTER XXXVIII

THE RECAPITULATION OF THE PROBLEMS

THE persistent endurance of Job, under the misery to which he had been exposed before the eyes of the heavenly hosts, solved the problem for which his suffering had been Divinely permitted. The Satan had indirectly challenged the Almighty to produce a man, who, in the person of Job, under the twofold extremities of penury and disease, would continue firm in his allegiance to God, and would not openly apostatise from faith in Jehovah.

"Does Job serve God for nought? Put forth Thy hand, and he will curse Thee to Thy face" (i. 11).

The trial, short of death, had been carried to the extremest limits. Reduction to penury and exposure to disease, involving agony of mind and torture of body, had been succeeded by temptation to suicide, originating in the despair of a loving wife, followed by false imputations of concealed guilt from the lips of his closest friends, as well as by the solemn words of the inspired prophet, convicting him of self-righteous utterances against the justice of the Almighty. But none of these things moved him to lose faith in God by openly apostatising from His worship, and thereby curse or reproach God to His face.

The trial itself caused to originate in his mind several subsidiary problems, the utterance of which are representative of the thoughts that spring up in the human mind under stress of want, and pain, and sorrow. They gave rise to vain attempts, on the part of his friends, to solve his inquiries. Their failure may be traced to their answers being based on the mistaken, though often accepted, view that all suffering should be attributed to some act of personal sin.

Thus Job, by the intensity of his anguish, was led to question the justice of God in bringing into existence a sentient being, who from the moment of his birth was subjected to suffering: "Why is light given to him that is in misery, and life unto the bitter in soul?" (iii. 20). The superficial reply of Eliphaz, that none ever perished being innocent (iv. 7), involving the doctrine that affliction is the result of an act of personal sin, does not meet the case, as Job's initial difficulty is witnessed in the case of a suffering babe utterly unconscious of right or wrong.

He then follows up his reasoning concerning the apparent hardship of the prolongation of life in those exposed to misery, for which no adequate reason can be advanced, unless the hidden cause be revealed and the unintentional transgressions freely pardoned: "Oh that it would please God to destroy me" (vi. 9). Bildad's affirmation of the traditional belief, that perversion of justice is impossible with God, again fails to explain why the cause should not be made known to the victim by an omniscient God (viii. 3).

Thus Job is further confronted with the certainty that "God destroyeth the perfect and the wicked" (ix. 22). Why then, he asks, does not God give man an opportunity for the adjudication of his suit by means of a mediator, who may interplead between the innocent sufferer and his Almighty Ruler, and explain the inconsistency of the condemnation of a good man to suffering with the revealed character of love, which is one of the attributes of omnipotence? (x. 6–12). Zophar's superficial assertion of the truism, that infinite wisdom can detect secret faults as well as open transgressions, affords no consolation to those who are unconscious of intentional guilt (xi. 6).

This gives rise in the mind of Job to the fresh problems; Why the existence of unavoidable sins originating in natural infirmity, and the certainty of future compensation in the Intermediate State, are not more clearly revealed: "Make me to know my transgression and sin" (xiii. 23). "If a man die, shall he live?" (xiv. 14). The attempt of Eliphaz to remind Job that human suffering is due to the general depravity of mankind, is no solace to the individual suffering apparently excessive misery (xv. 14).

Job, recognising that God is witness to the reality of his efforts to do right, naturally asks, Why all hope of relief appears to be relegated to the moment of death? (xvi. 19; xvii. 13). The attempt of Bildad to solve this problem, with the affirmation that failure of relief in the case of the perfect should be traced to the natural order of cosmic events, is of too materialistic a character to content the mind of a spiritual man such as the suffering patriarch (xviii. 4).

Job is therefore led to inquire further, Why the vindication of his integrity, doubts of which had been advanced by his friends, whereby his misery had been intensified, should not be assured prior to his departure into Sheol? (xix. 25–27). The mere reiteration by Zophar, that the wicked would ultimately be punished, fails to give relief to the suffering minds of the perfect (xx. 5).

It moreover gives rise to a deeper question in Job's mind, "Why God gives prosperity, both to the wicked and the perfect, without apparent discrimination?" (xxi. 7, 22–26). Such a question cannot be dismissed with the simple affirmation made by Eliphaz, that even in the perfect suffering must be attributed to the commission of some act of personal sin, unless its commission is clearly established.

U

The general accusation of sin only leads to a feeling of increased astonishment that the openly wicked should remain unpunished, whilst the perfect, without apparent reason, are exposed to the deepest afflictions (xxiii. 8–15). The ultimate punishment of the wicked is universally admitted (xxiv.).

The point of the problem lies in the unmerited afflictions of the good. Job naturally retorts, "Why, seeing times are not hidden from the Almighty, do not they who know Him, not see His days?" or, Why are they not permitted to see days of prosperity in which the justice of His Divine action is clearly manifested? (xxiv. 1). The plea advanced by Bildad, that the intrinsic imperfection of man by natural descent renders freedom from pain and sorrow impossible, though essentially true of the race, yet affords no consolation to the individual, when he contrasts the frequent immunity of the wicked from well-deserved punishment with the frequent exposure of the perfect to unmerited afflictions (xxv. 4).

The problem still remains unsolved, Why the amount of misery in life is not proportioned to the guilt of the sinner, or the degree of earthly happiness proportioned to the integrity of the righteous?

The arguments of the three friends, built upon the fallacious foundation that all suffering is the result of personal guilt, are opposed equally to reason and experience, and therefore failed of necessity to give support or consolation to the tortured patriarch.

The inspired prophet Elihu, who intervened at the conclusion of Job's discussion with his three friends, addressed his remarks against the attitude which Job allowed himself to assume towards the Almighty, without attempting to show that his suffering was sent as a punishment for sin. Yet he strongly affirms the impropriety of his claim to inherent innocence and absolute freedom from transgression (xxxiii. 8–12). He points out the impossibility that the righteousness of man can bear any comparison with that of God, and consequently that any pretence to self-justification is inappropriate to the standpoint of a created being (xxxv. 2). He shows how all the events of life in adversity, as well as in prosperity, are intended to be means of instruction for the guidance of his steps and the preservation of his life, and that contentment with his environment, and the right performance of his duty in magnifying God's work, constitute the sole business of man (xxxiii. 14–30).

Elihu, however, gives no direct solutions to the problems by which the mind of Job is agitated. On these points he was still left in ignorance, whereby his mind became the more open to hear the voice of God speaking from the whirlwind. By the words of the first voice he realised the intensity of his ignorance, in imagining that he could divert God from His purposes, and also the greatness of the sin which he had committed in venturing to doubt the wisdom of the Divine action (xl. 1–4).

A second time the voice was heard from the whirlwind, convincing Job of his utter inability to arraign the righteousness of the Divine will, and of the necessity for the entire surrender of himself into the hand of God. Self-abhorrence for his past impatience was at once followed by sincere repentance, and the humbling of himself in dust and ashes, whilst the victory over self was shown to be complete and perfect (xlii. 2–6). Yet still no response was given by God to any of his questions, whereby implicit acquiescence in the course of current events was revealed as the duty which is due from man to his Creator.

Though no direct answer was accorded to the thoughts that distracted the mind of Job, yet the problem, which had been propounded by the Satan in the Presence Chamber of the Almighty in the heavenlies, received its full solution in the continuous endurance with which he resisted all temptations to apostatise from faith in God, or to withdraw from his open allegiance to his Divine Ruler. The problem suggested by the Satan impugned not only the disinterestedness of Job, but also the power of God to create a man who would serve Him without hope of earthly reward: " Does Job serve God for nought?

Is not his uprightness and departure from evil due to the success and the wealth with which he has been blessed?" For the instruction of the heavenly hosts, and of the earthly men to whom the history should be made known, the Satan was permitted to tempt him to curse God by his exposure to the extremes of penury, and bodily as well as mental misery.

In this attempt to betray Job into apostacy the Satan signally failed, for though much impatience of language was displayed during the discussion, yet the thought of any denial of God as the Moral Ruler, to whose will all must bow in the profoundest submission, was not for a moment entertained in the mind of Job. In this Job became an imperfect type of the all-perfect Man, who alone has been able to do the will of God so as to be free from every blemish of thought, word, or deed. No reproach against His Heavenly Father's wish ever escaped the lips of the Lord Jesus. There was no trace of any attempt to free Himself from the restraint of the cradle, of the school, or of the workshop, in the prosecution of His high office as the Saviour of the world, until the moment revealed by the Father at the Jordanic baptism for the commencement of His ministerial work. To corroborate His teaching He made no spontaneous display of superhuman power in coercing the minds of those to whom He addressed Himself, witnessed in His refusal, at the temptation, to call to His assistance the angelic hosts by casting Himself in the sight of man from the pinnacle of the temple. When the occasion demanded the performance of miracles, He revealed that they were done with the sanction and at the command of the Divine Father who dwelt within Him and did the works (John xiv. 10). He shrank from no humiliation of body or mind in carrying out His prophetic office. The indifference of mankind, the enmity of foes, and the rejection of friends were borne without a murmur. At the approach of the last dread moment, when preparing Himself for the bitter conflict by the humble prayer for its prevention, the burden of His soul found expression in the perfect submission of His spirit: "Father, not My will, but Thine, be done." The malicious accusations of the Jewish priesthood, the unjust sentence of the Gentile ruler, the scorn and mockery of the abject rabble, and the torments inflicted by the cruel soldiery, failed to call forth a word of rebuke. The crown of thorns, the inhuman scourging, the nail-pierced hands, called from His lips no words of revenge. The despairing yet faith-enduring exclamation was alone heard, "My God, My God, why hast Thou forsaken Me?" The loud cry of perfect surrender, "Father, into Thy hands I commend my spirit," was the last human effort before the broken heart terminated our Lord's earthly sufferings.

The Apostle St. Peter witnesses to the perfection of the uncomplaining patience with which our Lord endured the sufferings to which He was exposed, as contrasted with the impatience of Job's language: "Who, when He was reviled, reviled not again; when He suffered, He threatened not; but committed Himself to Him who judgeth righteously." He also reveals the vicarious character of the sufferings of the perfect man in our Lord's all-sufficient sacrifice, "Who His own self bare our sin in His own body on the tree, that we, being dead to sin, should live unto righteousness." So also the vicarious nature of Job's sufferings are witnessed in the history as an encouragement to the Heavenly Hosts, and to Mortal Men in the performance of their respective duties.

The general idea, that struggle and effort are matters unknown in the work of the angelic hosts, appears incapable of proof in face of several events in the heavenlies recorded in the Scriptures. The war in Heaven, when Michael and his angels fought and prevailed over the devil and his angels, gives evidence of their intensified resistance to the power of the evil one (Rev. xii. 7–11). The same doctrine is revealed in the vision of Daniel, where the Divine Man clothed in linen is represented as being opposed by the disobedient angelic prince of the kingdom of Persia, and receiving assistance from Michael, one of the chief princes (Dan. x.). The ministrations of the holy Angels to those who are the heirs of salvation is affirmed by the writer of the Epistle to the Hebrews, and is apparently referred to by our Lord when speaking of the Guardian Angels of each believing little one of His flock, who always behold the face of the Father who is in heaven. Such ministrations are necessarily accompanied with exertion and prayer, together with preparation and learning, to enable them to be rightly carried out, whereby the resultant success will be proportionate to the qualifications of the angelic ministrants. The allusion of St. Paul to the Elect Angels, presupposes that their election to position in the heavenlies was due to the mode in which the function of their sacred offices had been performed (1 Tim. v. 21).

It is, therefore, possible that the instruction of the Heavenly Hosts in the endurance of temptation may have been one of the objects, for which the Satan was Divinely permitted to expose the holy patriarch to the dangers of apostacy from his allegiance to the Almighty, as an encouragement to them to continue firm in their obedience to the will of God, and thereby avoid a guilt to which some of the members of the angelic order had before succumbed, whereby they forfeited their first principality and lost their heavenly habitation, by which they were reduced for reservation in invisible chains under darkness to the judgment of the great day (Jude 6; Gen. vi.). Job thus became an example of patient endurance under temptation, not only to the whole Human Race, but also to those Higher Existences in the heavenlies by whom the Divine purposes throughout the universe are eternally being fulfilled.

On Job's perfected submission to the Divine will, the failure of the Satanic attempt to convict him of an hypocritical devotion to God's service with a view to obtain for himself earthly prosperity, and on its loss to further tempt him to apostatise from his allegiance to His worship, was thus evidently made manifest in the heavenly sphere. The subsequent publication of the history by the pen of an inspired writer has revealed to the members of the human race that a firm and enduring faith in the existence of a personal God, and in the doctrine that He is the rewarder of all who diligently seek Him, will sustain them under every trial, and will finally enable them to obtain the fulfilment of the Divine promise to make all things work together for good to those who love Him.

The history briefly closes with the exemplification of the truth of these doctrines in the deliverance of Job from his captivity, and in the reduplicated blessings with which he was subsequently Divinely endowed.

CHAPTER XXXIX

JOB'S RESTORATION TO PROSPERITY

(CHAP. xlii.)

AT the conclusion of the words which were spoken out of the whirlwind, and Job's full admission of his sin and entire repudiation of any claim to perfected righteousness, Jehovah is revealed as having addressed Himself to Eliphaz in words of stern rebuke in respect of the doctrines to which he and his two companions had given utterance: " My wrath is fiercely kindled against thee and thy two friends, for ye have not spoken concerning Me that, of which the truth can be established, as My servant Job has done " (xlii. 7). The underlying principle on which their arguments were based, and shown by experience to be incapable of proof, consisted in the assumption that all suffering must be traced to some act of personal sin, and that its alleviation was only to be expected when the sin had been discovered and corrected. In the majority of cases the validity of this view must be admitted, but besides these, there exists a vast amount of misery to which no such cause can be assigned. The new-born babe, who is utterly unconscious of right and wrong, is by heredity not exempt from pain, although perfectly innocent of any act of personal sin. In such instances the existence of the suffering can only be accounted for by its toleration, for some purpose which God, in His infinite wisdom, for a time conceals from the knowledge of man. It may be sent for spiritual training, for the promotion of watchfulness under future trials, or for the development of character. Instances of these causes are recorded in the sacred writings. The training of the Baptist for the right performance of his prophetic office was aided by the self-denial which was demanded by the provisions of the Nazarite vow, and by his ascetic life in the isolation of the hill-country of Judea. The distresses caused to St. Paul by the Satanically inflicted thorn in the flesh, and to Jacob by the shrunken sinew, preserved these holy servants of Jehovah from the danger of spiritual pride, which the supernatural revelations of the unseen mysteries which they had received might have engendered in their minds. The perfecting of our Lord's humanity, as the Author of our salvation, was manifested in the revelation of His learning obedience through the things that He suffered throughout the whole period of His earthly existence. In these cases their worldly misery could be traced to no act of personal sin. Much suffering is due to its vicarious character; many a mother has succumbed to the hand of death through contagious disease contracted in her loving care to free her infant from the pains of sickness, and many a father has been exposed to loss of health and paralysis of limb by overtaxing his bodily strength to support his starving family.

The hidden causes of suffering revealed in the history of Job also convey the deeper lesson, that at times men are Divinely elected to the extremes of earthly wretchedness, so that by their endurance of such trials, the works of God may be manifested in their bodies and His glory the more promoted by the revelation that man, the noblest product of the hand of God in the mundane system, while endowed with the fullest power in the exercise of his free will, is yet at the same time capable of surrendering himself implicitly to the will of God at the cost of every happiness, that the world was able to bestow upon him. Such causes of affliction are too often overlooked by the prosperous and ambitious men of the world, by the secular philosophic reasoners and by the shallow imaginations of ordinary members of society. The knowledge of the unseen operations of the Satanic opponent of God's will is, however, clearly shown by the history as one of the most powerful causes of human wretchedness. It is a knowledge which can only be derived from some inspired revelation such as that referred to by Elihu, when he points out to Job and his three friends, that inspiration from the Almighty alone gives man understanding in heavenly mysteries (xxxii. 8). St. Paul corroborates this doctrine, "that the natural man

JOB'S RESTORATION TO PROSPERITY

receiveth not the things of the Spirit of God: they are foolishness unto him; neither can he know them, because they are spiritually discerned" (1 Cor. ii. 14).

The sin of Eliphaz and his two companions consisted in their condemnation of Job without giving any reason for their accusation, or any solution of the problems to which he had drawn their attention (xxxii. 3). They were unable to show the falsehood of his claim to the conscientious performance of his duty; for, notwithstanding the impatience of his language, extorted by the extremity of his affliction, Job never relaxed his reliance upon God's mercy and wisdom, feeling convinced that the day would come when his integrity would be vindicated, and that after he had been tried he would come forth as gold purified in the fire. They were equally unable to disprove the correctness of his statement, that the perfect and the wicked are equally exposed to suffering in life; yet they hesitated not to accuse him of personal sin, without being able to assign any proof of its commission. Thereby they rendered themselves obnoxious to the action of a Divine law, which in later days was revealed to Moses, and which enacted that in cases of non-proven offences, the judges should condemn the false accuser to the same penalty to which he had endeavoured to subject an innocent person (Deut. xix. 18-21).

They had adjudged Job to be guilty of sin, and their restoration to the Divine favour was only to be procured through the intercession of the priestly patriarch whom they had wrongfully calumniated. They were now commanded by Jehovah to take the ancient patriarchal offering of "seven bullocks and seven harts or rams, and to go to Job that he might offer them on their behalf for a burnt offering, and make intercession for the forgiveness of their vileness, in not having spoken words which were capable of being established by reliable evidence" (xlii. 8). This they immediately did, and the Lord accepted the intercession of Job for the remission of their sin.

The prevalence of Job's intercession for his friends is indirectly corroborated by the prophet Ezekiel, in associating him with Noah and Daniel, as the most powerful intercessors with God in seasons of cosmic disturbance and national apostacy. To Noah was entrusted the resuscitation of the human species after its submergence under the waters of the flood. To Daniel was committed the office of arousing the imperial world-rulers to the necessity of re-establishing the worship of Jehovah, for the preservation of national prosperity, while Job was commanded to intercede for the forgiveness of the sins of those individual members of the human race with whom he was placed in the closest contact. The intercession of these three holy patriarchs represent the ministry of those elected into the Church of God, for her threefold work of the Catholic, National, and Individual restoration of the various classes of mankind to their objective recognition of God as the Moral Governor of the world.

The intercession of Job, at the command of God, was not only attended with acceptance on behalf of his friends, but also with the removal of his own captivity from the hand of the Satan, as well as by his restoration to reduplicated prosperity: "Jehovah gave Job twice as much as he had before." Those by whom he had been forsaken, under the dread of infection from his loathsome disease, are described as again resuming their intercourse with him. "There came to him his brethren, and all his sisters, and all his former acquaintance, and did eat bread with him in his house." The days of his social ostracism were ended, and they bemoaned with him and comforted him over all the evil that the Lord had brought upon him. Their words of consolation were followed by deeds of kindness. Every man gave him a kesitah or purse of money for the support of his life, and an earring, or nose-jewel of gold, for the adornment of his person, typical of things necessary for the body, as well as things pleasing to the mind. Nothing is revealed as to the amount of these gifts. The two gifts probably represent the minimum offering of each of his friends. Their intrinsic value must have been great, and proportionate to the high estimation in which he had been held before the days of his distress, and to the multitude of the companions by whom he had formerly been surrounded, when they recognised the goodness and mercy which made him the friend of all who resorted to his presence, as well as the wisdom with which as the princely Sheik he guided the counsels of the clan.

As years rolled on his wealth increased in accordance with the Divine assurance, that the blessing of the Lord maketh rich, whereby the number of his flocks and herds became doubled. There is no intimation that the reduplication of his worldly prosperity was of an instantaneous character. The supply of his earthly wants appears at first to have been entrusted to human agencies in the gifts of the kesitahs and golden ornaments of his friends. The hoarding of such treasures is the peculiar feature by which oriental races were enabled to amass their wealth in olden times, and its adoption is still continuous in modern days in Eastern countries, in preference to investment in national securities. The vast increase in his flocks and herds may equally be traced to natural causes, rendering them prolific by the additional protection of the Divine blessing, realised in their exemption from disease and sterility, such as was witnessed in the case of Jacob's herds, received in payment for his six years' servitude to his father-in-law, Laban: "So Jehovah blessed the latter end of Job more than his beginning, for he had fourteen thousand sheep and six thousand camels, and a thousand yoke of oxen and a thousand she-asses."

He had also seven sons and three daughters.

To these last he gave the names of Jemima, "fair, or clear as day;" Kezia, "fragrant as cassia or spices;" and Keren-happuch, "the horn which overthrows his enemies, or by others 'the horn of eye-paint, or stibium,'" emblematical of aggressive progress or of adornment by artificial means. In all the earth no women were found fairer than the daughters of Job, to whom their father gave an inheritance in the midst of their brethren.

"After this Job lived a hundred and forty years, and saw his sons, and the sons of his sons, even to four generations. Thus Job died an old man and full of days." His age therefore appears to have exceeded that of Abraham, who died when a hundred and seventy-five years old, from which period the ages of the succeeding patriarchs appear to have decreased in length, until they reached the limit of seventy or eighty years recorded by the Psalmist. Job must have been at least forty or fifty years old at the time of his trial, to allow for the position of his sons as individual possessors of houses, so as to enable them to give the weekly feast to their sisters. At the time of his death he would probably have completed some hundred and eighty or ninety years. This protracted age is another argument for the early date of the history.

In Job's restoration to health, with the additional grant of protracted age, and to his worldly prosperity the double of that of which he had been deprived, after being chosen to be a person through whom the glory of God should be promoted, is revealed the important doctrine, that in such cases compensation for losses in doing God's work will assuredly be vouchsafed to the sufferer. The period when it will be given, and the form which it may assume, rest with the Almighty. In the case of Job it was granted during the remainder of his life, under the form of increased wealth and restored health. The call of Abraham to leave his home and kindred in Chaldea, to preserve by the force of his example the knowledge of the true God amidst the Canaanitish, Hittite, and Egyptian nations, was rewarded with earthly riches and honourable position, united with the far greater blessing of deep communion with God, not only in his inner consciousness but also through objective visions. God's subjection of Moses to a forty years' exile in the land of Midian, necessitating the renunciation of his possible expectations, as the adopted son of Pharaoh's daughter, to the throne of Egypt, prior to his Divinely predestined elevation to the leadership of the Israelites, was followed by the enjoyment of a closer communion with Jehovah than ever before or since has been granted to man. The election of Paul to the Apostolate of the Gentiles, causing him to forfeit worldly wealth and legislative position as a member of the Jewish Sanhedrim, was compensated for by the mysterious visions of Paradise and the Third Heavens, together with the Divinely impressed conviction of the sufficiency of His grace for the direction of his life, notwithstanding his bodily weakness, through the audible voice of God.

But for the full realisation of the certainty of the glory to be granted to all who, in their election by God as subjects for the manifestation of His glory, are exposed to earthly suffering, attention must be fixed upon our Lord's call at the Jordanic baptism for the work of man's salvation. Throughout His whole earthly life He was subjected to the extremes of suffering. His compensation on earth consisted in the inner consciousness of perfect peace, and in the full communion which He held with His Heavenly Father. But His fullest glorification as the reward of His sacrificial work came to Him through the Resurrection and the Ascension, followed by the continual attraction of converts to faith in Him as their Redeemer, according to His prophetic words, " I, if I be lifted up, will draw all men unto Me." Thus does He see of the travail of His soul, and is satisfied, in the justification of many through the knowledge of His finished work, and in the worship which they will render to Him as He sits at the right hand of the throne in heaven. The principle of such compensation to all who are chosen by God for the promotion of His honour appears to be foreshadowed in our Lord's words, " When the Son of Man shall come in the glory of His Father, then will He reward every man according to his works."

CHAPTER XL

INDUCTIVE BIBLICAL CRITICISM

THE character of the numbers of Job's flocks has led some writers of the present century to advance the theory that the Book of Job cannot be supposed to recite a literal history, from the use of apparently symbolical numbers, in describing his flocks and his children, and from the fact, that after his restoration the latter were the same in number as before, while the former were exactly doubled, and that for this reason it is manifestly the studied product of the author's leisurely reflections. Such a theory is not only opposed to the doctrine of its inspiration, but also to the accepted idea that Job himself was an historical personage. It deprives mankind of the strongest proof of the revealed doctrine of the existence of a personal Satan, who, for some wise reasons, is permitted at times by God to afflict the members of the human race. The whole history is based on its being a revelation of the personality of the Satan, and also of other mysterious events in the Heavenlies, the occurrence of which can only be learnt by means of the direct inspiration of the Holy Spirit.

If these writers are correct in their averments, the

objective temptation of our Lord by the personal Satan may with equal force be regarded as a simple myth, and His words, that He beheld Satan as lightning having fallen out of heaven, may be also treated as having their origin in a delusion. The veracity of His statement is thereby impugned, and His teaching of the future condemnation of the devil and his angels to the eternal fire may also be regarded as a rhetorical utterance, to show the danger to which those expose themselves who neglect the wants of their fellow-creatures. The introduction of sin into the mind of man through the suggestions of the Serpent ceases to be reliable as an article of faith, and its origin, attended by its sad results of sorrow, disease, and death, may therefore be traced to the spontaneous evolution of inorganic matter, acted upon by some concealed force, the source of which is beyond the discovery of human reason. Such is the doctrine of the materialistic evolutionist, who denies the existence of the determining Will of an omnipotent Creator.

But other arguments of a deeper and wider reaching character have been advanced by modern criticism against the Book of Job, the acceptance of which imperils faith in its inspiration, and reduces it to the level of a mere dramatic poem, evolving as it is suggested out of the mind of a highly educated writer, who lived in a post-exilic age, whereby the correctness of the prophet Ezekiel's reference to the well-known character of Job as an historic fact is directly impugned, and the value of his example, as a real man labouring under the sharpest conceivable temptations of his Satanic opponent to apostatise from his allegiance to God, is minimised in its ceasing to show the power of man to endure aggravated misfortune. Thus one of the objects for which the history was published is frustrated.

The allegation that the literary power and form which the poem displays, as well as the development of the subject to which it relates in a regular progressiveness, are to be attributed to the individual talent of an uninspired author, living in an age when a very mature stage of mental culture had been reached, is subversive of faith in events which are recorded as having occurred in the sphere of the heavenlies, which, if there be any truth in the revelation, can only have been signified to the writer by accredited inspiration from the Spirit of God. The doctrine of the personality of Satan becomes open to doubt as being the dream of a poet, and the exposure of a real man to his objective attack is only to be regarded as the fable of a dramatist, parallel with the novel idea that the origin of the Antichrist legend of the dragon is to be traced to the fear produced on the mind of the savage at the sight of an Egyptian crocodile, or to what is equally probable, that of Prehistoric Man at the appearance of a Palæozoic Ichthyosaurus.

The suggestion that the speech of Elihu is either an interpolation or an afterthought of the writer becomes the rejection of the utterance of an inspired prophet, and opens the way to the rejection of "the sayings of other holy men, who spake as they were moved by the Holy Spirit," making the acceptance of their words dependent on the verifying faculties of their hearers, or of the readers of the books in which such utterances have been recorded. The hypothesis of a veil of inspiration, extended over the infallible veracity of the doctrines which they enunciated without being farther extended to the historic details of the events which they recorded, is also subversive of faith in the writings in which they are contained, for thereby it is left to such individual readers to determine what portion of the contents of the writing is or is not to be accepted as veracious.

The claim of Elihu to be an inspired prophet is the underlying principle of his authoritative pretension to address Job and his three friends in words of stern rebuke, and to stand before them in God's stead, to receive their defence of the errors to which they had given utterance, in a manner whereby they might be divested of the terror to which they would be subject on being called upon to make such defence in the immediate presence of the Almighty Jehovah (xxxiii. 4-7). As an interpolation or an afterthought of the writer the words of Elihu would cease to carry any weight with the reader, inasmuch as their actual utterance is denied, and they would express only the thoughts of an anonymous poet. The canonicity of the record would thus be invalidated, and the Church of God, from the period of its acceptance into the sacred canon, would be open to the charge of labouring under an illusion equally shared by the God-man from whom as the Incarnate Word the history originated.

The bald and unproven assertion, affirmed by some advanced critics, that "there was no Theophany," is in direct opposition to the words of the history. It states that "Jehovah answered Job from the whirlwind," and also to the words of Job himself: "I have heard of Thee by the hearing of the ear, but now mine eye hath seen Thee" (xxxviii. 1 : xlii. 5). In these words he affirms the reality of the voice, and also the historic fact of his vision of Jehovah. If the record is correct, the critic is in error. If the record is fallacious, the critic accuses the Church of faithlessness in the performance of her sacred duty as the keeper of Holy Writ, in having admitted an apocryphal record to be regarded as forming part of her sacred canon. The choice is left to the believer as to whose word he will render allegiance. The Word of God interpreted by the Church, or the Word of Man determined by Human Reason. The Word of God records the fact of the Theophany, the occurrence of which is declared to be incredible to Human

Reason, although no valid argument is advanced for its rejection as being unauthentic which might not, with equal force, be adduced against the Theophany appearing to Moses in the burning bush, or to that manifested to our Lord at the Jordanic baptism. All three are recorded in different portions of the same Scriptures which have for centuries been regarded as Divine revelations. By these and similar attacks upon the veracity of the sacred writings, the claim of revelation to be the outward expression of the will of God is exposed to depreciation, and man is tempted to unfaith in the only existing records whereby the certain knowledge of unseen heavenly mysteries has been conveyed to him.

The legal axiom, that a man cannot be ousted from his possession of an estate without the production of a prior title, is equally applicable to man's spiritual inheritance. Such a spiritual inheritance is the Faith which is held by believers in the inspired character of Holy Scripture, and consequently in the veracity of its contents. Outside the pages of the written Word man has no reliable knowledge of the origin of his existence, of the object for which he has been called into being, of what becomes of him after death, or even of the continuity of his life after the dissolution of the particles of which his body is compounded. Without this reliable revelation of the Word of God the heathen maxim would be the creed of the world: "Let us eat and drink, for to-morrow we die." The written Word is the alone Divinely authenticated record of the Resurrection of Christ, whereby this materialistic doctrine that death is the annihilation of all men can be confuted. Man, moreover, possesses no other knowledge of the occult causes which occasion a vast amount of the misery to which human life is exposed through the direct agency of the Satan, or of the means whereby it may be alleviated and compensation granted for its patient endurance. The solution of these problems forms the most important portion of the revelation which, from the days of Eden, has been handed down for the formation of man's hope of eternal life and for the regulation of his earthly conduct. Unless, therefore, the critics are in a position to offer for man's acceptance a history of God's dealing with the world since the creation of the Adam and the establishment of the human race upon the earth, accredited by objective proofs no less irrefragable than those by which its history as contained in the books of the Sacred Canon has been preserved, its claims for acceptance remain unimpaired.

But here it will naturally be asked, What is the nature of the history which these writers propose to offer in substitution for the Sacred Scriptures? Take one section of the Bible as an example, that of the Pentateuch. Since the establishment of the Israelites in Canaan it has ever been acknowledged to have been written by the hand or under the direction of Moses. After a lapse of some thirty-five centuries the correctness of this belief of the Jewish Church has been disputed, and a record under the new name of the Hexateuch has been declared to be the true history. The authorship of the Pentateuch as emanating from the pen of Moses is challenged, and the Hexateuch under the free handling of the critics becomes a species of literary Mosaic, compiled by certain unknown Jewish scribes during the Babylonish captivity. This theory is unsupported by any external accredited proofs, and dependent only for its acceptance on arguments based on the results of inductive criticism.

The theory advanced is that the Pentateuch is a history formed of excerpts taken from three or four archaic records, many of which extracts relate to laws and ceremonies posterior to the age of Moses, gradually evolving to meet the moral and ecclesiastical requirements of succeeding periods, but forming no part of the law originally given to Moses, the great lawgiver, who habitually communed with God face to face on matters connected with the legislation of the chosen people. Such a code is therefore posterior to the Mosaic record, and does not comply with the legal requirement, that dispossession of an estate is only effected by the production of a duly authenticated prior title. The fallacy of the theory is moreover accentuated by our Lord's quotations of various passages from the Pentateuch, in which He referred to Moses as their author, whereby the infallibility of our Lord's nature as the Incarnate Word is impugned.

In support of this theory recourse is had to the revival of the exploded doctrine of the limitation of our Lord's human knowledge to such a degree as to render Him liable to the enunciation of error. The Gospel of St. Luke reveals an ineffable self-imposed limitation of our Lord's human knowledge up to the moment of the Jordanic baptism, at which period He received the plenary and abiding unction of the Holy Spirit, and His solemn appointment to go forth as the Divine Son, the infallible Prophet to whose words all men were commanded to render obedience, affirmed by the audible voice of the Divine Father: "This is My beloved Son, in whom I am well pleased;" supplemented at the Transfiguration by the command to "Hear Him." Enunciation of error becomes an impossibility in one so plenarily anointed, and declared to be of the same nature as the Father.

The sandy foundation of this revived doctrine is mainly based on an expression used by our Lord in reference to His ignorance of the day of the Parousia: "Of that day knoweth no man, no not the angels, neither the Son, but My Father only." The words relating "to the Son," are omitted by St. Matthew (xxiv. 36), and are only found in St. Mark's Gospel (xiii. 32). Their omission by St. Matthew is in accordance with the acknowledged nature of our

Lord's Divine omniscience as " One with the Father." Their admission into St. Mark's Gospel should therefore be traced to human error in their transmission, as being an interpolation made by some copyist of the original autograph, otherwise the Evangelist would have exposed the doctrine of Unity of the Son with the Father to the charge of being open to doubt, unless the propounders of this theory are prepared to ascribe liability to the enunciation of error, not only to the Son, but also to the Father.

It is rather a rash proceeding in sacred things to build up a theory upon an isolated text uncorroborated by its admission into a parallel passage of a contemporary and equally accepted document on the same subject, and the more so, should the theory, if the words of such text be not an interpolation, appear to extend the period of the limitation of our Lord's human knowledge beyond the moment of His plenary endowment by the Holy Spirit at the Jordanic baptism. It appears similar to the suggestion of an archæologist, that owing to the discovery of one word in an ancient document, unsupported by its existence in another similar document bearing on the same event, equally accepted as authentic, the recognised interpretation of the contents of the entire mass of documents, of which these two form a part, should be regarded as unreliable. The improbability of the correctness of his proposal will be increased if it can be shown that such use of the word is directly opposed to the admitted character of the alleged speaker, and that it affects not only his admitted claims to fulness of knowledge but also to his veracity.

Such is the proposition which certain writers of the present day submit to our acceptance. On this isolated text they have built up a theory, that in the Sacred Scriptures place must be given to the recognition of the doctrine, that amidst a certain undefined amount of truth there is also an admixture of compilations, myths, allegories, idealisms, dramas, and other literary productions emanating from the minds of their respective authors, who make no claim to the reception of direct and accredited inspiration, and who are in many cases utterly unknown. The verification of what is infallible truth, and what are the fallible concepts of human reason, is left to the verifying faculty of each Biblical student, whatever may be his qualification for the task which he has undertaken.

The same arguments apply with equal force to the hostile criticisms which have been advanced against the historic accuracy of the Book of Job. In this case the objections raised are simply those of direct negation. No trace is found of any proposal to substitute any other record in contravention to its account of the marvellous occurrences therein related, and of the deep spiritual doctrines thereby revealed. Until the impugners of its inspiration and of its veracity are in a position to produce a written revelation of an earlier date, duly accredited by miraculous signs and inspired documentary evidence, declarative of mysterious events revealed as having taken place in the Presence Chamber of Jehovah in the Heavenlies, witnessing to the fallacy of the doctrine of the opposition of the Satan to the will of God, and of his persecution of some well-known historic personage whom he has been Divinely permitted to expose to accentuated misery, in order to tempt him from his allegiance to the Almighty, the claims of the Book of Job to man's acceptance remain unimpaired.

From the time when it was first published it has been regarded as an inspired record, witnessed by its position in the Jewish Canon. The words of the prophet Ezekiel, and of the evangelist St. James, testify that for more than twenty-five centuries it has been so regarded by the Church of God. The absence of any word of disapproval from the mouth of our Lord, of the estimation in which it was held by the Jewish Church in the days of His flesh, is corroborative of the correctness of her action, in allowing it to be numbered amongst the sacred writings, and conclusive as to the reality of Job's existence and of the truth of the doctrines which the history reveals. He thereby bears testimony to the personality of Satan and of his limited power at certain permitted times to afflict the children of God.

It should not be forgotten that the ordinary standpoint of Biblical inductive criticism is that of unfaith in the record, and its general character that of negation of its contents. Like the scalpel of the vivisectionist seeking to discover the source of life in a living subject, it is fatal to that of its victim, for the biologist, in tracing its origin to materialistic causes, denies its Divine source: "God breathed into man's nostrils the breath of life." To test the truth of revelation by its accordance with the conclusions of human reason is productive of unfaith, not only in the record in which it is preserved, but also in the Incarnation of the Word and its assurance of eternal life, for "These things were written that we might believe that Jesus is the Christ, the Son of God, and that believing we might have life through His name" (John xx. 31). Without revelation the doctrine of the Incarnation is beyond the conception of human reason.

Inductive criticism starts with the primeval interrogation, "Yea, has God said?" suggestive of doubt in the goodness of God in inculcating the superiority of implicit obedience to the will of God over the fallacious imaginings of human reason. For yielding to the suggestions of his free will, Adam was cast out of Paradise; whilst by faithful submission to the Divine Will, "I come to do Thy will, O God," the Second Adam caused the gate of Paradise to be opened for His re-admission. In our Lord's three temptations, the pretensions of science, the exercise of omnipotence, and the assumption of empire, were all controlled by His threefold appeal to the Sacred Scriptures. "It is written" was the threefold answer to the devil's challenge. The Satanic tempter was thereby foiled, and the salvation of mankind was secured, by our Lord's fulfilment of all things that had been written concerning Himself in the law of Moses, and in the Prophets, and in the Psalms, inclusive of the Book of Job, which is now asserted to be partially discredited. The noble-minded Berean inquirers were confirmed in their faith by their daily appeal to the Scriptures, whether the things which they had heard from the apostles were true, whilst the sceptical critic, appealing to worldly science, philosophy, and history, gradually loses faith in the Written Word. The Bereans criticised the words preached to them by the apostles, and obtained a solution of their doubts by an appeal to Holy Scripture. The inductive critic contends for the substitution of the fluctuating decisions of human reason for the authoritative and sacred canon of Holy Scripture, as the final court of appeal to determine what is the revealed will of God.

The true order of Biblical interpretation has been lost sight of. The Divine court of appeal is revealed by Isaiah to be "to the law and to the testimony; and where men speak not according to this Word, it is because they have no light in them." Instead of endeavouring to interpret the contents of Revelation so as to suit the ever-changing theories of science, the inconstant doctrines of philosophy, and the inaccurate statements of history, the attempt should be made to reconcile the discoveries of science, the conclusions of philosophy, and the impressions of history, with the immutable principles of Divine Revelation contained in the Written Word of God.

It is greatly to be feared that much of the scepticism which prevails amongst the intellectual classes is traceable to the unguarded statements and rash assumptions concerning the unscientific character and the historic inaccuracy of the sacred writings, which owe their acceptance more to the ecclesiastical position of the writers than to the inherent value of their theories. In a similar way the evil extends itself to the less highly educated classes, in consequence of the ill-considered expressions and confused suggestions which emanate from the Church's pulpits in matters pertaining to Scripture exposition. Our Lord's words, "If they hear not Moses and the prophets, neither will they be persuaded though one rose from the dead," convey a powerful warning that unfaith in the Written Word imperils also faith in the doctrine of His Resurrection, whereby men lose the assurance of admission into Life Eternal.

CHAPTER XLI

INSPIRATION OF SCRIPTURE

THE doubts which have been thrown out concerning the historic veracity and scientific accuracy of the Book of Job, and other portions of the Sacred Scriptures, is mainly traceable to the indefinite views which are held as to the nature and extent of their inspiration.

It is said that "the Church is not tied by any existing definition, and consequently there is no exact claim on any one's belief." Thus faith in the degree of inspiration is alone determined by the verifying faculty of the reader of Scripture, whatever be his qualification to decide. It is also affirmed that "the strongest believers in the inspiration of the Church see a Divine Providence in this absence of dogma, because now only since its foundation has the state of human knowledge been such as to admit of its being legitimately raised."

It appears, therefore, that for nearly nineteen centuries the Church of Christ is to be regarded as being destitute of sufficient Divine knowledge, to render her capable to perform the work for which she has been elected out of the world, in revealing to man the true character of her sacred writings, which were expressly given to enable him to become wise unto salvation.

The teaching of Scripture is somewhat opposed to this doctrine. In the case of the Jewish Church, her doctrines, her sacrificial system, and her ceremonial rites of worship were revealed to Moses by God personally, and through the dispensation of angels, and from him disclosed to the Church to be made known to the world. Under the Christian development of the Church of God a similar process is to be observed. Her fundamental doctrines and her essential sacramental ordinances were the means by which the Divine principles of doctrine, worship, and sacrifice, before revealed in the Jewish Church, were now to receive their fulfilment, but not their destruction, for Christ says, "I came not to destroy, but to fulfil." This is done by the adaptation of their details in the Christian Church to the doctrinal revelation which was given by our Lord in the Theophany on the Mount in Galilee, when He delegated to the eleven Apostles the threefold function "to disciple all nations, to baptize them into the name of the Father, and of the Son, and of the Holy Ghost, and to teach them to observe all things whatsoever He had commanded them."[1]

[1] Too little attention is paid to the character of our Lord's appearance on the Mount in Galilee. None but the eleven are recorded as being present (Matt. xxviii. 16). The meeting had been foretold to the eleven by our Lord on the road to Gethsemane,

Both of these developments of the Church owe their origin to the Word of God, as the Rock upon which the Church of God is built. The word, spoken by the Lord God in Eden in the promise that "the Seed of the woman should bruise the serpent's head," is the fundamental rock on which she is built. The promise given to Abraham, that "in him should all the families of the earth be blessed," is a development of the original promise depictive of the family through whom the Seed should come. The command given to Moses to "build a sanctuary, that the Lord God should dwell amongst them," is a fresh development of the original

when they alone were present with Him: "After I am risen I will go before you into Galilee" (Matt. xxvi. 32; Mark xiv. 28). The first command given by the angel to the women from the empty tomb was, that they should go and tell His disciples and Peter that He goeth before them into Galilee, and there they should see Him, as He said to them (Matt. xxviii. 7; Mark xvi. 7). Our Lord Himself reiterated the same command to the other Mary and Salome, as He met them going to tell the disciples, although in His Divine omniscience He must have known that He was about to meet them on the evening of the Resurrection in Jerusalem (Matt. xxviii. 9). The appearance in Galilee was therefore one of a special nature. The particular mountain had been pre-appointed (Matt. xxviii. 16). Our Lord had been seen and recognised by the disciples on three antecedent occasions, yet when He thus appeared in Galilee, it is recorded that though they saw Him and worshipped Him, yet some doubted. The cause of their hesitation should be traced to their incapability of believing in the identity of the risen Christ with an appearance of so glorious a character as to compel their brother apostles to offer Him Divine worship, and to receive the Divine announcement, that "all power had been given unto Him in heaven and in earth." The sole explanation of the difficulty lies apparently in refusing to regard this mysterious event as a Theophany.

promise, as to the mode whereby its blessings might be apprehended by the chosen race.

The Christian Church, as taught by our Lord Himself, is founded on the words revealed by the Father to St. Peter: "Thou art the Christ, the Son of the living God." Of this doctrine of the Incarnation Christ says: "On this rock I will build My Church." Christ, as revealed by St. Paul, writing to the Corinthians, is the rock. The same word *petra* is used in both passages, and the dogma revealed is that of "the Word made flesh." The public inauguration of the Church at Pentecost originates with the Word revealed to St. Peter, and accredited by the gift of tongues: "Let all the house of Israel know assuredly that God hath made this same Jesus whom ye have crucified both Lord and Christ."

In these four great epochs of the Church's history, her origin and her renewed developments are Divinely revealed as being built upon the Divinely spoken Word of God, subsequently committed to writing by men whose claim to inspiration has been universally admitted by the Church. They were Moses, the two apostles Matthew and Peter, with the evangelist Luke, the writer of the Acts.

According to the modern theory, believers in the inspiration of the Church, seeing a Divine providence in the absence of a dogma presumably in the matter of the inspiration of the Sacred Scriptures, as distinguished from the inspiration of the Church, appear to affirm that there is no certainty as to whether the writings containing the revelations of these four events were or were not inspired, and that therefore the Church is incapable of determining whether these histories are or are not correct. The first record which contains the promise of the Seed has already been relegated to the position of a myth. The history of the fall ceases by some to be regarded as veracious, whereby the doctrine of the personality of the Satan, described as the Serpent by St. Paul and St. John, and recognised by our Lord as the Devil, becomes open to doubt. Thus the state of Biblical knowledge, which has only of late become sufficiently advanced to allow the doctrine of inspiration to be accurately defined, is apparently on the road to deprive mankind of faith in a large portion of the sacred writings, which have hitherto been regarded as veracious because they have been inspired.

Similarly in dealing with Mosaic history and its recorded laws and ordinances of Divine worship, it is suggested that, instead of emanating from the pen of Moses, writing under the inspiration of God, it is a collection of extracts made during the exile in Babylon by certain unknown Judaic scribes from three or four archaic records, such as the Elohistic and Jehovistic sections, the Book of the Covenant, the Book of Origins, or the Priests' Code, many of which extracts were long posterior to the age of Moses, and that the composition owes itself to an unconscious idealising of history in reading into past records of ritual development, statements which are really later. The consistency of such idealism with absolute truth is incredible, and is utterly opposed to the generally admitted idea of inspiration, in its relation to a revelation universally believed to have been given to man by the Omniscient Father for the direction of His chosen people. The inspired origin of the Jewish Church is thus supplanted by a history which derives its gradual evolution out of the mind of man, notwithstanding our Lord's claim to have fulfilled all things written concerning Himself in the law of Moses, and in the Prophets, and in the Psalms, all of which writings were in His days universally accepted as containing the inspired utterances of the Almighty. As inspired writings, our Lord's appeal to the necessity of their fulfilment by Himself is easy of apprehension, but as uninspired writings, or compilations of uninspired archaic documents, such appeal becomes divested of its true character as the expression of the Divine will. In the case of the Book of Job, the various problems which presented themselves to his mind, as to the causes of suffering, are typical of the problems which presented themselves to our Lord's human soul while enduring the sufferings to which, in His perfected humanity, He was exposed, which He successfully combated by His uncomplaining submission to the Divine will, whereby He became an all-perfect example to suffering humanity.

In order to weaken the claims to direct inspiration which have hitherto been generally, if not universally, admitted to attach to the Word of God, it is affirmed that "mankind is not tied by any existing definition of the character of the inspiration to which the Sacred Scriptures owe their origin," and this in face, not only of our Lord's words quoting from the 110th Psalm, as one spoken by David in or under the influence of the Holy Spirit, but also of His reference to the prophet Daniel, foretelling the elevation of the abomination of desolation in the holy place. Modern criticism thus directly impugns our Lord's knowledge of the authorship and inspiration of the Psalm, regarding His words as a mere colloquialism, thereby charging Him who is the Truth with the enunciation of error, not to say falsehood, by His utterance of words which would thus convey a mistaken impression.

His mention of the name of the prophet Daniel is attributed to an interpolation by some officious copyist, whereby its prophetic character is discredited, on the plea that the passage of the book in which it is found is a mere secular history of the reign of Antiochus Epiphanes, and that the entire book itself is the production of one of the chasidim, or pious men of the Maccabean age.

The affirmation, that such silence in respect of the definitive dogma of inspiration owes itself to the inspiration of the Church, savours of the Roman doctrine, that the oral tradition of the Church is to be preferred to the direct teaching of the Word of God. Revelation has ever been antecedent to the decrees of the Church, which are only based on their accordance with the revealed Word. Thus the inspiration of the Word is the only principle on which the Church, as a corporate body, can support her pretension to the possession of direct inspiration. Her claim to inspiration, in her silence as to the character of the dogma of inspiration, is therefore declarative of failure in the right interpretation of the Sacred Scriptures.

On two occasions, under the direct inspiration of the Holy Spirit, the Church defined doctrine, in the matter of the binding power of Mosaic law upon Gentile converts, and in that of the ethical treatment of an incestuous Corinthian. In neither case was her decision antagonistic to the revealed teaching of Scripture. Her solemn decree did not free Judaic converts from obedience to the Mosaic law, and her excommunication of the incestuous Corinthian was in accordance with the law, "that the soul which doeth ought presumptuously shall be cut off from among His people" (Acts xv.; 1 Cor. v.; Num. xv. 31).

These are apparently the only two instances of inspired conciliar action recorded in the New Testament. Since the last of the six œcumenical councils of the Church, it is doubtful if any universal authoritative claim to direct conciliar inspiration can be sustained. The succeeding councils are not regarded as œcumenical, and their decrees are only binding on her members in the localities with which they were connected. The breach between the Churches of the East and West is fatal to the promulgation of any œcumenical decree binding on the Catholic Church, while those of the Lambeth council are equally exposed to non-acceptance by any except the members of the Anglican communion.

The pretentious claim of certain nineteenth century critics to "the possession of knowledge never before possessed by man, so as to admit of the dogmatic character of inspiration being legitimately discussed," is infinitely more opposed to human reason, than that of the Roman Church to enforce the acceptance of her dogma, that the oral tradition of the Church is equally if not more binding than the teaching of the Sacred Scriptures. The dogmatic teaching of the Church of Rome is to a certain degree conditioned by her subservience to the decrees of an ecclesiastical, though not of an œcumenical council. The dogmatic teaching of the critics consists only of the segregated affirmations of a number of intellectual, but owing to the abeyance of the legislative and judicial functions of the Church, irresponsible theologians, few if any of whom are members of the apostolate to which order alone Christ on the Galilean Mount delegated the control of His Church.

The value of such defective and informal decisions

may be tested by their result. The elevation of the oral tradition of the Church to an equality with the inspired Scriptures was provocative of the Reformation, which gradually led to the loss of the temporal power of the Papacy, and to the preposterous decree affirming the infallibility of the personal Pope. The effects which may probably follow the depreciation of the inspired Scriptures, on the ground of their historic or scientific inaccuracy advanced by modern criticism, are at present inchoate. Their tendency, however, points to socialistic movements of the Robert Elsmere school, or philanthropy originating in human emotion as contrasted with faith in the doctrine of a future Resurrection, accredited by that of the crucified Son of Man, and also to the substitution of materialistic science and secular philosophy, based on unlimited Darwinian evolution and Spencerian speculation, for revealed knowledge emanating from the Divine Wisdom.

The Traditional View.

The traditional doctrine of the inspiration of the Scriptures dates from the days of Adam. It originates in the certainty that every utterance of Jehovah, from His essential nature, is infallibly true. His earlier utterances from the period when they were made, have been preserved by means of oral tradition, or of written documents compiled by Moses into one record, that of Genesis. The whole of the Pentateuch has hitherto been universally admitted to have been written by the pen or under the direction of Moses. Its inspiration as containing the will of God, not only for the governance of the chosen race, but also for the instruction of all mankind, is necessitated by the character of its contents. Amidst a certain amount of historic details capable of being recorded by the seer independent of inspiration, the bulk of its contents relate to matters which, without the inspiration of the writer, could never have been absolutely determined by the mind of man. They refer to heavenly mysteries, to secular occurrences anterior to the formation of man, and to other future events, whose fulfilment took place years and even centuries posterior to their revelation, as well as to others which remain as yet unfulfilled. The doctrine of the inspiration of the fulfilled portions is avouched by their fulfilment, by which the certainty of the inspiration of the other as yet unfulfilled portions is placed beyond dispute.

The safeguarding of the Pentateuch is generally accepted without hesitation till the death of Joshua, who is revealed as having been magnified in the sight of all Israel by a miracle of so stupendous a character as to cause him "to be feared, as the people feared Moses, all the remaining years of his life" (iv. 14). At its close he wrote a history of the events which accompanied the conquest of the land, and its apportionment amongst the twelve tribes, as a supplement to be incorporated in the original book of the Law of God (xxiv. 26). The contents of that book of the Law, according to our Lord's words (Luke xxiv. 44) were not confined to the precepts of the law, but comprehended the events of the history of the nation in their relation to His work. History and Law were contemporaneously recorded as they were developed and revealed in the early ages.

The days of the Judges, all of them Divinely appointed to their offices, were marked by periodical relapses into idolatry, followed by national restoration to the faithful worship of Jehovah. The history relates Divine revelations, accredited by miracles, with repeated references to the survival of ceremonial rites amongst a godly though possibly a segregated remnant, who were enabled to become agents for the restoration of the national worship of Jehovah, witnessing to the preservation of the written law of Moses, whereby in a greater or less degree it could be rendered acceptable to the Almighty.

The days of Samuel were marked by a revival of open visions and miraculous revelations. In the record of his life not a trace is found that the book of the law of Moses, and its supplements in the Books of Joshua and the Judges, were ever regarded as unveracious records, or as being devoid of inspiration. The establishment of Samuel to be a prophet by his visions of Jehovah, and his full acceptance as such by the entire nation, witnesses to the inspired character of these national archives, the preservation of which was further safeguarded by the formation of the schools of the prophets, as additional guardians of the laws originally committed to the priests.

The continuous chain of inspired prophets in the persons of David, "the man after God's own heart," Nathan and Gad, "to whom the word of Jehovah came," bears similar witness to the veracity and inspiration of the two Books of Samuel, carrying us on to the days of Solomon, the builder of the temple, and himself a recipient of Divine visions. It is needless to show that the establishment of the temple, its building and its sacrificial worship, were not only based on their accordance with the law of Moses, but even the details of the building, its courts, its priestly courses, and its Levitical work, had been given to David by the Spirit, and by him communicated to his son Solomon for his execution of them (1 Chron. xxviii. 12). On the completion of the work the Divine approval was manifested to the assembled multitudes at its dedication by the visible descent of the Shekinah of glory.

Thus far not a loophole exists to show that the united body of the Israelitish nation ever doubted the truth or the inspiration of their national archives, whose veracity from the days of Moses had been continuously corroborated by a chain of inspired prophets, priests, and kings.

The death of Solomon was followed by the disruption of the nation. The temple and its courts, with their sacred contents, remained with the tribe of Judah, and its services were continuously—though at times imperfectly—observed until the time of the Babylonish Captivity. This lengthened period was, however, marked by alternations of national corruption and reformation. The Book of the Law and its concurrent history—the national archives—appear at times to have been lost to sight, only to be again recovered at the moments of national reformation. Their preservation appears to owe itself to their being hidden in troublous times in the recesses of the temple by some pious priest, who, like Jehoiada, concealed Joash, the rightful heir to the throne, from the murderous attempts of Athaliah. Such appears to be the solution of the discovery of the Book of the Law in the reign of Josiah. These national archives may possibly have been hidden in some of the treasuries of the temple in the early days of the apostacy of Manasseh, followed by the Assyrian invasion, and their very existence and place of concealment forgotten until the reformation by Josiah, when they were recognised and authenticated by Huldah, the inspired prophetess.

From the days of Rehoboam to the close of the Babylonish Captivity, there is a continuous chain of some thirty-one recorded inspired prophets, the writings of sixteen of whom belong to the sacred canon. By none of these is a shadow of doubt thrown against the inspiration and consequently historic veracity of the Books of the Kings and Chronicles. These two sets of contemporaneous documents, like all other historic books of the two Testaments, make no claim to be regarded as consecutive history. They are only collections of certain salient events happening respectively in Israel and Judah, which appear to have been selected under Divine inspiration for revealing the principles, whereby the lives primarily of the Israelites, and afterwards of the members of all other nations, should be regulated under their threefold social, political, and religious aspects. If the inspiration of these Scriptures is questioned, their value for this object is lessened by the reduction of their dogmatic teaching to the level of empirical judgments based on human reason. This was the sin of the fall. The test of experience at the devil's suggestion supplanted direct obedience to Divine commands.

The conservation of these national archives on the return from Babylon is attested by three post-exilic inspired prophets, whose words are incapable of being understood, unless their agreement with the original law of Moses, commanded to him in Horeb, with the statutes and judgments, together with its supplementary increments of national history, is fully admitted. Malachi, the last of the prophets, not only commands the Israelites to remember the law of Moses, but also accompanies his message with

z

a prophecy of the return of Elijah, the greatest of the prophets, with a view to their national conversion, and further pronounces a curse upon the earth on pain of disobedience.

In the Maccabean age the Apocryphal books teem with allusions to the restoration of the temple services, in accordance with the requirements of the law of Moses, whilst its conservation to the time of our Lord becomes fully established from the various quotations which He makes from its writings. Its inspiration is equally certified by our Lord's words to His disciples, that "all things must be fulfilled which are written in the law of Moses, and in the Prophets, and in the Psalms, concerning Him." Unless these writings had been inspired, the prophecies which they contained could not have been adduced by Him as witnessing to their fulfilment in His Divine and Human nature, in their having been uttered in a continuous succession during a period of some four thousand years anterior to His incarnation, from the days of Adam to those of Malachi.

The same arguments hold good as to the preservation and inspiration of the other two divisions of the Old Testament, the Prophets and the Psalms, referred to by our Lord. The prophetical books were universally accepted by the Jews as Divine records of words spoken by inspired men, conveying a knowledge of future events incapable of attainment except from miraculous sources. The objective voice of a Theophany, messages from the Heavenlies conveyed through angelic ministration, secret intuitions of coming events accredited as Divine by external signs,—these and other agencies were the modes by which holy men of old recognised that they were commissioned to give utterance to such communications as they were moved by the Holy Spirit.

The future is alone known unto God, and to those to whom He entrusts it for revelation to man. This was the office of the Prophet. He foretold the future under Divine influence. To describe a prophet as only a man possessed of extraordinary insight into human character, or of great intuition of political probabilities, is a degradation of his sacred office as the revealer of Divine mysteries communicated to him by the Holy Spirit. These may form part of his office as a preacher of the Word, in which case his efficiency is conditioned by his intellectual and spiritual attainments. They only represent his unrecorded utterances. But in his prophetic utterances he is the voice of One crying in the wilderness. The man is but the unconscious instrument by whose voice the Word of God is conveyed, as the sound of the note from the wire of a harp.

Oftentimes the prophets knew not the meaning of the words they uttered, and the contents of the books in which they were recorded were at times sealed to their own understanding. Without inspiration, therefore, the Prophet becomes an impossibility.

Our Lord's words to the apostles, in reference to His fulfilment of the utterances of the prophets, become a direct affirmation that the writings in which they are found are not only veracious, but are also inspired.

Our Lord, in thus speaking to His disciples, witnessed to His acceptance of the Jewish Tripartite division of the Sacred Scriptures, as the Law, the Prophets, and the Psalms, whose provisions, long before foretold, He teaches them that He came to fulfil. His words apply equally to the third division, that of the Psalms, as to the other two. They are thus equally stamped with our Lord's imprimatur of their veracity and inspiration. The appellation, " the Psalms," is collective, including not only those commonly so called, but also the three Solomonic writings of the Proverbs, Ecclesiastes, and the Canticles, as well as the Books of the Chronicles, Ezra, Nehemiah, Esther, Job, and Daniel.

The majority of Christians accord their fullest assent to the inspiration of the Book of the Psalms, in accordance with our Lord's affirmation that David speaks in or under the influence of the Holy Spirit in the case of the 110th Psalm. Our Lord's words appear to stamp with the seal of Inspiration the remaining Psalms of the collection. Without this His reference to their prophetic character, in respect of His sufferings, would be rendered unintelligible. The Psalms foretold the devotional feelings which would exist in His human mind during His earthly life, as well as the spiritual temptations to which His human soul would be exposed in the endurance of His vicarious sufferings, by resistance to which our Lord vindicated His claim to the perfected humanity that was the special characteristic of the righteous Servant of Jehovah. His words apply with equal force to the other Scriptures of which the collective body of the Hagiographa, or third section called the Book of the Psalms, is composed. They all relate to events foretold hundreds of years before our Lord's advent, which He affirms He came to fulfil. As prophecies their inspiration is therefore assured. When referred to by Himself in support of His mission, their veracity is established beyond doubt.

In the case of the Solomonic writings, these views are supported by the essential character of their contents. They all claim to originate with the pen of Solomon. The truth of this, in reference to the Book of Proverbs, is verified by their compilation by the men of Hezekiah, and their relegation to the period of the Wisdom literature of later days would falsify the statement that they were accepted as writings of Solomon in the days of Hezekiah. The motive of our Lord's appeal to His fulfilment of its contents reveals its essential character. It is a compendium of the intrinsic principles Divinely ordained for the regulation of man's secular life under its individual, social, civic, and commercial aspects, revealed long ages before His advent, the fulfilment of which, in the daily practice of His secular life, constituted one of the claims which He advanced to be regarded as the Light of the World, or man's example in ordinary life.

Ecclesiastes claims to have been written by the son of David, the king of Israel. No other before or since the days of Solomon has possessed the position, or opportunity, or wisdom, sufficient to test by personal experience the matters of which it treats. The writer is the pessimistic revealer of all the metaphysical and materialistic doubts by which the human mind is tempted to abjure faith in the Divine wisdom and love. It represents a psychical temptation originating in the innermost springs of the human intellect, without being exposed to which our Lord's humanity might have been open to the charge of imperfection by its absorption into His Divinity, so as to exclude the possibility of His Divinity becoming conditioned by His assumption of the humanity. As a Divine being, the idea of intellectual temptation is precluded. As the perfect Man, His voluntary obedience to the will of God is shown to proceed from the volition of His human will. Thus he reveals Himself as the infallible Koheleth, or preacher, who by His own personal experience, in having successfully overcome the temptation to yield to materialistic and metaphysical doubts, is able to teach man the fallacy of such intellectual reasoning, and to assist him in preserving his faith in God as the Moral Governor of the world. These two prophetic writings foretold two essential temptations, to which our Lord would be exposed in His practical and intellectual life, in order that by their fulfilment the perfection of His humanity should be revealed to all coming ages.

The Song of Songs, or the Canticles, stands on a different footing. No adequate interpretation of this Divine poem has yet been given. The cause apparently lies in the restriction of its interpretation to the Earthly sphere, as representative of the love of Christ for His Church antecedent to her consummated glory in the Heavenlies.

The poem claims to originate from the mind of Solomon. It reveals, under the sublimest form of spiritualised symbolism, that love for His Church therein foretold as about to be fulfilled and resident in the deepest recesses of our Lord's human mind. Glimpses of our Lord's human love for the individual and collective members of His Church were revealed when He dwelt on earth; but even this perfection of love fails to correspond with the mystical character of that foretold in the Song. It is a love that transcends the limitation of earthly feeling or expression. Its consummation can only be attained when the earthly humanity of her Divine Spouse had been glorified in the Heavenlies.

The continuity of our Lord's human life did not terminate with the death on the cross. As Man,

His human soul went to Hades, and preached to the spirits in the safe guardianship of the Intermediate State. As Man, in the glorified condition of the resurrected body, He returned to earth; and lastly, as Man, in the resplendent radiancy of the spiritualised body, He ascended to the right hand of the throne of God. From thence, as the glorified Son of Man, He rules over the universe; and as the human Head of His Church, He invisibly directs her action on earth and in Hades.

The burden of the Song is of a far more mysterious character than any which pertains either to Earth or to Hades. It is only in the faintest outlines that its sublime symbols can be apprehended. It describes the unutterable love of the Church's Divine Spouse, and the ineffable joy with which He regards her gradual emancipation from her Earthly trammels, as He welcomes her approach to the Heavenly vineyard. It represents the correspondent transport with which the Church prepares herself for His advent, and looks forward to the time when her earthly isolation shall be ended, and her eternal union with her Divine Lord shall be consummated in the Heavenlies.

These mysteries are beyond the imagination of man in his fleshly condition. The mortal must put on immortality before they can be apprehended. Yet in Christ, according to His own words, all must be fulfilled. The time may be distant, but their consummation is certain. To attribute such a revelation to the uninspired pens of the Judaic Wisdom literati is as irrational as the placing the fancies of Dante or of Milton on a level with the Apocalyptic revelation of Jesus Christ, given to Him by God and signified by His angel to His servant John.

So also, according to our Lord's words, He was to fulfil the provisoes of the Book of Job as one of the constituent parts of the Hagiographa, or Book of the Psalms. The perfectioning of His humanity requires the fulfilment of the antecedent prophecies of the miseries to which, as Man, He was exposed in the conservation of faith in His Heavenly Father. Of these the Book of Job is the most exhaustive revelation whereby our Lord's words bear witness to the veracity of the writing and to its inspiration.

The contents of the Books of Ezra and Nehemiah, which have also to be fulfilled in their connection with our Lord's sufferings, equally require the test of inspiration to enable them to bear witness to the problems which agitated His human soul in the re-establishment of the sacrificial, ecclesiastical, and political institutions of His chosen people, and to His enduring resistance to adopt any measures which were inconsistent with the revealed will of the Divine Father, whereby He fulfilled His claim to the perfected Humanity of the Elect One in whom Jehovah's soul delighteth.

The Book of Esther stands in the same category. Its acceptance into the Hagiographa before our Lord's advent precludes its exclusion, from the force of His words, that He came to fulfil its contents. They foretell the Divine method by which Gentile despotism and intellectual Heathenism would be overruled by the leavening influences of the Jewish Church, fulfilled under the evangelising action of her Christian development, motived by the direction of her Divine Head. Esther, the star, represents the collective angels, or evangelists of the Church, held in the hand of the glorified Christ. The visions of Daniel, similar in character to those of Zechariah, are distinctly prophetic, and unless their inspiration be admitted, the Jewish Church would stand convicted of the admission of Apocryphal writings into her sacred Canon. These visions represent problems, which presented themselves before our Lord's human soul in His contest with the Antichristian world-power, influenced by the Satanic opponent of God's will. By resistance to the Devil's temptation to avail Himself of the principles of government foreshadowed in these visions for the recovery of the kingdom of the world, our Lord in His perfected Humanity established His infinite claim to be accepted as King of kings and Lord of lords.

History witnesses to the progressive fulfilment of Christ's operations throughout the world, in accordance with the prophetic revelations contained in the law of Moses, and in the Prophets, and in the Psalms, concerning Himself. The veracity of such fulfilled portions and their inspiration are thereby established beyond doubt, and the fullest assurance is also given that the portions, as yet unfulfilled, are stamped with the same Divine characteristics.

Our Lord's acceptance of the Jewish Canon becomes an infallible proof of the Inspiration of the Books of the Old Testament, and the refusal to receive His decision impugns the correctness of His judgment and the extent of His knowledge.

Nothing need be added concerning the traditional belief in the inspiration of the New Testament. It is an accepted fact by all Christians, and the revival of the exploded theory of the limitation of our Lord's human knowledge, beyond the period of His plenary unction with the Holy Spirit at the Jordanic baptism, appears to originate in the difficulty of interpreting the sacred text, so as to make the existent discoveries in science and in the readings of Assyrian cylinders and Egyptian papyri harmonise with the Biblical record. The process adopted to arrive at a solution would seem to be fundamentally erroneous. Revelation, by its essential nature, as the Word spoken by God, or indirectly revealed to the mind of man, accredited by miraculous signs, must be immutably true. The scientific fact of to-day, however, is liable to be superseded by the scientific fact of to-morrow, witnessed in the supersession of the Ptolemaic system by that of Copernicus, proportioned by the ever-increasing advances into the depths of scientific knowledge. The records of archaic history are infinitesimally few in number compared with the period over which they range, and their interpretation is uncertain, from the difficulty which attends the decipherment of their alphabetical symbols.

The theory that pronounces the superior accuracy of scientific or historic knowledge over the revealed Word of the Sacred Scriptures is distinctly opposed to our Lord's utterance, that the Scripture cannot be broken (John x. 35). The doctrine of degrees of inspiration, whose value is to be determined by human reason, is equally opposed to St. Paul's assertion, that "All Scripture (is) God breathed or inspired, and profitable for teaching," and also antagonistic to the doctrine of St. Peter, that "holy men of God spake as they were moved by the Holy Spirit."

The generally received idea of the great age, to which St. John attained, is one of the strongest proofs to the veracity and inspiration of the Books of the New Testament. All these would appear to have been written before his death. It is therefore beyond belief that he should have been unacquainted with any of the writings of the New Testament extant before that event, falsely claiming to be inspired, without exposing the falsity of their claims.

The doubts which have been thrown out against the veracity and inspiration of large portions of the Sacred Scriptures may possibly cause comparatively little danger to faith when emanating from neologians of other countries; but how far such destructive criticism is consistent with the terms of the ordination oath, respecting faith in the canonical Scriptures of the Old and New Testaments, is open to grave consideration, and the more so that the number and names of these Books have remained unaltered by any authoritative Act of the Church of England since the ratification of the Articles in 1571.

We, who are ordained ministers of the Church, would do well to lay to heart the warning words of the Divine vision of "the dragon, great and fiery, having seven heads and ten horns, and upon his heads seven diadems" (Rev. xii. 3). The dragon is revealed as identical with the old Serpent, the cause of man's fall (Gen. iii.); his mode of action, that of a Devil, or an accuser of man's sin before Jehovah (Zech. iii.); his essential character, that of the Satan, or resister of God's loving purposes for man's restoration revealed in Christ (Ps. cix. 4).

His sphere of action is revealed in the universal power with which he energises the world-powers of the age, symbolised by his seven heads (Rev. xvii. 9), through the agency of his ten horns or aggressive legislative enactments, of which ten is the numerical symbol (Zech. i. 21; Deut. v. 21). The diadems or objective symbols of authority are bound upon his seven heads through the agency of those over whom he rules. The power of Satan originates from man yielding to his advice to disobey God (Gen. iii.; Jas. iv. 7).

"His tail drags after it a third part of the stars of the heavens, and casts them to the earth." The prophet Isaiah (ix. 15) defines the tail as "a prophet teaching falsehood." The stars are the angels, or evangelists of the Church (Rev. i. 20). Their true work lies in the heavenlies, of which three is the Divine symbol. Their casting down to the earth reveals their expulsion from their heavenly office, and their abasement to secular pursuits.

The vision appears to reveal the attraction exercised by false philosophy, in causing those who have been elected to be the evangelists of heavenly things, and deriving their knowledge from words which the Holy Spirit teaches in comparing spiritual things with spiritual, to dedicate themselves to secular intellectual studies, and to substitute materialistic science and rationalistic philosophy for the wisdom of God hidden in mystery, and contained in the Written Word of God (1 Cor. ii. 7).

THE END

Printed by BALLANTYNE, HANSON & Co.
Edinburgh & London

SELECT LIST OF BOOKS
DEVOTIONAL AND PRACTICAL

PUBLISHED BY

JAMES NISBET & CO., LIMITED.

A complete list will be forwarded, post free, on application to the Publishers.

PREACHERS OF TO-DAY.

A SERIES OF CHEAP VOLUMES OF SERMONS BY POPULAR WRITERS.

Small crown 8vo, 1s. paper covers; 1s. 6d. cloth.

BRIEF SERMONS FOR BUSY MEN. By the Rev. R. F. HORTON, M.A., D.D.

SIN AND ITS CONQUERORS. By the Very Rev. Dean FARRAR.

THE ENDLESS CHOICE. By the Rev. W. J. DAWSON.

THE GLORY OF THE LORD. By Canon EYTON.

THE NEW LAW. By Archdeacon SINCLAIR.

STATUTES AND SONGS. By the Rev. F. B. MEYER, B.A.

THE ASSURANCE OF LIFE. By the Rev. E. A. STUART, M.A.

JAMES NISBET & CO.'S
NEW AND RECENT PUBLICATIONS.

By the Rev. ANDREW MURRAY.
THE MINISTRY OF INTERCESSION. A Plea for more Prayer. Small crown 8vo, 1s. 6d.

THE LORD'S TABLE. A Help to the Right Observance of the Holy Supper. Pott 8vo, 1s.

WAITING ON GOD. Extra pott 8vo, 1s.; roan, gilt edges, 2s.

By the Rev. E. A. LITTON.
THE CHURCH OF CHRIST. Revised and re-written from an earlier work. With an Introduction by the Rev. F. J. CHAVASSE. Extra crown 8vo, 5s.

By the Rev. A. T. PIERSON, D.D.
Author of "The New Acts of the Apostles," &c.

SEVEN YEARS IN SIERRA LEONE. The Story of the Work of WILLIAM A. B. JOHNSON, Missionary of the Church Missionary Society from 1816 to 1823, in Regent's Town, Sierra Leone, Africa. Crown 8vo, 3s. 6d.

By JOHN R. MOTT.
STRATEGIC POINTS IN THE WORLD'S CONQUEST. The Universities and Colleges as related to the Progress of Christianity. Specially designed for Christian Students. With Map. Crown 8vo, gilt top, 3s. 6d.

By R. A. TORREY,
Author of "How to Bring Men to Christ," &c.'

HOW TO OBTAIN FULNESS OF POWER. Crown 8vo 1s. 6d.

By EDWIN HODDER.
THE LIFE OF LORD SHAFTESBURY: As SOCIAL REFORMER. With Portrait. Crown 8vo, 2s. 6d.

By S. F. HARRIS,
Author of "Earnest Young Heroes."

A CENTURY OF MISSIONARY MARTYRS. A Series of Biographical Studies in Missionary Work. With Frontispiece. Crown 8vo, 2s. 6d.

Published by James Nisbet & Co., Limited.

NEW AND RECENT PUBLICATIONS—*Continued.*

By the Bishop of ROCHESTER, Bishop BARRY, Archdeacon SINCLAIR, Canon SCOTT-HOLLAND, Canon NEWBOLT, Professor RYLE, and the Rev. T. B. STRONG.

THE FAITH OF CENTURIES. A Series of Essays and Lectures by well-known Writers and Preachers, re-stating and explaining in a form both scholarly and popular the Essential Doctrines of the Christian Faith. Edited by the Rev. W. E. BOWEN. Extra crown 8vo, 7s. 6d.

By Canon GIRDLESTONE.

OLD TESTAMENT SYNONYMS. New and Revised Edition. Demy 8vo, 12s.

By the Rev. GEORGE EVERARD, M.A.,
Author of "Strong and Free," &c. &c.

FIGHT AND WIN. Talks with Lads about the Battle of Life. Pott 8vo, 1s.
LINED WITH LOVE. Pott 8vo, 1s.

By the Rev. J. R. MILLER, D.D.,
Author of "Making the Most of Life," &c.

GLIMPSES THROUGH LIFE'S WINDOWS: Selections from the Writings of the Rev. J. R. MILLER, D.D. Small crown 8vo, with Portrait, gilt top, 2s. 6d.
GIRLS: FAULTS AND IDEALS. A Friendly Talk, with Quotations from Young Men's Letters. Crown 8vo, 6d.
YOUNG MEN: FAULTS AND IDEALS. A Friendly Talk, with Quotations from Girls' Letters. Crown 8vo, 6d.
These two booklets bound together in cloth, 1s.

By Mrs. FRANCES BEVAN.

HYMNS OF TER STEEGEN AND OTHERS. Second Series. Crown 8vo, 1s. 6d.

By Canon McCORMICK, D.D.

WHAT IS SIN? A Volume of Select Sermons preached before the University of Oxford. Crown 8vo, 2s. 6d.

By the Rev. H. W. WEBB-PEPLOE,
PREBENDARY OF ST. PAUL'S CATHEDRAL.

THE LIFE OF PRIVILEGE. With Portrait. Extra crown 8vo, 3s. 6d.
THE VICTORIOUS LIFE. Extra crown 8vo 3s. 6d.

By the Rev. J. REID HOWATT.

THE CHILDREN'S PREACHER. A Year's Addresses and Parables for the Young. Extra crown 8vo, 6s.

A NIGHT IN BETHLEHEM FIFTY YEARS AFTER. Freely Rendered. Long fcap. 8vo, 1s. sewn; 1s. 6d. cloth.

THE CHILDREN'S PEW. Sermons to Children. Extra crown 8vo, 6s.

THE CHILDREN'S PULPIT. A Year's Sermons and Parables for the Young. Second Edition. Extra crown 8vo, 6s.

THE CHILDREN'S ANGEL. Being a Volume of Sermons to Children. Crown 8vo, 2s. 6d.

FAITH'S STRONG FOUNDATIONS. Small crown 8vo, 1s.

YOUTH'S IDEALS. Small crown 8vo, 1s.

"So bright and cheerful, so clever and well written, yet so full of deep Christian earnestness, that we would like to see it circulated by tens of thousands."—*The New Age.*

AFTER HOURS; or, The Religion of Our Leisure Time. With Appendix on How to Form a Library for Twenty Shillings. Small crown 8vo, 1s.

AGNOSTIC FALLACIES. Crown 8vo, 1s.

"Mr. Howatt has succeeded remarkably well in the five lectures before us. They are plain, straightforward, logical, and eminently to the point."—*Literary Churchman.*

THE CHILDREN'S PRAYER BOOK: Devotions for the Use of the Young for One Month. Cloth extra, pott 8vo, 1s.

LIFE WITH A PURPOSE. A Book for Girls and Young Men. Crown 8vo, 1s.

By Miss NUGENT.

THE PRINCE IN THE MIDST. Jesus our Centre. Extra pott 8vo, 1s.

By R. A. TORREY,

SUPERINTENDENT OF MR. MOODY'S BIBLE INSTITUTE, CHICAGO.

HOW TO OBTAIN FULNESS OF POWER. Crown 8vo, 1s. 6d.

HOW TO BRING MEN TO CHRIST. Crown 8vo, 1s. 6d.

HOW TO STUDY THE BIBLE FOR GREATEST PROFIT. Crown 8vo, 1s. 6d.

THE BAPTISM WITH THE HOLY SPIRIT. Crown 8vo, 1s.

THE VEST POCKET COMPANION FOR CHRISTIAN WORKERS. In Leather, 1s.

Published by James Nisbet & Co., Limited.

By the Rev. GEORGE MATHESON, D.D.

MOMENTS ON THE MOUNT. A Series of Devotional Meditations. Second Edition. Crown 8vo, 3s. 6d.

VOICES OF THE SPIRIT. Small crown 8vo, 3s. 6d.

By EDITH RALPH.

STEP BY STEP THROUGH THE BIBLE. PART I. **2s. 6d. each Part**
FROM THE CREATION TO THE DEATH OF JOSHUA. A Scripture History for Little Children. With a Preface by CUNNINGHAM GEIKIE, D.D., LL.D., and Twelve Illustrations. Crown 8vo, 2s. 6d. Suitable for Use in Schools and Families.

Part II. FROM DEATH OF JOSHUA TO END OF THE OLD TESTAMENT. A Scripture History for Little Children. Revised and recommended by CUNNINGHAM GEIKIE, D.D., LL.D. Twelve Illustrations. Crown 8vo, 2s. 6d.

"No sweeter, wiser, or more Christian story of the Scriptures could be given to a little child or read to it."—*Christian Commonwealth.*

"Just the thing for Sunday afternoon."—*Word and Work.*

Part III. BEING A LIFE OF CHRIST FOR CHILDREN. Recommended by Rev. CUNNINGHAM GEIKIE, D.D., LL.D. With Twelve Illustrations. Crown 8vo, 2s. 6d.

"Sound in doctrine, and at the same time simple in style, and attractively illustrated, this book should have a large sale and do a good work."—*Methodist Recorder.*

By the Rev. JAMES WELLS, M.A.

BIBLE OBJECT LESSONS. Addresses to Children. With Illustrations. Crown 8vo, 3s. 6d.   **3s. 6d. each**

BIBLE ECHOES. Addresses to the Young. Small crown 8vo, 3s. 6d.

BIBLE CHILDREN. Studies for the Young. With Illustrations. Small crown 8vo, 3s. 6d.

BIBLE IMAGES. With Illustrations. Crown 8vo, 3s. 6d.

By the Rev. A. T. PIERSON, D.D.

6s. THE NEW ACTS OF THE APOSTLES. Second Edition. Being Lectures on Foreign Missions delivered under the Duff Endowment. With Coloured Chart, showing the Religions of the World and the Progress of Evangelisation. Extra crown 8vo, 6s.

"Ought to create a new enthusiasm in missionary work."—*Christian Commonwealth.*

"As a repertory of missionary facts and arguments, this work is as deeply interesting as the style is truly enthusiastic, and we bespeak for it a wide circle of readers, whom it will assuredly stimulate to increased zeal in sending the Gospel throughout the world."—*Christian.*

"Such a work as this ought greatly to help in the evangelisation of the whole world."—*Sword and Trowel.*

"Emphatically the handbook of Missions."—*Presbyterian.*

3s. 6d. each THE CRISIS OF MISSIONS; OR, THE VOICE OUT OF THE CLOUD. Small crown 8vo, 3s. 6d.

"A book full of the right kind of inspiration. A book emphatically for the times."—*Christian Commonwealth.*

THE ONE GOSPEL; OR, THE COMBINATION OF THE NARRATIVES OF THE FOUR EVANGELISTS IN ONE COMPLETE RECORD. Crown 8vo, 3s. 6d.

"It is a skilful mosaic of the four Gospels in one design."—*Rock.*

By FREDERICK A. ATKINS,

Editor of "The Young Man," and Hon. Sec. of the National Anti-Gambling League.

1s. each ASPIRATION AND ACHIEVEMENT. A Young Man's Message to Young Men. Small crown 8vo, 1s.

Dr. R. F. HORTON writes: "I have rarely read a more salutary book."

MORAL MUSCLE: AND HOW TO USE IT. A Brotherly Chat with Young Men. By F. A. ATKINS, Editor of "The Young Man." With an Introduction by Rev. THAIN DAVIDSON, D.D. Small crown 8vo, 1s.

Dr. CLIFFORD writes:—"It is full of life, throbs with energy, is rich in stimulus, and bright with hope."

FIRST BATTLES, AND HOW TO FIGHT THEM. By F. A. ATKINS, Editor of "The Young Man." Small crown 8vo, 1s.

"Another of Mr. Atkins' capital little books for young men."—*British Weekly.*

HOW TO STUDY THE BIBLE. By Dr. CLIFFORD, M.A.; Professor ELMSLIE, D.D.; R. F. HORTON, M.A.; Rev. F. B. MEYER, B.A.; Rev. C. H. WALLER, M.A.; Rev. H. C. G. MOULE, M.A.; Rev. C. A. BERRY; Rev. W. J. DAWSON. Third Edition. Small crown 8vo, 1s.

"In this little book we have the choicest counsels of men who are themselves successful students of the Word. We very earnestly commend this volume. All those who desire to know how to study the Scriptures with the utmost profit should secure it at once."—*Christian Advocate.*

www.ingramcontent.com/pod-product-compliance
Lightning Source LLC
Chambersburg PA
CBHW030359230426
43664CB00007BB/665